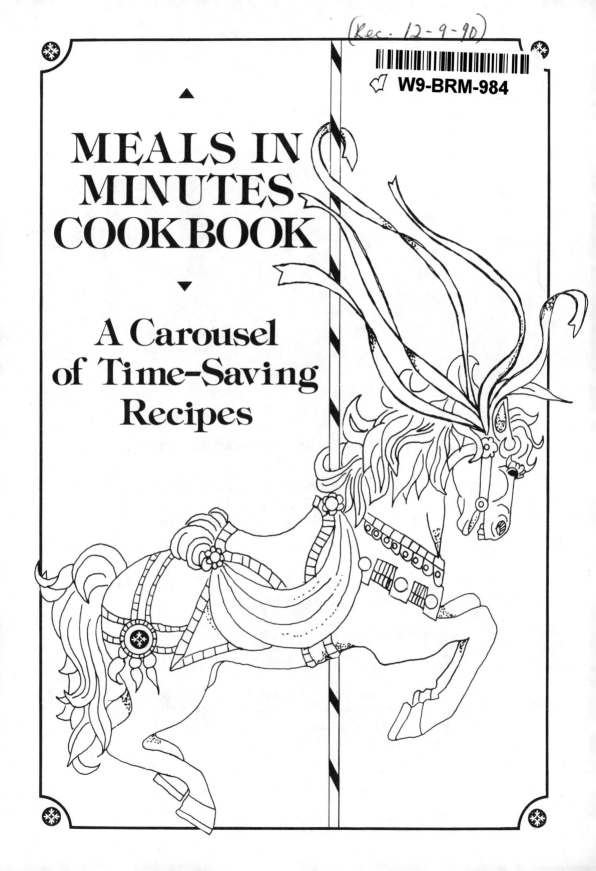

MEALS IN MINUTES COOKBOOK

A Carousel of Time-Saving Recipes

Great American Opportunities, Inc./Favorite Recipes® Press

Editorial Manager: Mary Jane Blount
Editors: Georgia Brazil, Mary Cummings, Jane Hinshaw, Linda Jones,
Marian Sherman, Mary Wilson
Typography: Pam Newsome, Sara Anglin

This cookbook is a collection of our favorite recipes which
are not necessarily original recipes.

Library of Congress Catalog Number is: 89-25939
ISBN: 0-87197-266-2

Manufactured in the United States of America
First Printing 1990

Contents

GREEN PEPPER STEAK AND RICE

1½ lb. sirloin steak
1 tsp. paprika
2 cloves of garlic, crushed
2 tbsp. butter
1 c. sliced green onions
2 green peppers, slivered

2 tomatoes, chopped
1 c. beef broth
2 tbsp. cornstarch
2 tbsp. soy sauce
3 c. hot cooked rice

Cut sirloin into ¼ inch thick strips. Sprinkle with paprika. Let stand for several minutes. Sauté steak and garlic in butter in skillet until steak is brown. Add green onions, green peppers, tomatoes and broth. Simmer, covered, for 15 minutes or until steak is tender. Combine ¼ cup water, cornstarch and soy sauce in small bowl. Stir into steak mixture. Cook until thickened, stirring constantly. Serve over rice. Yield: 6 servings.

Shortcuts to Meals in Minutes

Today's busy lifestyles mean that homemakers must make every minute count. We are concerned with providing our families with the best in nutrition and taste but find our time limited because of activities outside the home—careers, community work, sports, etc. Even on tight schedules, the homemaker can master the art of quick cooking yet still maintain the quality of "homemade."

The key to planning nutritious meals in minutes is "flexible organization." Flexible organization means adjusting your total cooking environment and schedule. Organize your time, as well as your kitchen, with precision. Keep your kitchen uncluttered so everything will be ready for quick meal preparation. Invest in time-saving appliances—microwave ovens, blenders, food processors. All of these can save valuable time and money. Be careful not to limit your creativity. The goal should be flexible organization, which is structured, yet fits *your* lifestyle.

Organize Your Time

Your most effective resource is your ability to plan ahead. Start by planning menus for the whole week. Follow this menu plan closely as you make your shopping list. Be sure to add staples that are running low. This preparation for shopping may seem time-consuming at first but will save time and eliminate the need for return trips to the supermarket. In addition, shop only once a week, take your shopping list and stick to it.

As you plan your shopping day, always allow extra time *after* shopping for advance preparations that will ease your workload at mealtime. Divide large quantity packages and store in meal-sized portions; cook meat before storage whenever possible; brown ground beef, then store in packages for chili, meat sauces, and casseroles; cook chicken and package for casseroles and salads. Shape ground beef into patties, or mix and shape for meat loaves or meatballs before freezing. Grate cheese, and store tightly covered to use as needed. Chop onions, green peppers, and celery to freeze so they are ready when you need them. Squeeze citrus fruit and freeze the juice in ice trays. Store in plastic bags in the freezer until needed. The rind may be grated and stored in small plastic bags in the freezer as well.

These ideas for advance preparation will take extra time on shopping day, but will save you double the time when you are preparing a meal in a hurry at the end of a busy day. And, as you use these, creative ideas of your own will continue to increase the time you save.

Minute Savers

- As you prepare a casserole, double the recipe. Place half in a foil-lined baking dish, and cover tightly with foil. Place in the freezer. When frozen solid, lift out of the baking dish. When you need a fantastic meal in a hurry, remove from freezer, and place in the same dish for baking.

- Plan a meal with several dishes that can be baked at the same time to save both time and energy.

- Freeze chili in ice cube trays, then transfer to plastic bags for storage. Thaw and heat as needed.

- Use leftover gravy or cream soup instead of sauces in casseroles.

- Use your double boiler for maximum effectiveness by cooking vegetables in the bottom while you prepare white sauce or cheese sauce in the top.

- Use aluminum foil whenever possible to save clean-up time as well as to seal in flavor and moistness.

- Butter French bread slices, and season with garlic. Freeze slices on cookie sheet, then store in a plastic bag. Remove from freezer, and heat in the oven as needed.

- When preparing a main dish casserole that is mixed in one bowl, mix it in the baking dish instead—saves clean-up time.

- Place stale bread or crackers in blender container. Process until reduced to crumbs. Store in a covered container to use as needed.

- For a quick cake "frosting," place chocolate candy bars on top of hot cake. Let stand for several seconds, then spread evenly with a knife. Another easy topping is a sprinkling of confectioners' sugar.

- Eliminate extra trips to the pantry during meal preparation by assembling all ingredients before starting.

- Plan your meal preparation according to length of time each dish requires. Start with the dish that takes the longest, working the others in during cooking time. This will save time, and all the foods will be served at their best.

- When making waffles, prepare an extra recipe, and freeze the extras. Place frozen waffles in a hot oven for several minutes for fresh-tasting waffles at any time.

- When a recipe for sauces or custards calls for scalded milk, use cold milk instead. It blends just as well with less danger of curdling. A smoother product is the result, and you save the time you'd spend scalding milk and cleaning up the pan.

- Combine 1 cup confectioners' sugar and 2 tablespoons frozen lemonade, and mix until smooth. Use as dessert topping on cakes, puddings or custards. Topping may be stored in refrigerator or freezer.

- To cook frozen vegetables in the oven, remove frozen block from its package and place it on a square of foil. Place two pats butter on top; season with salt, pepper, and herbs as desired. Fold foil over, making tight seal, leaving room inside for steam expansion. Bake at 425 degrees for 30 to 40 minutes—no messy pans and so easy.

- Always label packages and containers for the freezer. Include the name of the item and the date frozen. This will save time in finding what you want and also eliminate waste.

- To eliminate extra cleanup when using the food processor, start with dryer ingredients and work through to moister ones.

- Fill cooking pans immediately with hot water to soak. Use cold water for cereal, egg and milk dishes.

Organize Your Kitchen

Take an inventory of your kitchen equipment—including all utensils. Get rid of items that you never use, and store or give away duplicate items. Think about where you use certain items, and plan their storage accordingly. Dishes should be near the eating area or dishwasher, pots and pans near the stove, and food staples near your work area. The time you spend rearranging your kitchen will be saved over and over as you prepare meals.

Plan several meals that can be prepared from canned goods and other convenience foods. With thoughtful planning these can be nutritious meals also. Add these items to your grocery list, in addition to your normal week's groceries. Store emergency items together, and DO NOT use them unless an emergency arises. When you do need them, be sure to make a note to replenish the supply on your next shopping trip. This way, you'll always be ready for any occasion.

A Pantry Shelf For Quick Meals

- Canned chunk chicken, ham, tuna and salmon; canned shrimp, crab, lobster and sardines
- Canned ham, corned beef, pressed meat, corned beef hash, dried beef, potted meats, chili and stews
- Packaged dinner and main dish mixes
- Quick-cooking rice
- Macaroni, spaghetti, spaetzle and noodles
- Packaged seasoned noodle, macaroni and rice mixes
- Canned vegetables, fruits and juices
- Canned bean and potato salads, marinated artichoke hearts and mushrooms
- Canned tomatoes, tomato sauce and tomato paste
- Instant potatoes and seasoned potato casserole mixes
- Canned soups and instant soup mixes
- Dried fruits
- Packaged biscuit, pancake, corn bread, muffin and pizza mixes
- Packaged tortillas and taco shells
- Cracker crumbs and bread crumbs
- Packaged sauce, marinade, gravy, dip, salad dressing and seasoning mixes
- Bottled sauces such as spaghetti, pizza, barbecue, chili, teriyaki, sweet and sour, Worcestershire and Tabasco
- Bottled pickles, mustards, sandwich spreads, olives, catsup, lemon juice, pimento and salsas
- Cereals, granola, wheat germ and bran; instant hot cereals
- Canned evaporated, whole and sweetened condensed milk
- Instant dry milk powder, buttermilk mix and coffee creamer
- Packaged pudding, cake, cookie, cheesecake, frosting and pie crust mixes
- Prepared pie crusts and canned pie filling
- Chocolate chips, candy bars, marshmallows and ice cream toppings
- Herbs, spices, seasonings, bacon bits and dried vegetable flakes
- Instant coffee, tea and flavored drink mixes

Quick Fix Recipe Finder

The Microwave Fix

The One-Dish Meal Fix

Breakfasts & Brunches

BREAKFAST
FOR TWO

Cranberry Juice Cocktail
*Breakfast Schnitzel
*Quick Bran Muffins
Spiced Crabapples

A SKILLET BREAKFAST
FOR FOUR

Sliced Peaches and Cream
*German Farmer's Breakfast
*Quick Buttermilk Biscuits
Butter Curls • Apple Butter

A BURRITO BREAKFAST
FOR FOUR

Papaya with Lime Wedges
*Apple Burritos
Brown and Serve Sausage Links
Sour Cream or Honey Yogurt

EASTERN SHORE BREAKFAST
FOR THREE TO SIX

Grapefruit Halves
*Stray Crab Strut with Broccoli
Cherry Tomatoes
Café au Lait

SUNDAY BREAKFAST
FOR SIX

Chilled Honeydew Melon Wedges
*Scrambled Eggs Supreme
Canadian-Style Bacon
*Cinnamon-Sugar Bowknots

EASY BREAKFAST
FOR EIGHT

Nectarines and Blueberries
*Welsh Rarebit
Toasted Wheat or Cheese Bread
Grilled Tomato Halves

Breakfasts & Brunches

QUICK BREAKFAST
FOR SIX TO EIGHT

Clam-Tomato Juice
*Ham and Egg Sandwiches
with Cheese Sauce
*Ambrosia Yogurt

BRUNCH IN A JIFFY
FOR FOUR

Chilled Juice
*Corned Beef Hash Stacks
*Five-Cup Fruit Salad
Toasted Bagels with Cream Cheese

A BREAKFAST
FOR A BUNCH

Melon Balls in Pineapple Juice
*Broiled Ham Sandwiches
Sliced Hard-Boiled Eggs
Frozen Hashed Brown Potato Patties

AN ELEGANT BRUNCH
FOR FOUR

Raspberry-Blackberry Cup
*Eggs Florentine
Croissants
Butter Curls • Strawberry Jam

OVEN BRUNCH
FOR THREE

Cranapple Juice
*Eggs Baked in Green Peppers
Toasted English Muffins
Spread with Deviled Ham
Pineapple Rings

A HEARTY BRUNCH
FOR SIX

Orange-Grapefruit Juice
*Omelets with Spanish Sauce
*Potato Pancakes
*Microwave Apple Crisp

Lunches

A POCKET LUNCH
FOR THREE

*Pita Chicken Sandwiches
Fresh Fruit
*No-Bake Fudge Cookies
Apple Juice

LUNCH OLÉ
FOR EIGHT

*Chili Sandwiches Supreme
*Avocado Salad
Corn Chips
*Easy Peanut Butter Cookies

SATURDAY LUNCH
FOR SIX

*French Hamburgers
Potato Chips
Carrot and Celery Sticks
*Championchip

SOUP AND SANDWICH LUNCH
FOR FOUR

*Clam Chowder
*Corned Beef Pocket Sandwiches
Ice Cream with Fresh Fruit
Hot Cocoa

SALAD LUNCHEON
FOR FOUR

*Mushroom-Tuna Medley
*Poppy Seed Muffins
*Sautéed Rainbow Fruit Cup
Iced Tea

LUNCH AL FRESCO
FOR SIX

*Pasta Salad
*Easy Herbed Bread
Fruit and Cheese Platter with Cookies
Capuccino

Lunches

A NUTRITIOUS LUNCH
FOR SIX

*Cream of Carrot Soup
*Cheesy Peanut Sandwiches
Apple and Pear Wedges
Oatmeal Cookies

SOUP AND SALAD LUNCHEON
FOR FOUR

*Asparagus and Crab Bisque
*Scandanavian Luncheon Salad
*Pita Breadsticks
*Microwave Chocolate Fondue

PARTY LUNCHEON
FOR FOUR

*Shrimp Savannah
Patty Shells
*Fresh Broccoli and Tomato Salad
*Persian Peaches

MICROWAVE LUNCHEON
FOR SIX

*Microwave Chicken Divan
*Peach Halves Delight
Hot Rolls
*Microwave Pecan Bars

LINGUINE LUNCHEON
FOR SIX

*Linguine with Smoked
Salmon Sauce
*Italian Green Beans
*Creole Garlic Bread
Lemon Ice • Cookies

BRIDGE LUNCHEON
FOR EIGHT

*Broiled Open-Faced Sandwiches
Tossed Salad
Spiced Apple Rings
*Fast Blintzes
Iced Tea

Dinners

BUSY-NIGHT SUPPER
FOR SIX

*Microwave Chili Chicken
Mixed Green Salad
Corn Muffins
*Chocolate Macaroons

A SKILLET SUPPER
FOR FOUR

*Tuna-Rice Curry Skillet
Chutney
*Mystery Rolls
*Microwave Peach Crisp

AN EASY DINNER
FOR TWO

*Crab Louis
*Chinese Almond Chicken
*Brandied Fruit Fondue
Hot Green Tea
Fortune Cookies

A SUNDAY DINNER FOR
SIX TO EIGHT

*Ham-Broccoli Rolls
*Microwave Sweet Potatoes
Apple Salad
Rolls
*Microwave Cherry Cobbler

A COMPANY DINNER
FOR FOUR

*Chicken and Artichoke
Hearts Supreme
Marinated Mushrooms
*Special Rice Pilaf
*Hot Raspberry Soufflé
Tea or Coffee

A HOLIDAY DINNER
FOR EIGHT

*Favorite Oyster Stew
*Microwave Apricot Chicken
*Cran-Mandarin Toss
*Microwave Scalloped Potatoes
*Nippy Green Bean Casserole
*Quick Herb Rolls
*Microwave Cherry Cheesecake Cups

Dinners

A STIR-FRY DINNER
FOR FOUR

Won-Ton Soup
*Stir-Fry Dinner
*Fried Rice
Fortune Cookies

AN ELEGANT DINNER
FOR FOUR TO SIX

*Italian Chicken Soup
*Veal Piccata
*Caesar Salad
*Fettucini Alfredo
Lemon Ice • Crisp Cookies

A BAVARIAN DINNER
FOR FOUR

Potato Soup
*Microwave Smoked Pork Chops
Rye Bread
Bakery Strudel
Apple Cider

A QUICK DINNER
FOR SIX

*Steak Polynesian
Steamed Rice
Broiled Tomato Halves
*Pineapple Sherbet with Raspberries
Beverage of Choice

A SOUP SUPPER
FOR SIX

*Microwave Taco Soup
Tossed Salad
Corn Chips
Sour Cream
Chocolate Pudding

A CURRY DINNER
FOR SIX

*Curried Chicken
*Austrian Cucumber Salad
Hot Rice
*Ginger Carrots
Sherried Grapefruit

Dinners

A LIGHT MEXICAN SUPPER
FOR SIX

*Cheese Enchiladas
*Orange-Avocado Salad
Salsa
*Microwave Lemon Bundt Cake
Mocha Coffee

A SEAFOOD DINNER
FOR SIX

*Cream of Corn Soup
*Creole Haddock
Microwave Baked Potatoes
*Broccoli with Sour Cream Sauce
*Bananas Foster

A JAMBALAYA SUPPER
FOR SIX TO EIGHT

*Shrimp Jambalaya
Spinach and Orange Salad
*Corn Bread Ring
Vanilla Ice Cream
Caramel Sauce and Pecans

A LIGHT DINNER
FOR FOUR

*Coquille St. Jacques
Fresh Fruit Salad
*Artichoke Hearts and Pecans
Crusty Hard Rolls
Lemon Sorbet

THE 30-MINUTE TRIP TO THE
GROCERY STORE

You can pick up small amounts of chopped vegetables and toppings for salads and stir-frying at the salad bar. The deli counter has delicious fully-cooked lean meats, roasted chickens, barbecue, bagels, prepared salads and cheesecake. Look for time-saving items in the frozen food case such as chicken breast filets, vegetable and pasta combos, bread dough, cakes, fruits, waffles, pancakes, French toast and hashed browns.

Breakfasts & Brunches

BREAKFAST PICANTE
FOR SIX

Orange and Watermelon Cup
*Chili-Cheese Eggs
Warm Tostados
Hot Chocolate

A BRUNCH
FOR TWELVE

Tangerine-Apple Cup
*Crab Pie
Asparagus Spears
Coffee

AN OVEN BREAKFAST
FOR EIGHT

Cran-grape Juice
*Breakfast Casserole
Grilled Sausage Links
*Orange-Glazed Apples

A PEACHY BREAKFAST
FOR FOUR

Orange-Peach Compote
*Impossible Quiche
Bacon Curls
Hot Spiced Tea

A SKILLET BREAKFAST
FOR FOUR

Fresh Figs in Cream
*Brittany Skillet
*Pluck-It Coffee Cake
Beverage of Choice

A TEENAGER'S BREAKFAST
FOR EIGHT

Orange Juice
Blueberries with Yogurt
*Breakfast Pizza
Milk Shakes

Breakfasts & Brunches

SUNDAY BRUNCH
FOR SIX

Orange-Apricot Juice
*Blintz Soufflé
Crisp-Cooked Bacon
Coffee or Tea

A FAMILY BREAKFAST
FOR FOUR

Tomato Juice on the Rocks
*Cheese and Egg Wedges
*Blueberry Muffins
Butter and Jam

A CASSEROLE BREAKFAST
FOR EIGHT

Apricot Nectar
*Baked Egg and Cheese Dish
*Apple-Cinnamon Delights

AN EASY BREAKFAST
FOR SIX

Grapefruit Juice with Orange Sherbet
*Oven Omelet
*Apple Kuchen Coffee Cake

A SOUTHERN BREAKFAST
FOR SIX

Sliced Pears and Strawberries
*Cajun Cheese Grits
Grilled Ham Slice
Biscuits

A BRUNCH
FOR EIGHT TO TEN

Melon Cup with Lime Wedges
*Spinach Squares
*Bacon Curls
*Yogurt Coffee Cake

Lunches

A TEEN-SET LUNCH
FOR SIX

*Favorite Taco Salad
Catalina Dressing
Sour Cream • Guacamole
*Fruit Pizza

PRESTO LUNCH
FOR FOUR TO SIX

*Avocado Soup
*Taco Crescents
Salsa
*Apricot Bars

SATURDAY LUNCH
FOR FOUR TO SIX

*Quick and Easy Potato Soup
*Saturday Sandwiches
Carrot and Celery Sticks
*Self-Filled Cupcakes

A SUMMER LUNCH
FOR SIX

*Spiced Walnut Fruit Salad
*Parmesan Cheese Bread
*Coconut Magic Pie
Lemonade

A SOUP AND SANDWICH
LUNCH FOR SIX

*Classic Onion Soup
*Stroganoff Sandwiches
Fruit and Cheese
Iced Tea

WINTER PICNIC LUNCH
FOR FIFTEEN

*Fireside Sandwiches
Potato Chips
*Super Pizza Cookie
Hot Chocolate

Lunches

BUSINESS LUNCH
FOR FOUR

*Golden Cauliflower Soup
*Chicken Piccata
Hot Rice
*Easy Cheesecake Pie

AN EASY LUNCHEON
FOR FOUR

*Easy Chicken and Rice
Cranberry Sauce
Broccoli Spears
*Marble Fudge Pudding

BUSY-DAY LUNCH
FOR FOUR

*Macaroni-Corned Beef
Buttered Peas
*Sally Lunn
Fresh Fruit Cups

AN OVEN LUNCH
FOR SIX

*Curried Salmon
*Cheese Pinwheels
*Confetti Coleslaw
*Blonde Brownies

A SALAD LUNCH
FOR TWO TO FOUR

*Delicious Cold Soup
*Hearty Shrimp Salad
Assorted Crackers
*Pecan Dream Bars

LASAGNA LUNCH
FOR NINE

*Vegetarian Lasagna
*Sicilian Tomato Salad
Italian Bread
*Pistachio Ice Cream

Dinners

SUPPER
FOR TWO

*Saucy Chicken
Hot Spaghetti
Buttered Italian Bread
Spumoni

AN OVEN DINNER
FOR EIGHT

*Shrimp Rockefeller
Honeydew Melon Wedges
*Parmesan Cheese Bread
*Easy Chocolate Roll-Up

SATURDAY SUPPER
FOR FIVE

*Chicken and Broccoli Potpies
Fresh Fruit Salad
Buttered Carrots
*Cream Cheese Quickie

BAYOU SUPPER
FOR SIX

*Ham Jambalaya
Broccoli Salad
*Quick Corn Bread
*Crunchy Apricot Cake

A SUMMER DINNER
FOR SIX

*Microwave One-Step Lasagna
Tossed Salad
*Garlic Bread
*Butter-Brickle Ice Cream Pie

AN ELEGANT DINNER
FOR TWO

*Citrus Poached Chicken Breasts
*Orange and Carrot Timbales
Spiced Apple Rings
*Fresh Fruit Torte

Dinners

A FAMILY DINNER
FOR SIX

*Cranberry Pork Chops
*Corn Salad
Green Peas and Onions
*Southern Spoon Bread
*Apple Pie Cake

A COMPANY DINNER
FOR SIX

*Beef and Mushroom Stroganoff
Hot Buttered Noodles
*Beets with Pineapple
*Popovers
*Individual Baked Alaskas

THANKSGIVING FRIDAY
DINNER FOR SIX

*Crunchy Turkey Strata
*Spinach Salad
*Confetti Bread
*Turtle Cake

SOUP AND SALAD SUPPER
FOR SIX

*Sour Cream-Potato Soup
*Apple-Salmon Salad
*Goody Biscuits
*Rocky Road Ice Cream

PATIO DINNER
FOR SIX

*Barbecued Whitefish in Foil
*Zucchini in Cream
Corn on the Cob
*French Bread Monterey
*Lemon Pie

ALL-AMERICAN DINNER
FOR TWO

*Mini Meat Loaves
*Microwave-Baked Potatoes
Buttered Peas
*Onion-Topped Bread
*Strawberry Shortcut Cake

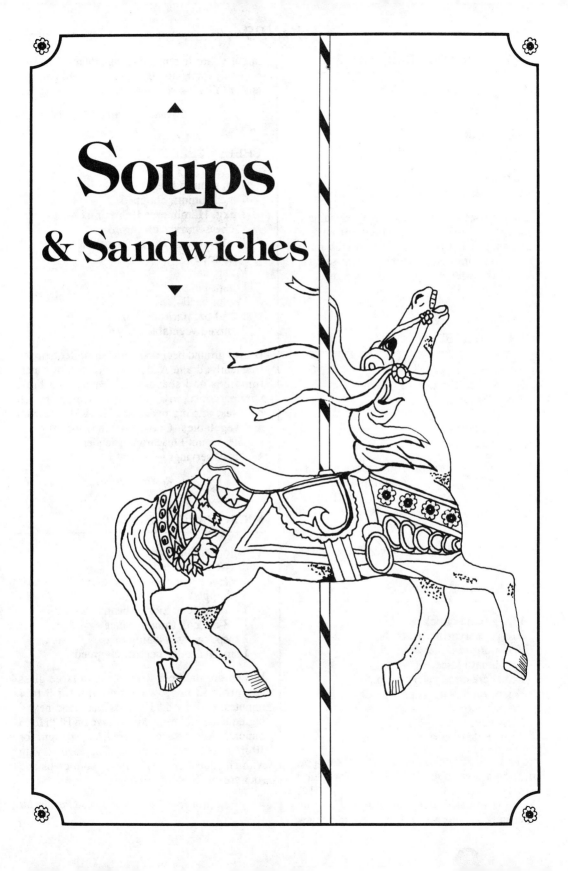

Soups
& Sandwiches

ASPARAGUS AND CRAB BISQUE

1 can mushroom soup
1 can asparagus soup
1 c. cream
1½ c. milk
¼ tsp. seafood seasoning
1 c. crab meat
Salt to taste
½ c. Sherry

Combine soups, cream, milk and seasoning in saucepan. Cook over low heat for several minutes, stirring frequently. Add crab meat. Heat to serving temperature. Stir in salt and Sherry. Top with chives. Yield: 6 servings.

Mabel O. Walters, Baltimore, MD

AVOCADO SOUP

4 ripe avocados
3 c. cold chicken broth
2 tsp. lime juice
½ tsp. salt
⅛ tsp. garlic powder
2 c. cream, chilled

Place avocados, broth, lime juice, salt and garlic powder in blender container. Process until smooth. Stir in cream. Chill in refrigerator. Pour into soup bowls. Garnish with lemon slices. Yield: 6 servings.

Zunny McLellan, Alberta, Canada

BURGER BEEF SOUP

1 lb. ground chuck
3 tbsp. margarine, melted
¼ c. minced onion
3 c. tomato juice
2 cans cream of celery soup
¼ tsp. each pepper, garlic salt
1 tsp. sugar
1 bay leaf
2 c. shredded carrot

Brown ground chuck in margarine in soup pot, stirring until crumbly. Add onion. Cook until lightly browned, stirring occasionally. Combine tomato juice and soup with 1 cup water in bowl; mix well. Add to ground chuck mixture. Stir in remaining ingredients. Simmer, covered, for 15 to 20 minutes or until carrot is tender. Yield: 4 servings.

Cynthia A. Cirelli, Ellwood City, PA

CHEESY BEEF SOUP

1 lb. ground beef
1 med. onion, chopped
1 pkg. Hamburger Helper mix for cheeseburger macaroni
1 16-oz. can whole tomatoes, chopped
¼ tsp. salt
⅛ tsp. pepper
¼ tsp. basil
1 10-oz. package frozen mixed vegetables

Brown ground beef and onion in skillet, stirring frequently; drain. Add sauce mix, 5 cups water, tomatoes and seasonings. Bring to a boil, stirring constantly. Simmer, covered, for 10 minutes, stirring occasionally. Add macaroni and vegetables. Cook, covered, for 10 to 15 minutes or until macaroni is tender. Yield: 10 servings.

Rosemary Brown, Corsicana, TX

MICROWAVE TACO SOUP

¾ lb. ground beef
½ c. chopped onion
1 16-oz. can stewed tomatoes, chopped
1 16-oz. can kidney beans
1 8-oz. can tomato sauce
2 tbsp. taco seasoning mix
1 sm. avocado, peeled, chopped

Brown ground beef with onion in large glass casserole in microwave on High for 3 to 4 minutes; drain. Add 1¼ cups water and next 4 ingredients; mix well. Microwave on High for 5 minutes. Microwave, covered, on Medium for 10 minutes. Stir in avocado. Top each serving with shredded Cheddar cheese, corn chips and sour cream. Yield: 6 servings.

Marilyn Jean Mancewicz, Grand Rapids, MI

CABBAGE PATCH SOUP

1 lb. ground beef
1 sm. onion, chopped
3 cans chicken broth
3 cans ranch-style beans
1 can tomatoes
1 sm. head cabbage, shredded
1 c. chopped celery
½ tsp. cuminseed
½ tsp. chili powder

Sauté ground beef and onion in skillet until beef is crumbly. Combine with remaining ingredients in 4-quart saucepan. Simmer until vegetables are tender. Yield: 8 servings.

Deanna Reeves, Granite, OK

GOLDEN CAULIFLOWER SOUP

2   10-oz. packages frozen cauliflower
½ c. chopped onion
¼ c. butter
½ c. flour
2 tbsp. instant chicken bouillon
2 c. shredded mild Cheddar cheese
2 c. milk
⅛ to ¼ tsp. ground nutmeg
Chopped fresh parsley
Paprika

Cook cauliflower in 1 cup water in medium saucepan until tender; drain, reserving liquid. Reserve 1 cup cauliflower. Place remaining cauliflower and reserved liquid in food processor or blender container. Process until smooth; set aside. Sauté onion in butter in large heavy saucepan until tender; stir in flour. Add 1 cup water and bouillon gradually. Cook until well blended and thickened, stirring constantly.Stir in processed cauliflower, reserved flowerets and cheese. Cook until cheese melts; add milk and nutmeg. Cook until heated through. Garnish with parsley and paprika. Yield: 6 servings.

Olivia Howe, Chicago, IL

CREAM OF CARROT SOUP

1 lb. carrots, pared, sliced
½ c. chopped onion
1 bay leaf
1 tbsp. instant chicken bouillon
¼ c. butter
¼ c. all-purpose flour
1 tsp. salt
Dash each of pepper, nutmeg
2¾ c. milk

Place carrots, onion, bay leaf, 1½ cups water and chicken bouillon in 3-quart saucepan. Bring to a boil; cover. Simmer for 15 to 20 minutes or until tender. Melt butter in 2-quart saucepan. Blend in flour, salt, pepper and nutmeg, stirring constantly, for 2 minutes. Remove from heat; stir in milk gradually. Bring to a boil over medium heat, stirring constantly. Boil for 1 minute, stirring constantly. Remove bay leaf from carrots; pour carrots with cooking liquid into blender container. Process just until coarsely chopped. Combine carrot mixture and cream sauce; heat just to boiling. Top with parsley.

DELICIOUS COLD SOUP

1 can chicken and rice soup
1 tsp. curry powder
1 sm. can evaporated milk
Juice of ½ lemon

Combine all ingredients in blender container. Process until smooth. Chill in refrigerator. Pour into soup bowls. Yield: 2 servings.

Erma M. Bischoff, Louisville, KY

ITALIAN CHICKEN SOUP

7½ to 10 c. chicken broth
4 eggs, well beaten
10 tbsp. Parmesan cheese
5 tbsp. bread crumbs
Salt, pepper and nutmeg to taste
Italian bread

Bring broth to a boil in 3-quart saucepan. Mix eggs, 10 tablespoons Parmesan cheese and next 4 ingredients in small bowl. Pour slowly into boiling broth, stirring vigorously. Heat over very low heat, stirring often. Serve immediately with additional cheese and Italian bread. Yield: 4-6 servings.

Jacqueline M. Torri, Washington D.C.

CORNY CHICKEN-NOODLE SOUP

1 can cream of chicken soup
½ c. noodles
½ c. frozen corn

Blend soup and 2 soup cans water in saucepan. Bring to a boil over medium heat. Add noodles and corn. Cook until noodles are tender. Yield: 4 servings.

Kandee Graham, Hershey, PA

CREAM OF CORN SOUP

1 can creamed corn
1 qt. milk
1 onion
1 tsp. flour
¼ c. butter, softened
Salt and pepper to taste

Combine corn, milk and onion in double boiler. Bring to a boil. Blend flour with butter in small bowl. Stir into corn mixture with seasonings; blend well. Bring to a boil. Remove onion before serving. Yield: 8 servings.

Anita Mullins, St. Louis, MO

CLAM CHOWDER

1 can cream of potato soup
1 can cream of onion soup
1 soup can milk
1   10-ounce can minced clams

Blend soups and milk in saucepan. Add clams and juice. Heat to serving temperature, stirring frequently. Serve with crusty bread. Yield: 4-6 servings.

Rose Stafford, Medford, MA

HAM CHOWDER

2½ c. chopped cooked ham
1 c. chopped onion
2 c. sliced potatoes
⅔ c. sliced carrots
1 tbsp. butter
1 env. buttermilk farm-style
    salad dressing mix
2 c. milk

Sauté ham, onion, potatoes and carrots in butter in large skillet for 6 minutes or until vegetables are tender. Add 2 cups water. Simmer, covered, for 15 minutes. Combine salad dressing mix and milk in bowl; mix well. Stir into ham and vegetables. Simmer, covered, for 5 minutes. Ladle into soup bowls. Garnish with chopped parsley. Yield: 6 servings.

Anne Dale, Gadsden, AL

FISH CHOWDER

1½ lb. haddock fillets
1 lg. onion, sliced
¼ c. butter
3 cans cream of potato soup
Salt to taste
3 qt. milk
Crackers

Cook haddock in a small amount of salted water in saucepan until haddock flakes easily. Sauté onion in butter in skillet. Add to fish. Stir in soup, salt and enough milk to make of desired consistency. Simmer until heated through. Place 1 warm cracker in each chowder bowl. Pour chowder over cracker. Garnish with paprika. Yield: 8 servings.

Sally Riley, Wheaton, IL

FAVORITE OYSTER STEW

1 pt. oysters with liquid
10 oz. clam juice
½ tsp. each salt, pepper
¼ c. butter
1 pt. half and half
Paprika (opt.)

Combine oysters, clam juice, salt, pepper and butter in 2-quart saucepan. Cook over medium heat until edges of oysters start to curl. Add half and half. Heat to serving temperature. Do not boil. Serve immediately sprinkled with paprika. Yield: 6 servings.

Emily R. Hill, Annapolis, MD

KIELBASA SOUP

1 lb. kielbasa, sliced ½-inch thick
2 c. sliced frozen carrots
¼ tsp. caraway seed
2 c. cream of celery soup
½ head cabbage, finely shredded

Brown kielbasa in heavy saucepan. Add remaining ingredients and 2 soup cans water; mix well. Simmer for 10 minutes or until cabbage is tender. Yield: 4-6 servings.

Mary Gamble, Huntsville, AL

CLASSIC ONION SOUP

4 c. thinly sliced sweet onions
1 clove of garlic, finely chopped
¼ c. butter
½ c. dry Sherry (opt.)
8 tsp. instant beef bouillon

6 slices ¾-inch thick French
   bread, toasted
6 slices Swiss cheese, cut in half

Sauté onions and garlic in butter in large saucepan until onions are golden brown. Add 5½ cups water, Sherry and bouillon. Bring to a boil; reduce heat. Simmer for 30 minutes to blend flavors. Pour soup into 6 ovenproof soup bowls. Place toast slice in each bowl; top with cheese slice. Broil until cheese melts. Serve immediately. Yield: 6 servings.

Maria Lucarini, Buffalo, NY

QUICK AND EASY POTATO SOUP

4 slices bacon, chopped
1 pkg. frozen potatoes O'Brien
4 c. milk
Salt and pepper to taste

Fry bacon in soup pot until crisp. Add 1½ cups water. Bring to a boil. Add potatoes. Cook until potatoes are tender. Stir in milk, salt and pepper. Heat to serving temperature, stirring constantly. Garnish with croutons.
Yield: 4 servings

Liz Barrows, Payne, OK

SOUR CREAM-POTATO SOUP

3 c. diced potatoes
½ c. each finely chopped celery, onion
2 c. scalded milk
2 or 3 chicken bouillon cubes
3 tbsp. butter
1 c. sour cream
1 tbsp. flour
2 tsp. salt
⅛ tsp. pepper

Combine potatoes, celery and onion with 3 cups water in medium saucepan. Cook, covered, until potatoes are tender. Add milk, bouillon cubes and butter; mix well. Mix sour cream with flour in small bowl until smooth; add to soup mixture. Cook until thickened and bouillon cubes are dissolved, stirring constantly. Stir in salt and pepper.
Yield: 6 servings

Nancy Coles, Auburn, AL

BROILED HAMBURGER-ON-A-BUN

1 lb. ground beef
½ c. milk
¼ c. catsup
1 tbsp. each mustard,
    Worcestershire sauce
1 tsp. vinegar
1 tsp. sugar
10 hamburger buns, split

Mix first 7 ingredients in bowl. Spread thin layer of ground beef mixture on each bun half. Place on broiler rack. Broil for 5 minutes. Yield: 10 servings.

Stella Heath, Oklahoma City, OK

BUFFALO CHIPS

1½ lb. ground beef
1 lb. sausage
2 tsp. oregano
1 tsp. red pepper
½ tsp. each salt, garlic salt
1 lb. Velveeta cheese, cut into chunks
Rye bread

Brown ground beef and sausage in skillet, stirring until crumbly; drain. Add seasonings and cheese, mixing well. Cook over low heat until cheese melts. Serve on rye bread. Yield: 10 servings.

Marcia Johnson, Prescott, AR

BURRITO FILLING

1 lb. ground beef
½ onion, chopped
1 tsp. chili powder
⅛ tsp. Tabasco sauce
1 tbsp. flour
¾ tsp. salt
¼ tsp. garlic powder
1   16-oz. can whole tomatoes, drained

Brown ground beef with onion in skillet, stirring until crumbly; drain well. Add remaining ingredients, mixing well. Cook until heated through. Serve in flour tortillas or taco shells. Yield: 6 servings.

Clara Carroll, Des Arc, AZ

CHEESY BACONBURGERS

2 lb. ground beef
6 to 8 slices crisp-fried bacon, crumbled
1 sm. onion, chopped
1 c. catsup
1   2-oz. jar sliced mushrooms, drained
Salt and pepper to taste
2 c. shredded Cheddar cheese
8 hamburger buns, split

Brown ground beef in large skillet; drain. Stir in bacon, onion, catsup, mushrooms, salt and pepper. Cover skillet. Simmer for 10 to 15 minutes. Sprinkle cheese over top. Heat until cheese melts. Serve on hamburger buns. Yield: 8 servings.

Janet Baker, Knoxville, TN

CHILI SANDWICHES SUPREME

1 loaf French bread, cut in half
    lengthwise
2   12-oz. cans chili
2   12-oz. cans cream-style corn
1   6-oz. can pitted ripe olives, drained
5 slices American cheese,
    cut into 10 triangles

Place bread cut side up on baking sheet. Heat chili in 2-quart saucepan. Layer hot chili, corn and olives over bread. Arrange cheese over top. Bake at 350 degrees until cheese melts. Cut each loaf into 4 equal parts. Serve with corn chips. Yield: 8 servings.

Mark Williams, Cleveland, OK

FRENCH HAMBURGERS

½ lb. lean ground beef
1 tsp. salt
2 tsp. mustard
1½ tbsp. chili sauce
1 tbsp. each finely chopped onion,
    green pepper
2½ oz. Velveeta cheese, cut
    into ¼-in. cubes
3 hamburger buns, split

Mix first 7 ingredients in bowl. Spread evenly over bun halves, covering completely. Place on baking sheet. Bake at 350 degrees for 15 minutes. Yield: 6 servings.

Ruth Brasfield, Pelham, NY

HAMBURGERS DELUXE

1 lb. ground beef
1 tbsp. parsley flakes
1 med. onion, finely chopped
½ tsp. each seasoned salt, garlic salt
1 tsp. thyme
5 drops of Worcestershire sauce
3 drops of Tabasco sauce

Combine all ingredients in bowl, mixing well. Shape into 4 patties. Place on broiler rack. Broil to desired degree of doneness, turning once. Serve on buns, if desired.
Yield: 4 servings.

Helen L. Rattray, Frankfort, OH

MEXICAN BEEF HEROES

½ lb. ground beef
1 onion, chopped
1   4-oz. can green chilies, chopped
¼ c. sliced ripe olives
¼ c. catsup
½ tsp. each salt, chili powder
6 slices Colby cheese
6 slices crisp-cooked bacon
6 slices Muenster cheese
6 sm. French bread loaves, split

Brown ground beef with onion in skillet, stirring until crumbly. Add next 5 ingredients, mixing well. Cook for 5 minutes longer, stirring occasionally. Layer Colby cheese, ground beef mixture, bacon and Muenster cheese on bottom halves of loaves. Top with remaining loaf halves. Bake, wrapped in foil, at 375 degrees for 10 minutes. Yield: 6 servings.

Judith A. Herman, Dublin, CA

PIZZA BURGERS

1   8-oz. can tomato sauce
1 clove of garlic, minced
¼ tsp. oregano
½ tsp. pepper

1 tsp. salt
1 lb. ground beef
3 hamburger buns, split
6 slices mozzarella cheese

Combine first 3 ingredients and half the pepper in saucepan; mix well. Cook for 5 minutes. Mix remaining pepper, salt and ground beef in bowl. Shape into 6 patties. Place on rack in broiler pan. Broil 3 inches from heat source for 5 minutes; turn. Place 1 tablespoon sauce on each patty. Broil for 3 minutes longer. Place patties on bun halves. Top with cheese. Broil for 2 minutes longer or until cheese is melted.
Yield: 6 servings.

Bernita Wessel, Glouster, OH

PIZZAWICHES

1½ lbs. ground beef
½ c. grated Cheddar cheese
1 tbsp. chopped onion
1   3-oz. can black olives, sliced
1 can tomato soup
½ tsp. oregano
¾ tsp. garlic salt
1   12-count pkg. hamburger buns
Grated mozzarella cheese

Brown ground beef in skillet, stirring until crumbly; drain. Combine next 6 ingredients in bowl. Add ground beef; mix well. Spread mixture on hamburger bun halves. Place on baking sheet. Bake at 250 degrees for 5 minutes. Sprinkle with mozzarella cheese. Broil until cheese melts. Yield: 24 servings.

Diann L. Fowlkes, Newman Grove, NE

SLOPPY JOES

2 lb. ground beef
1 tsp. salt
1 can tomato soup
1 can onion soup
1 can celery soup

Brown ground beef in skillet. Add remaining ingredients; mix well. Simmer for 30 minutes. Spoon into buns. Yield: 12 servings.

Tammy M. Loudermelk, Taylorsville, NC

SPOON BURGERS

2 lb. ground beef
1 med. onion, chopped
2 tsp. salt
½ tsp. pepper
¼ c. flour
1 tsp. Worcestershire sauce
1½ c. catsup
16 hamburger buns

Brown ground beef in skillet; stir until crumbly. Mix in onion, salt and pepper. Cook until onion is tender. Add flour, mixing well. Mix in 2½ cups water, Worcestershire sauce and catsup. Simmer for 15 minutes, stirring frequently. Serve on buns. Yield: 16 servings.

Betty L. Blackburn, Broken Arrow, OK

STUFFED ROLL

1 lb. ground beef
½ onion, chopped
1 can cream of mushroom soup
½ tsp. salt
½ tsp. pepper
10 sourdough rolls

Brown ground beef with onion in skillet, stirring frequently. Add soup and seasonings; mix well. Simmer for 5 minutes. Cut rolls in half crosswise. Scoop out inside of rolls, reserving shells. Crumble half the scooped-out bread into ground beef mixture. Spoon mixture into reserved bread shells. Place on baking sheet. Bake at 350 degrees for 15 to 20 minutes or until heated through. Yield: 20 servings.

Jane Smith, Lakeland, FL

TACO CRESCENTS

¾ lb. ground beef
1 sm. onion, minced
1 pkg. taco seasoning mix
1   3-oz. can minced ripe olives, drained
2 eggs, beaten
2 pkg. refrigerator crescent rolls
½ to ¾ c. grated Cheddar cheese

Brown ground beef with onion in skillet, stirring frequently; drain. Stir in taco seasoning mix and olives; cool. Mix in eggs. Separate rolls into triangles. Place a small amount of cheese and 1½ tablespoons ground beef mixture on each triangle. Roll to enclose filling. Shape into crescents on baking sheet. Bake at 375 degrees for 15 minutes or until brown. Serve with salsa or hot mustard. Yield: 16 servings.

Ivy Webb, Yolo, CA

TACO LOAF SANDWICHES

1 lb. ground beef
1 pkg. taco seasoning mix
2 loaves French bread
1 can refried beans
12 oz. jalapeño pepper cheese, sliced

Prepare ground beef with seasoning mix, using package directions. Slice top fourth from each loaf. Hollow out bottom, leaving shell. Spread beans over bottoms of shells. Spoon ground beef mixture over beans. Top with cheese. Replace loaf tops. Bake, wrapped in foil, at 350 degrees for 20 to 30 minutes or until heated through. Yield: 12 servings.

Doris W. Larke, Peoria, IL

UPSIDE-DOWN SANDWICHES

½ c. bread crumbs
1 tbsp. chopped onion
½ c. milk
1 lb. ground beef
1 egg, beaten
6 slices bread
¼ c. butter

Combine bread crumbs, onion and milk in bowl. Let stand for 15 minutes or until liquid is absorbed. Add ground beef and egg; mix well. Sauté one side of each bread slice in butter in skillet until golden brown. Spread beef mixture on other side. Place beef side down in skillet. Cook until beef is browned. Serve hot. Yield: 6 servings.

Lila Warrell, Muncie, IN

Tip: Perk up hamburgers with Chinese sweet and sour sauce, Japanese teriyaki sauce or German hot mustard.

WIMPIES

1½ lb. ground beef
1 lg. onion, chopped
1 can tomato soup
1 tbsp. Worcestershire sauce
1 tbsp. brown sugar
9 pita-bread rounds, cut into halves

Brown ground beef with onion in skillet; drain. Add soup, ½ soup can water, Worcestershire sauce and brown sugar; mix well. Bring to a boil. Simmer, covered, for 30 minutes, stirring occasionally. Serve in pita-bread.
Yield: 8 servings.

Doris Teufel, Pomona, NY

CHICKEN SANDWICH NEOPOLITAN

1   4¾-oz. can chunky chicken spread
2 sandwich rolls, split
2 slices mozzarella cheese
2 slices red onion
1 tomato, sliced
4 fresh spinach leaves

Spread chicken on bottom of each roll. Top with remaining ingredients in order listed. Cover with remaining roll halves.
Yield: 2 servings.

Belinda Olson, Montgomery, AL

CHICKEN DOLITTLES

1 can chunky chicken spread
⅓ c. chopped apple
½ tsp. honey
½ tsp. mayonnaise
4 slices whole wheat bread
Lettuce

Combine chicken, apple, honey and mayonnaise in small bowl; mix well. Spread on 2 slices of bread; top with lettuce. Cover with the remaining bread slices. Yield: 2 servings.

Tricia Wilcox, Phoenix, AZ

Tip: *Use canned chunk chicken for sandwich spreads and salads.*

CORNED BEEF SANDWICHES

1   12-oz. can corned beef, chopped
1 c. shredded longhorn cheese
½ c. chopped green olives
¼ c. chopped green onion (opt.)
½ c. catsup
2 tbsp. Worcestershire sauce
12 sm. sandwich buns

Combine corned beef, cheese, olives and onions in bowl. Add catsup and Worcestershire sauce; mix lightly. Spoon onto buns. Wrap in foil. Bake at 375 degrees for 15 minutes.
Yield: 12 servings.

Doris Patterson, Collinsville, IL

CORNED BEEF POCKET SANDWICHES

½ c. mayonnaise
2 tbsp. prepared mustard
2   3-oz. packages thinly sliced
    corned beef, slivered
2 pita-bread rounds, cut into halves
Sliced pickles
Shredded Swiss cheese
Lettuce

Mix mayonnaise and mustard in bowl. Add corned beef, stirring to coat. Spoon into pita-bread pockets. Top with pickles, cheese and lettuce. Yield: 4 servings.

Melanie Clampet, Vallejo, CA

BROILED OPEN-FACED SANDWICHES

8 slices cooked turkey breast
8 slices cooked ham
8 slices tomato
8 spears broccoli, cooked
4 English muffins, split
1   1¼-oz. package Hollandaise sauce mix

Layer turkey, ham, tomato and broccoli on muffin halves on baking sheet. Prepare Hollandaise sauce, using package directions. Spoon over sandwiches. Broil for 2 minutes.
Yield: 8 servings.

Carrie Young, Alfalfa, OK

BROILED HAM SANDWICHES

8 oz. Velveeta cheese, cubed
1 lb. bacon, crisp-fried, crumbled
1 lb. ham, ground
Mayonnaise
10 English muffins, split

Combine cheese, bacon and ham in bowl. Add enough mayonnaise to moisten; mix well. Spread on muffin halves. Place on baking sheet. Broil until bubbly. Yield: 20 servings.

Lois Lawler, Cedar Rapids, IA

HAM AND EGG SANDWICH WITH CHEESE SAUCE

1 can Cheddar cheese soup
¼ c. milk
¼ tsp. mustard
6 slices ham
3 hard-boiled eggs, sliced
6 slices buttered toast

Blend soup, milk and mustard in saucepan. Heat to serving temperature, stirring occasionally. Layer ham and egg slices over buttered toast. Spoon sauce over top. Yield: 6 servings.

Kathy Krejsek, Grant, OK

HAM ROLLS

18 brown and serve finger rolls, split
6 tbsp. butter
⅓ lb. boiled ham, ground
3 hard-boiled eggs, ground
1 tsp. grated onion
2 tbsp. catsup
¼ tsp. salt
2 tbsp. salad dressing

Spread rolls with butter. Combine ham, eggs, onion, catsup, salt and salad dressing in bowl; mix well. Spread on bottom rolls and replace tops. Wrap in foil. Bake at 300 degrees until heated through. Yield: 6 servings.

John Curtis Temples, Saluda, SC

Tip: Grind or chop leftover meats to use as sandwich spreads.

SATURDAY SANDWICHES

18 finger rolls
¼ c. butter, softened
2 tbsp. mustard
2 tsp. poppy seed
2 tbsp. finely chopped onions
18 thin slices boiled ham
Swiss cheese, sliced

Brush insides of rolls with butter. Mix mustard, poppy seed and onions in bowl. Spread on rolls. Place ham and cheese on rolls. Place rolls in roll pans. Bake, wrapped in foil, at 325 degrees for 20 minutes. Yield: 6 servings.

Phyllis West, Wendell, NC

FIRESIDE SANDWICHES

8 oz. sharp cheese
1 lb. hot dogs, coarsely chopped
2 hard-boiled eggs, chopped
4 green onions, sliced
½ c. sliced stuffed olives
½ can tomato paste
2 tbsp. mayonnaise
15 hot dog buns, split

Cut cheese into ½-inch cubes. Combine cheese, hot dogs, eggs, onions and olives in bowl. Blend tomato paste and mayonnaise together. Add to hot dog mixture. Spoon into buns. Wrap each bun in foil. Place on baking sheet. Bake at 350 degrees for 15 to 20 minutes or until heated through. Yield: 15 servings.

Mary C. Hooker, Knoxville, TN

CHEESY PEANUT SANDWICHES

2 c. shredded Cheddar cheese
½ c. chunk-style peanut butter
½ c. sour cream
¼ c. raisins
2 tbsp. orange juice
1 tsp. grated orange rind
12 slices whole wheat or rye bread

Combine first 6 ingredients in bowl; mix well. Spread between bread slices.
Yield: 6 sandwiches.

Photograph for this recipe on page 25.

PITA CHICKEN SANDWICHES

1 6-oz. can chunk-style chicken,
  drained
1 carrot, grated
2 sm. unpeeled apples, grated
½ c. fresh bean sprouts
½ sm. head lettuce, shredded
¼ c. yogurt
½ tsp. curry powder
Salt and pepper to taste
3 pita-bread rounds

Combine chicken, carrot, apples, bean sprouts
and lettuce in bowl. Blend yogurt and curry
powder. Add to chicken mixture; toss lightly.
Season with salt and pepper. Cut pita rounds to
form pockets. Spoon chicken mixture into pita
pockets. Yield: 3 servings.

Missy Morton, Clarskville, TN

PITAS WITH FRUIT SALAD

½ c. whipping cream
¼ c. mayonnaise
1 tbsp. honey
1 red apple, chopped
1 tbsp. chopped walnuts
1 banana, cut into chunks
1 c. fresh pineapple chunks
3 pita-bread rounds
3 frilly lettuce leaves

Whip cream in large bowl until thickened.
Blend in mayonnaise and honey. Fold in apple,
walnuts, banana and drained pineapple. Cut
pita round into halves; open to form pockets.
Line pockets with lettuce; fill with fruit
mixture. Yield: 3 servings.

Lorna Roberts, Springfield, MO

MICROWAVE PITA POCKETS

1 onion, chopped
1 clove of garlic, minced
1½ tsp. paprika
½ tsp. Tabasco sauce
1 tsp. salt
1 lb. ground beef, crumbled
1 tomato, finely chopped

2 tbsp. minced parsley
3 pita-bread rounds

Microwave first 5 ingredients in covered baking
dish on High for 4 minutes, stirring once. Add
ground beef, tomato and parsley. Microwave,
uncovered, for 3 minutes, stirring once.
Microwave pita rounds on Medium for 1
minute. Cut each round in half and open to form
pockets. Spoon ground beef mixture into
pockets. Yield: 6 sandwiches.

Margaret Betts, Redwater, TX

STROGANOFF SANDWICHES

1 lb. ground beef
1 onion, chopped
½ green pepper, chopped
1 tsp. salt
¼ tsp. garlic powder
1 tbsp. mustard
1 c. sour cream
6 individual loaves French bread
6 to 12 green pepper rings
6 to 12 tomato slices
6 slices sharp cheese, cut into triangles

Brown ground beef with onion and green
pepper in skillet, stirring frequently; drain. Add
salt, garlic powder, mustard and sour cream.
Cook until heated through, stirring constantly.
Do not boil. Slice tops from loaves; scoop out
to form shallow shells. Spoon ground beef
mixture into shells. Arrange green pepper rings,
tomato and cheese over ground beef. Place
sandwiches and tops cut side up on baking
sheet. Bake at 350 degrees for 10 minutes or
until heated through. Broil until cheese bubbles
if desired. Replace tops; place on serving plate.
Yield: 6 sandwiches.

Blanche Gaphart, Bloomington, IN

*Tip: A quick and easy way to add
interest to sandwiches is to
vary bread selections. Try rye
bread, pumpernickel bread,
Kaiser rolls, pita rounds,
tortillas or onion buns.*

BROADWAY COMBO

1   4½-oz. can deviled ham
½ c. shredded Swiss cheese
4 slices whole wheat bread
2 thin slices red onion
2 lettuce leaves

Combine deviled ham and cheese in bowl; mix well. Spread on 2 slices bread. Top with onion, lettuce and remaining bread. Yield: 2 servings.

Jane Koonce, Golf, IL

CHIPPER BARBECUE

1 lb. chipped ham, chopped
1 c. catsup
1 med. onion, chopped
⅓ c. sugar
4 tsp. mustard
⅛ tsp. pepper
½ c. vinegar
4 tsp. Worcestershire sauce

Combine ham, catsup, onion, sugar and seasonings in saucepan; mix well. Simmer for 30 minutes. Yield: 4 servings.

Alice Fae Jones, Fairmont, WV

DAGWOOD'S DEVILICIOUS FAVORITE

1   4½-oz. can deviled ham
4 slices white bread
1 cucumber, sliced
1 tomato, sliced
1 hard-boiled egg, sliced
2 tbsp. blue cheese dressing

Spread deviled ham on 2 slices bread. Arrange next 3 ingredients over top. Top with remaining bread spread with blue cheese dressing. Yield: 2 servings.

Freida McIntyre, Fort Smith, AR

DELI TAKE-OUT SPECIAL

1   4½-oz. can corned beef spread
4 slices rye bread
2 slices Muenster cheese
⅔ c. coleslaw

Spread corned beef spread on 2 slices bread. Top with cheese, coleslaw and remaining bread. Yield: 2 servings.

Justine Burleson, Charlotte, NC

DIPWICHES

16 slices white bread
1   5-oz. jar cheese and olive spread
2   12-oz. cans corned beef, chilled
3 eggs
⅔ c. milk
1 tbsp. prepared mustard
2 tsp. caraway seed
2 to 4 tbsp. butter

Spread bread with cheese spread. Slice each can corned beef into 4 slices; place on half the bread slices. Top with remaining bread. Dip each sandwich in mixture of eggs, milk, mustard and caraway seed. Brown on both sides in butter in skillet. Yield: 8 sandwiches.

VEGETABLE BURRITOS

12 flour tortillas
1 c. chopped broccoli
1 c. shredded carrots
1 c. chopped onion
1 c. shredded cabbage
1 c. alfalfa sprouts
1 c. sliced avocado
2 tbsp. chopped dill pickle
¼ c. salad dressing

Wrap tortillas in damp cloth. Warm in oven for 15 minutes. Combine broccoli, carrots, onion and cabbage in glass bowl. Microwave until tender-crisp. Add alfalfa sprouts, avocado and dill pickle; mix gently. Spread tortillas with salad dressing. Spoon vegetable filling into tortillas. Roll tightly to enclose filling. Wrap in plastic wrap. Eat like sandwich.
Yield: 24 servings.

Carol McLennan, Lawton, OK

Salads

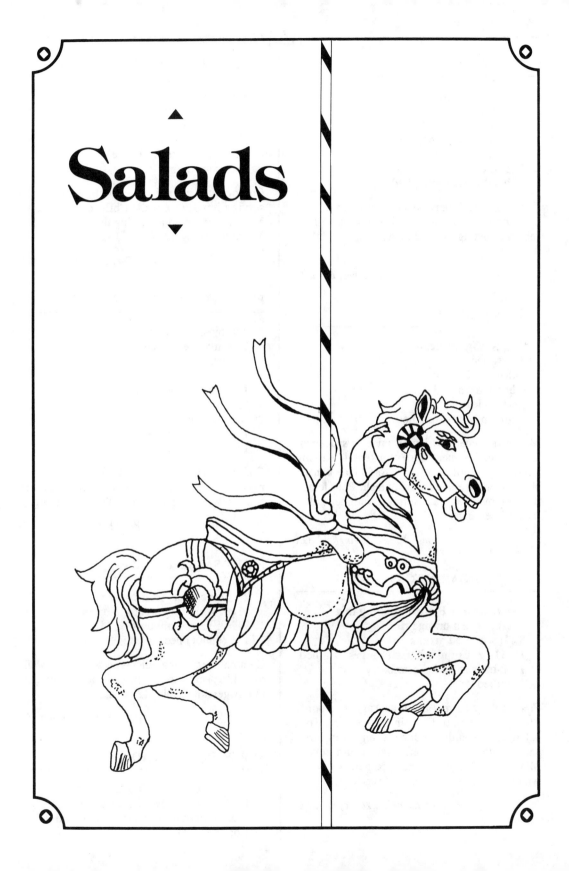

APPLE SALAD

2 apples, chopped
1 banana, sliced
12 red grapes, seeded
2 stalks celery, chopped
½ c. salad dressing
¼ c. milk
½ head lettuce, chopped

Combine first 4 ingredients in bowl. Mix salad dressing and milk in small bowl. Add to fruit mixture; mix lightly. Add lettuce; mix lightly. Yield: 8 servings.

Helen Daws, Lena, IL

BANANA SALAD

2 eggs, slightly beaten
1 c. sugar
Juice of 2 lemons
6 bananas, sliced
Lettuce leaves
Salted peanuts, crushed

Mix eggs, sugar and lemon juice in saucepan. Cook over low heat until thickened, stirring constantly. Chill in refrigerator. Place banana slices on lettuce-lined serving dish. Pour lemon dressing over bananas. Sprinkle with peanuts. Yield: 6 servings.

Betty P. Lee, Springfield, GA

CRAN-MANDARIN TOSS

1 env. creamy French dressing mix
½ tsp. grated orange rind
8 c. torn salad greens
1 11-oz. can mandarin oranges, drained
1 8-oz. can jellied cranberry sauce, chilled

Prepare dressing mix using package directions. Stir in orange rind. Chill in refrigerator. Toss salad greens and mandarin oranges in large salad bowl. Cut cranberry sauce into cubes. Mix with salad green mixture gently. Serve with chilled dressing. Yield: 8 servings.

Terri McLaughlin, Yanceyville, NC

FIVE-CUP FRUIT SALAD

1 c. mandarin oranges, drained
1 c. crushed pineapple, drained
1 c. coconut
1 c. miniature marshmallows
1 c. fruit cocktail, drained
½ c. sour cream

Combine all ingredients except sour cream in serving bowl; mix well. Chill in refrigerator. Mix in sour cream at serving time. Yield: 8 servings.

Kelly Tanner, Creedmoor, NC

FRESH FRUIT SALAD

2 apples, chopped
1 orange, sectioned
1 c. grapes
½ c. raisins
1 grapefruit, sectioned
½ c. mayonnaise
¼ c. honey
1 tbsp. lemon juice
1 tsp. celery seed

Combine fruit in serving bowl. Mix mayonnaise, honey, lemon juice and celery seed in small bowl. Serve over fruit. Yield: 6 servings.

Betty Petty, Wetmore, CO

FRUIT SALAD ROYALE

2 16-oz. cans fruit cocktail, drained
½ pt. whipping cream, whipped
½ bag marshmallows
1 c. (about) pecans

Combine first 3 ingredients in bowl; mix well. Sprinkle pecans over top. Chill for 45 minutes in refrigerator. Yield: 12 servings.

Rosemary Rios, Snyder, TX

SUPER FRUIT SALAD

1 9-oz. carton whipped topping
1 3-oz. package mixed fruit gelatin
1 can pineapple chunks, partly drained
1 banana, sliced

2 apples, chopped
1 orange, sectioned
½ c. grapes, halved
½ c. chopped pecans
1 c. miniature marshmallows

Blend first 2 ingredients in large salad bowl. Stir in fruit. Fold in pecans and marshmallows. Chill for 30 minutes or longer. Yield: 6 servings.

Anjanette Cureton, Elgin, TX

ORANGE-AVOCADO SALAD

2 California avocados, peeled, sliced
3 oranges, peeled, sliced
Iceberg lettuce
¾ c. mayonnaise
¼ c. orange juice
½ tsp. paprika
½ tsp. salt

Alternate slices of avocado and orange on lettuce leaves. Combine remaining ingredients; mix well. Drizzle over salad. Yield: 6 servings.

Sarah Windsor, Wheeling, WV

PEACH HALVES DELIGHT

1   3-oz. package cream cheese, softened
2 to 3 tbsp. salad dressing
¼ c. chopped pecans
4 lg. peach halves, drained

Blend cream cheese and salad dressing in bowl until smooth and creamy. Stir in pecans. Spoon into each peach half. Serve on lettuce-lined plates. Yield: 4 servings.

Monica B. Patterson, Sanford, NC

SPICED WALNUT FRUIT SALAD

2 tsp. butter
⅔ c. California walnuts
1 tbsp. sugar
½ tsp. cinnamon
4 c. shredded crisp lettuce
1 lg. red apple, cut into small wedges
½ c. cranberry halves
1 c. red grapes, seeded

1 c. mayonnaise
2 tbsp. orange juice
¼ tsp. grated orange rind

Melt butter in skillet. Add walnuts. Sprinkle with sugar and cinnamon. Cook over medium heat until walnuts are lightly toasted; cool. Place lettuce in chilled salad bowl. Arrange walnuts and fruits on top. Serve with mixture of mayonnaise, orange juice and rind. Yield: 6 servings.

Annelle Dickson, Indianapolis, IN

CHICKEN SALAD

1 lb. chicken, cooked, chopped
20 grapes, sliced
½ c. chopped pecans
2 or 3 stalks celery, chopped
½ to ¾ c. mayonnaise

Combine all ingredients in bowl; mix well. Chill until serving time. Yield: 4 servings.

Ellen H. Debaugh, Baltimore, MD

SCANDINAVIAN LUNCHEON SALAD

1½ c. mayonnaise
1 tsp. curry powder
½ c. whipping cream, whipped
2 c. cooked rice
2 to 3 c. chopped cooked chicken
2 hard-boiled eggs, cut into wedges
2 med. tomatoes, cut into wedges
2 lg. dill pickles, chopped
½ c. chopped celery
1   16-oz. can peas, drained

Mix mayonnaise and curry powder in bowl; mix well. Fold in whipped cream. Combine remaining ingredients in large bowl. Add half the mayonnaise mixture; mix gently. Turn into lettuce-lined serving dish. Top with remaining mayonnaise mixture. Yield: 8 servings.

Marlene Banttari, St. Paul, MN

Tip: For a quick fruit salad dressing, mix a little honey with yogurt in a flavor chosen to enhance the salad.

FAVORITE TACO SALAD

1 lb ground beef
1 pkg. taco seasoning mix
1 head lettuce, torn
2 tomatoes, chopped
1 green pepper, chopped
1 onion, chopped
2 c. shredded Cheddar cheese
1 pkg. corn chips
1 bottle of Catalina salad dressing

Brown ground beef; drain. Add taco mix using package directions. Combine lettuce, tomatoes, green pepper, onion and cheese in large bowl. Spoon taco sauce over top. Add corn chips and salad dressing just before serving; toss to mix. Yield: 6 servings.

Charles Hodges, Tillman, OK

SALAD FLORENTINE

1   12-oz. can Spam,
    cut into ½-inch cubes
3 tbsp. oil
¼ c. vinegar
1 tbsp. sugar
¼ tsp. pepper
¼ tsp. onion salt
9 c. fresh spinach leaves

Brown Spam in oil in skillet. Add 2 tablespoons water and remaining ingredients except spinach. Simmer for 2 minutes, stirring constantly. Pour over spinach, tossing lightly. Garnish with tomato slices and sliced hard-boiled eggs. Yield: 5 servings.

Debbie Perkins, Okeene, OK

CRAB LOUIS

½ head lettuce, separated
1   6-oz. can claw crab meat,
    drained, mashed
3 hard-boiled eggs, mashed
½ c. mayonnaise
Chili sauce to taste
6 or 8 ripe olives

Arrange lettuce on small serving plate. Spread crab meat and eggs on lettuce. Combine mayonnaise and chili sauce in bowl; mix well. Spoon over crab. Garnish with olives. Yield: 2 servings.

Vivian Jean Brown, San Antonio, TX

APPLE-SALMON SALAD

4 apples
3 pink grapefruit, peeled, sectioned
1 head lettuce, shredded
1   16-oz. can salmon
½ c. chopped celery
¼ c. chopped walnuts
⅓ c. mayonnaise

Core, but do not peel, 3 apples; cut into 12 slices each. Alternate apple slices and grapefruit sections, flower-fashion on bed of lettuce. Combine salmon, remaining ingredients and diced apple; mix well. Core, peel and dice remaining apple. Mound salmon mixture in center of fruit flower. Serve with additional mayonnaise, thinned with a small amount of lemon juice. Yield: 4-6 servings.

Photograph for this recipe below.

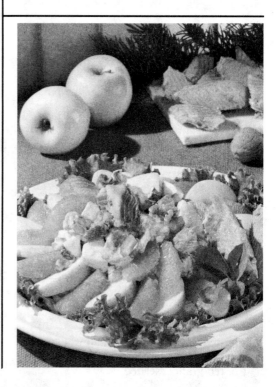

HEARTY SHRIMP SALAD

1 15-oz. can pineapple chunks
½ c. salad dressing
¼ tsp. curry powder
½ tsp. salt
1½ c. shell macaroni, cooked, drained
¾ c. sliced celery
½ c. chopped sweet pickle
½ c. cubed American cheese
2 c. boiled shrimp

Drain pineapple, reserving 2 tablespoons juice. Blend reserved juice with salad dressing, curry powder and salt in small bowl. Mix with macaroni in large bowl. Chill for 1 hour or longer. Stir in celery, pickle, cheese, shrimp and pineapple chunks. Chill until serving time. Yield: 4 servings.

Barbara S. Cribb, Georgetown, SC

JAVA SALAD

1 8-oz. bottle of Green Goddess
salad dressing
3 c. hot cooked rice
¼ c. minced onion
¼ c. raisins
⅔ c. sliced celery
⅓ c. chopped chutney
1 2-oz. can chopped pimento
2 6½-oz. cans tuna
¼ c. each chopped green pepper, parsley
⅓ c. cashews
Honeydew melon slices

Mix salad dressing, rice, onion and raisins in bowl. Chill in refrigerator. Add next 6 ingredients; toss lightly. Sprinkle with cashews. Arrange melon slices on top. Yield: 6-8 servings.

Janice F. Stripes, Spokane, WA

MUSHROOM-TUNA MEDLEY

½ c. oil
¼ c. cider vinegar
2 tsp. celery seed (opt.)
1 tsp. onion powder
1 tsp. salt
¾ tsp. garlic powder
⅛ tsp. pepper
½ lb. fresh mushrooms, sliced
12 cherry tomatoes, halved
1 c. sliced celery
½ lg. red onion, sliced
2 7-oz. cans tuna, drained, flaked

Combine oil, vinegar, celery seed, onion powder, salt, garlic powder and pepper in small bowl. Stir to blend; set aside. Combine mushrooms with tomatoes, celery and onion in large bowl. Add tuna; toss gently. Pour just enough dressing over the salad to coat completely. Serve in lettuce-lined bowl. Refrigerate remaining dressing in covered jar. Yield: 4 servings.

Janie Burke, Franklin, TN

SEACOAST SALAD

1 7½-oz. package macaroni
and cheese dinner
1 8½-oz. can green peas
1 6½-oz. can tuna, drained
¼ c. sweet pickle relish
2 tbsp. chopped onion
1 c. salad dressing

Prepare macaroni and cheese dinner according to package directions. Combine with peas, tuna, relish and onion in bowl. Stir in salad dressing. Chill until serving time. Serve on lettuce-lined plates.

Ben H. Martin, Pickens, SC

TUNA SHOESTRING SALAD

1 6-oz. can tuna, drained
1 c. shredded carrots
1 c. chopped celery
¼ c. minced onion
¾ to 1 c. mayonnaise
1 4-oz. can shoestring potatoes

Combine first 5 ingredients in bowl; toss to mix. Add potatoes just before serving; toss lightly. Yield: 4 servings.

Betty Paul, Stockton, CA

MACARONI SALAD

1   8-oz. package macaroni, cooked
1 c. cubed Cheddar cheese
½ c. chopped sweet pickles
¼ c. minced onion
½ c. chopped celery
½ c. mayonnaise
1 tbsp. mustard
1 tbsp. sugar
Salt to taste
1 c. peas, drained

Combine first 5 ingredients in bowl. Mix mayonnaise with mustard and sugar in bowl. Add to macaroni mixture, mixing well. Stir in salt and peas. Yield: 4 servings.

Lisa R. Barber, Newton, NC

PASTA SALAD

1 lb. pasta twists
1½ c. sliced tomatoes
½ c. sliced mushrooms
1 c. frozen peas
1 c. chopped green onions
¾ c. Parmesan cheese
6 tbsp. pesto sauce
1 stick butter, melted
½ c. cream
Salt and white pepper to taste

Cook pasta in boiling salted water in saucepan for 8 to 10 minutes; drain. Rinse with cold water. Mix with vegetables and Parmesan cheese in bowl. Heat pesto sauce in saucepan. Stir in butter and cream. Pour over salad; toss to coat. Sprinkle with salt and pepper. Serve immediately. Yield: 6 servings.

Gina Loduca, San Joaquin, CA

FAVORITE RICE SALAD

3 c. cooked minute rice, cooled
4 hard-boiled eggs, chopped
¼ c. chopped pimento
½ c. chopped onion
½ c. chopped green pepper
1 c. mayonnaise
1 tbsp. sugar
1 tsp. salt
¼ tsp. pepper
1 tsp. prepared mustard

Combine rice, eggs, pimento, onion and green pepper in large bowl. Combine mayonnaise, sugar, salt, pepper and mustard in small bowl; blend well. Pour over rice mixture; toss lightly to mix. Chill until serving time. Serve on lettuce-lined plates with garnish of tomato wedges and ripe olives. May add 8 ounces tuna, chicken, turkey or ham, if desired.
Yield: 6-8 servings.

Betty Shields, Knoxville, TN

ARTICHOKE SUPPER SALAD

1 pkg. chicken Rice-A-Roni
2 c. cooked rice, chilled
2 green onions, chopped
½ c. chopped green pepper
2 jars artichoke hearts, drained, chopped
Oil from 1 jar artichoke hearts
8 stuffed olives, chopped
½ c. chopped walnuts (opt.)
1 can mushrooms, chopped
¼ tsp. curry powder (opt.)
1 can shrimp
⅛ tsp. salt
Pepper to taste
¾ to 1 c. mayonnaise

Prepare Rice-A-Roni according to package directions. Combine all ingredients except mayonnaise in 2½-quart bowl; mix well. Fold in mayonnaise. Serve on lettuce-lined plates. Yield: 6 servings.

Steve Reckers, Colusa, CA

AVOCADO SALAD

2 lg. ripe avocados, chopped
Juice of 2 limes
¼ tsp. pepper
3 tbsp. finely minced onion
¼ c. mayonnaise

Combine avocado and lime juice in bowl. Mix pepper, onion and mayonnaise in bowl. Add to avocado mixture, tossing lightly. Spoon onto lettuce-lined serving plates. Yield: 4 servings.

Judith C. Beard, Fayetteville, NC

SPICY AVOCADO SALAD

1 lg. ripe avocado
1 lg. firm tomato
1 med. onion
Pepper and garlic salt to taste

Chop avocado, tomato and onion; place in serving bowl. Sprinkle with seasonings; mix well. Chill until serving time. Salad will make its own dressing. Yield: 4 servings.

Carol Sassin, Beeville, TX

KIDNEY BEAN SALAD

2 c. canned kidney beans
1 c. firmly chopped celery
¾ c. chopped sweet pickle
5 hard-boiled eggs, chopped
½ c. Hellmann's mayonnaise
½ c. chopped peanuts

Rinse kidney beans; drain well. Combine kidney beans with remaining ingredients; mix well. Serve in lettuce-lined bowl.
Yield: 5 servings.

Natalie Gross, Orlando, FL

PINTO BEAN SALAD

1   15-oz. can Old El Paso pinto beans,
   drained
¼ c. chopped onion
3 tbsp. chopped pickle
2 tbsp. Old El Paso chopped green chilies
¼ c. salad dressing

Combine all ingredients in bowl; mix well. Chill in refrigerator. Spoon into lettuce-lined salad plate. Yield: 4 servings.

Photograph for this recipe on page 60.

BROCCOLI SALAD

1 lg. head broccoli
1 pkg. Hidden Valley Ranch
   Dressing mix
Pinch each of parsley, basil, dillweed
Lemon juice to taste

1   6-oz. can pitted ripe olives,
   drained, sliced
1 sm. red onion, chopped
½ lb. fresh mushrooms, sliced

Cut broccoli into bite-sized flowerets. Prepare ranch dressing using package directions. Add seasonings and lemon juice. Combine broccoli, olives, onion and mushrooms in large bowl. Toss with dressing.

Catherine Smith, Miami, FL

FRESH BROCCOLI AND TOMATO SALAD

1 bunch fresh broccoli
1 carton cherry tomatoes, halved
6 slices crisp-cooked bacon, crumbled
1 bottle Green Goddess salad dressing
Garlic powder to taste
Juice of ½ lemon

Cut broccoli into bite-sized flowerettes. Toss broccoli, tomatoes and bacon in bowl. Combine remaining ingredients in small bowl, blending well. Add dressing just before serving.

Celeste Kelley, Enterprise, AL

CABBAGE AND PINTO BEAN SALAD

1 c. cold cooked cabbage
1 c. cold cooked pinto beans
1 tbsp. pimento slices
2 tbsp. each olive oil, vinegar
½ tsp. salt
¼ tsp. each pepper, onion powder
Dash of crushed hot pepper

Combine cabbage and beans in bowl. Add pimento; mix well. Mix remaining ingredients in jar; shake to blend. Pour over vegetables; toss until well mixed. Yield: 4-6 servings.

Sally O'Malley, Dallas, TX

Tip: Pick up chopped fresh vegetables at the supermarket produce section or salad bar for quick stir-fries and salads.

CONFETTI COLESLAW

4 c. shredded cabbage
½ c. shredded carrot
1 tsp. salt
1 tsp. sugar
½ c. mayonnaise
1 tbsp. vinegar
1 tbsp. milk
1 sm. red apple, chopped

Combine cabbage and carrot in bowl. Sprinkle with salt and sugar. Mix mayonnaise, vinegar and milk in small bowl. Add to cabbage mixture; mix well. Chill in refrigerator. Stir in apple just before serving. Yield: 8 servings.

Sharon Huey, Seattle, WA

CAESAR SALAD

3 med. heads romaine
2 eggs
8 flat anchovies
⅛ to ¼ tsp. salt
⅛ to ¼ tsp. freshly ground pepper
6 tbsp. lemon juice
Dash of Tabasco sauce
Dash of Worcestershire sauce
½ to ¾ c. olive oil
1½ c. grated Parmesan cheese
14 to 18 garlic croutons

Separate romaine, discarding largest outer leaves. Wash under cold running water; tear large leaves but leave small inner leaves intact. Dry thoroughly with paper towels; wrap in dry kitchen towel. Chill. Cook eggs in rapidly boiling water for 10 seconds. Place anchovies in large salad bowl; mash to make smooth paste. Add salt, pepper, lemon juice, Tabasco sauce, Worcestershire sauce and olive oil; mix well. Add eggs; toss to mix. Add romaine; toss until each piece is well coated. Sprinkle with Parmesan cheese. Scatter croutons over top. Serve immediately. This salad must be assembled at the last minute but eggs can be cooked, romaine washed and base of dressing can be made in advance.

Helen Crain, Nashville, TN

CAULIFLOWER SALAD

1 head cauliflower, cut into flowerets
1 green onion with tops, chopped
2 stalks celery, chopped
1 lg. tomato, chopped
2 hard-boiled eggs, chopped
2 oz. Cheddar cheese, diced
1 c. mayonnaise
1 tbsp. white vinegar
2 tbsp. sugar
1 tsp. salt
¼ tsp. pepper

Combine all ingredients in bowl; mix well. Chill until serving time. Yield: 6-8 servings.

Pamela M. Herndon, Camp Lejeune, NC

LUSCIOUS SALAD

1 head cauliflower
1 bunch broccoli
6 or 7 green onions
1 green pepper
1 c. sour cream
1 c. salad dressing
⅓ c. sugar
1 tbsp. wine vinegar
Dash of Tabasco sauce
Dash of Worcestershire sauce

Cut vegetables in bite-sized pieces; place in large bowl. Combine remaining ingredients; mix well. Pour over vegetables; toss well. Yield: 10 servings.

Joan Carsrud, Carbondale, IL

CORN SALAD

1   16-oz. can whole kernel corn, drained
1   16-oz. can red kidney beans, drained
1 green pepper, chopped
1 red pepper, chopped
1 tsp. sugar
1 c. wine vinegar
1 stalk celery, chopped
½ c. chopped green onion
2 cloves of garlic, minced
1 tsp. lemon juice
Salt and pepper to taste

Combine corn and beans in large bowl. Add remaining ingredients; mix well. Chill thoroughly. Serve on lettuce leaves. Yield: 6-8 servings.

Mabel O. Walters, Baltimore, MD

AUSTRIAN CUCUMBER SALAD

1 c. yogurt
2 tbsp. lemon juice
1 tsp. sugar
½ tsp. salt
Pepper to taste
1 cucumber, peeled, thinly sliced

Combine first 5 ingredients in bowl; mix well. Stir in cucumber gently. Chill until serving time. Yield: 2 servings.

Beth Johnson, Windsor, CO

MUSHROOM SALAD

1 lb. fresh mushrooms, sliced
8 oz. Swiss cheese, diced
2 bunches green onions, thinly sliced
½ c. oil
¼ c. red wine vinegar
1 tbsp. all-purpose Greek seasoning

Combine mushrooms, cheese and green onions in serving bowl. Add mixture of oil, vinegar and seasoning; mix well. Chill until serving time. Yield: 8 servings.

Barbara Morrison, Crescent City, CA

QUICK POTATO SALAD

¼ lb. bacon
2 tbsp. flour
½ c. vinegar
1 tsp. salt
⅛ tsp. pepper
1   16-oz. package frozen
    French-fried potatoes
½ c. thinly sliced onion
1 c. thinly sliced celery
¼ c. chopped parsley

Fry bacon in skillet until crisp. Remove bacon and chop coarsely. Reserve ¼ cup drippings.

Blend flour into reserved drippings in skillet. Add vinegar, ½ cup water and seasonings; mix well. Cook until thickened, stirring occasionally. Add potatoes. Simmer, covered, for 10 minutes. Add onion and celery. Cook for 2 minutes longer. Toss with parsley and crisp bacon. Spoon onto serving plate. Yield: 4-5 servings.

Kathy Blount, Atlanta, GA

SPINACH SALAD

½ bunch spinach
3 slices crisp-cooked bacon, crumbled
2 eggs, chopped
½ c. sliced fresh mushrooms
½ c. olive oil
¼ c. vinegar
⅛ tsp. garlic powder
1 tbsp. prepared mustard
Salt and pepper to taste

Combine spinach, bacon, eggs and mushrooms in wooden salad bowl. Chill in refrigerator. Mix olive oil, vinegar and seasonings in jar with lid. Shake until well mixed. Just before serving, pour enough dressing over salad to coat ingredients and toss to mix. Yield: 4 servings.

Susan D. Commons, Knoxville, TN

SICILIAN TOMATO SALAD

4 med. tomatoes, sliced
1 med. red onion, sliced
Lettuce leaves
½ c. shredded mozzarella cheese
1 tbsp. olive oil
1 tbsp. red wine vinegar
1¼ tsp. crushed basil
1 anchovy fillet, minced
¼ tsp. salt
1 clove of garlic, crushed

Arrange tomato and onion slices on lettuce-lined serving platter. Sprinkle with cheese. Combine remaining ingredients in bowl; mix well. Pour over salad. Let stand for 15 minutes or longer before serving. Garnish with additional anchovies. Yield: 4-6 servings.

Leeane Murphree, Houston, TX

MARINATED TOMATO SALAD

2 c. chopped tomatoes
½ c. sliced pimento-stuffed olives
¼ c. sliced green onions
⅓ c. French dressing
1 avocado, sliced

Combine tomatoes, olives, green onions and salad dressing in bowl. Chill, covered, in refrigerator. Spoon onto lettuce-lined plates. Arrange avocado slices on top.
Yield: 4 servings.

Helen Heath, Muncie, IN

TOMATOES ROSÉ

4 lg. tomatoes
½ c. Rosé wine
⅓ c. oil
3 tbsp. wine vinegar
¼ c. finely chopped celery
¼ c. thinly sliced green onions
1 env. Italian salad dressing mix

Slice tomatoes thinly; arrange in shallow dish. Combine remaining ingredients in covered jar; shake vigoursly. Pour over tomatoes. Chill, covered, until serving time. Arrange tomato slices on serving platter; garnish with celery leaves. Serve with dressing. Yield: 6 servings.

JoAnn J. Kresky, Lansing, MI

FRESH GRAPEFRUIT-SPINACH SALAD

½ c. oil
2 tbsp. fresh lemon juice
2 tbsp. vinegar
1 tsp. sugar
1 tsp. grated lemon rind
½ tsp. each salt, dry mustard
1   10-oz. package fresh spinach
3 grapefruit, peeled, sectioned

Combine first 7 ingredients in jar; shake vigorously. Wash spinach; pat dry. Tear into bite-sized pieces. Combine spinach and grapefruit in salad bowl. Add prepared dressing; toss lightly. Serve immediately.
Yield: 6 servings.

HOMINY SALAD

2 cans hominy, drained
¼ c. chopped celery
¼ c. chopped green pepper
¼ c. shredded carrots
¼ c. chopped green onions
½ c. sour cream
¼ c. mayonnaise
2 tbsp. vinegar
1 tbsp. mustard

Combine hominy and vegetables in serving bowl. Blend sour cream, mayonnaise, vinegar and mustard in small bowl. Add to hominy mixture; mix well. Chill until serving time.
Yield: 8 servings.

Prexy Pegram, Boerne, TX

WILTED LETTUCE SALAD

4 slices bacon, chopped
3 eggs, beaten
¼ c. cider vinegar
2 tsp. sugar
¼ tsp. salt
⅛ tsp. pepper
½ tsp. dried dillweed (opt.)
4 c. shredded leaf lettuce
⅓ c. chopped green onions

Fry bacon in 10-inch skillet. Beat eggs with vinegar, sugar, salt, pepper and dillweed. Add to skillet. Cook for several minutes until heated through, stirring constantly; remove from heat. Add lettuce and green onions. Toss until wilted. Spoon into serving dish. Serve immediately.
Yield: 4 servings.

Norma Grace Bauer, Altamont, IL

Tip: *Carving a head of lettuce with a knife causes the surrounding area to discolor more quickly. Leave core intact or remove by striking core end on kitchen counter and twisting out core with fingers.*

Meats

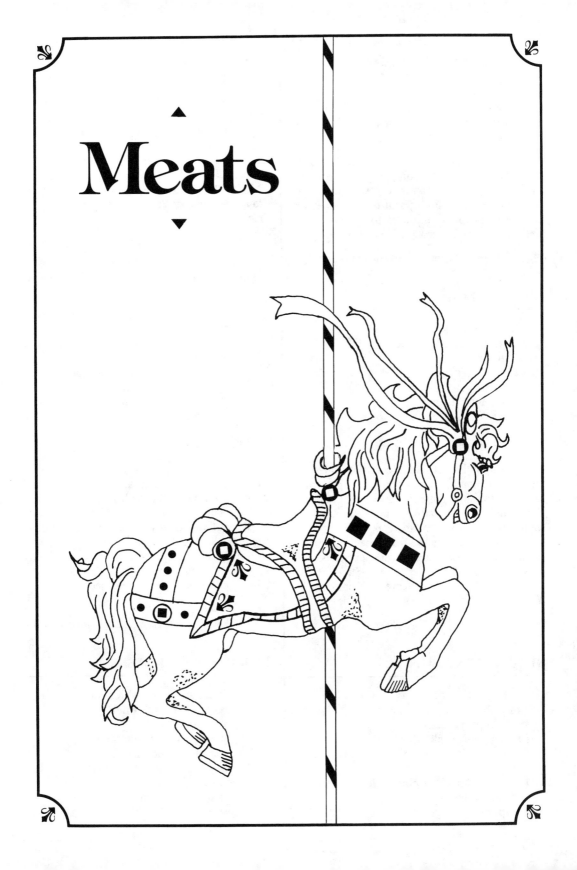

CALIFORNIA ROUND STEAK

1 lb. round steak
Salt and pepper to taste
1 can cream of mushroom soup
1 pkg. dry onion soup mix

Place steak in baking pan. Season with salt and pepper. Spoon mushroom soup over steak. Sprinkle dry onion soup mix over top. Cover pan completely with foil; seal tightly. Bake at 350 degrees for 45 minutes to 1 hour or to desired degree of doneness. Yield: 4 servings.

Tonya Cuthbertson, Monroe, NC

LONDON BROIL

1 lb. flank steak
2 med. onions, thinly sliced
¼ tsp. salt
1 tbsp. butter
2 tbsp. oil
1 tsp. lemon juice
2 cloves of garlic, crushed
½ tsp. salt
¼ tsp. pepper

Place steak on broiler rack. Score both sides of steak in diamond pattern, ⅛ inch deep. Sauté onions with salt in butter in skillet until tender. Set aside, keeping warm. Combine remaining ingredients in bowl. Brush steak with half the sauce. Broil 2 to 3 inches from heat source for 5 minutes. Turn steak and brush with remaining sauce. Broil for 5 minutes longer. Slice across the grain into thin slices. Serve with onions. Yield: 4 servings.

Doris Stiles, Louisville, KY

STEAK POLYNESIAN

6 cube steaks
2 tbsp. butter
¼ c. chopped onion
1 green pepper, sliced
½ tsp. salt
⅛ tsp. pepper
1   20-oz. can sliced pineapple
⅓ c. soy sauce
3 tbsp. brown sugar

1 tsp. ginger
2 tbsp. cornstarch

Brown steaks in butter in skillet. Add onion, green pepper, salt and pepper. Brown lightly. Add pineapple, soy sauce, brown sugar and ginger. Heat through. Arrange steak, pineapple slices and green pepper on serving platter. Stir cornstarch blended with ⅓ cup cold water into skillet. Cook until thick, stirring constantly. Pour over cube steaks. Serve over rice. Yield: 6 servings.

Joan Wilson, Springfield, OH

EASY PEPPER STEAK

1½ lb. sirloin steak, cut into thin strips
1 tbsp. paprika
2 cloves of garlic, crushed
2 tbsp. butter
1 c. sliced green onions with tops
2 green peppers, cut into strips
2 lg. tomatoes, chopped
1 c. beef broth
2 tbsp. cornstarch
2 tbsp. soy sauce
3 c. cooked rice

Sprinkle steak with paprika; let stand for several minutes. Brown steak with garlic in butter in skillet. Add green onions and green peppers. Cook until vegetables are tender-crisp. Stir in tomatoes and broth. Simmer, covered, for 15 minutes. Stir in mixture of cornstarch, soy sauce and ¼ cup water. Cook until thickened, stirring constantly. Serve over rice. Yield: 6 servings.

Brenda D. Long, Richlands, VA

STIR-FRY PEPPER STEAK

1 lb. flank steak, sliced diagonally
    cross grain ⅛ inch thick
¼ c. peanut oil
2 lg. green peppers, chopped
2 lg. tomatoes, chopped
⅓ c. soy sauce
2 tbsp. dry Sherry
1 clove of garlic, minced
Cornstarch

Cut steak into 2½ to 3-inch strips. Preheat oil in wok to 325 degrees for about 2 minutes. Add beef slices, ⅓ at a time. Stir-fry for 1 minute after each addition. Stir-fry for 2 minutes longer. Make well in center; add green peppers and tomatoes. Stir-fry for about 2 minutes. Make well in center; add soy sauce, Sherry, garlic and enough cornstarch to thicken. Bring to a boil without stirring. Cook for 1 minute longer or until thickened, stirring constantly. Yield: 4 servings.

May Lee Barstow, Cleveland, OH

STIR-FRY BEEF AND SNOW PEAS

1 tbsp. cornstarch
¾ tsp. sugar
1 tsp. soy sauce
2 tsp. Sherry
½ lb. lean beef, thinly sliced cross grain
½ tsp. salt
1 wedge fresh ginger, crushed
3 tbsp. oil
½ lb. snow peas
¼ c. stock
Dash of pepper

Combine 1 teaspoon cornstarch, ¼ teaspoon sugar, soy sauce and Sherry in bowl. Add beef; toss to coat. Stir-fry salt and ginger in 1½ tablespoons oil in wok for several seconds. Stir in snow peas until oil-coated. Add stock. Cook, covered, over medium heat for 30 seconds. Remove snow peas and pan juices. Stir-fry beef in remaining 1½ tablespoons oil until brown. Add snow peas and juices. Stir-fry until heated through. Stir in mixture of remaining 2 teaspoons cornstarch, ½ teaspoon sugar, pepper and 2 teaspoons water. Cook until thick, stirring constantly. Yield: 4 servings.

Pat Becker, Wild Rose, WI

STIR-FRY BEEF WITH BROCCOLI

4 tbsp. oil
1 tbsp. cornstarch
1 tbsp. soy sauce
1½ lb. round steak, thinly sliced
2 green onions, sliced
1 bunch fresh broccoli, chopped

Combine 1 tablespoon oil, cornstarch and soy sauce in bowl. Add steak slices; mix well. Brown onions in 2 tablespoons oil in skillet. Add steak, cooking until brown. Add remaining oil and broccoli. Stir-fry for 3 to 5 minutes. Yield: 6 servings.

Jo Burroughs, Trinity, NC

STEAK AND ZUCCHINI SUPPER

1 lb. round steak, cut into thin strips
1 tbsp. oil
1 10½-oz. can mushroom gravy
½ env. spaghetti sauce mix
   with mushrooms
3 med. zucchini, sliced 1½-inch thick

Brown steak in hot oil in skillet. Stir in gravy, ½ cup water and spaghetti sauce mix. Simmer, covered, for 20 minutes, stirring occasionally. Add zucchini. Cook for 10 to 20 minutes longer or until zucchini is tender-crisp. Serve over noodles or rice. Yield: 4 servings.

Kathleen Monteiro, San Diego, CA

QUICK BEEF STEW

1½ lb. ground beef
1 pkg. stew seasoning mix
1 16-oz. can tomatoes
1 lg. onion, chopped
6 potatoes, peeled, cubed
1 lg. package frozen mixed vegetables
½ tsp. salt

Combine ground beef, seasoning mix, tomatoes, onion and water in to cover in soup pot; mix well. Simmer for several minutes. Add potatoes. Bring to a boil. Add vegetables and salt; mix well. Cook until vegetables are tender. Yield: 6 servings.

Christy Kennedy, Osage, OK

Tip: Cooking frozen beef without pre-thawing saves time and the beef also retains more flavor, more juices and more nutritive value.

BEEF AND MUSHROOM STROGANOFF

3 lb. sirloin, trimmed,
    cut into small cubes
1¼ c. Sauterne
1 can beef bouillon
1 tsp. garlic salt
1 tsp. seasoned pepper
¼ tsp. dried dillweed
3 tbsp. flour
½ lb. mushrooms
½ c. chopped green onion
½ c. shortening
1½ c. sour cream

Brown sirloin in large heavy saucepan. Remove sirloin; set aside. Stir 1 cup wine and bouillon into pan drippings. Add garlic salt, pepper and dillweed. Return sirloin to saucepan. Simmer, tightly covered, until tender. Blend flour with ¼ cup wine; stir into pan juices. Cook for 10 minutes or until thickened, stirring constantly. Sauté mushrooms and onion in shortening in skillet until tender; drain. Add to sirloin. Stir in sour cream before serving. Yield: 6-8 servings.

Celeste Holman, Mena, AR

BEEF AND GREEN BEAN CASSEROLE

1 lb. ground beef
1 can French-style green beans,
    drained
1 sm. can sliced mushrooms,
    drained
1 sm. package slivered almonds
1 can cream of celery soup
1 can cream of mushroom soup
1 sm. package Tater Tots

Sauté ground beef in skillet until lightly browned; drain. Toss ground beef with green beans, mushrooms and almonds in bowl. Combine soups with 1 soup can hot water in bowl; mix well. Pour over green bean mixture; toss lightly. Spoon into casserole. Arrange Tater Tots over top. Bake at 350 degrees for 25 minutes or until brown. Yield: 6 servings.

Mrs. Brett W. Slusser, Agra, OK

DORITO CASSEROLE

1 lb. ground beef
1 sm. can chopped green chili peppers
1 can enchilada sauce
1 can cream of mushroom soup
1 can cream of chicken soup
1 pkg. Doritos
1 pkg. Monterey Jack cheese, grated

Brown hamburger in skillet, stirring until crumbly. Pour off drippings. Add next 4 ingredients; mix well. Cook until bubbly. Spread Doritos in baking dish. Spoon soup mixture over Doritos. Top with cheese. Bake at 400 degrees until cheese melts.
Yield: 6 servings.

Mary Lue Reed, Spiro, OK

QUICK TACO CASSEROLE

½ lb. lean ground beef
1 sm. onion, chopped
1 sm. can ripe olives,
    drained, sliced
1   12-oz. can tomato paste
1 pkg. taco seasoning mix
1   8-oz. package tortilla chips
2 c. grated mild Cheddar cheese

Brown ground beef and onion in skillet, stirring frequently. Add olives, tomato paste and 3 paste cans water. Stir in seasoning mix. Simmer for 5 minutes. Layer tortilla chips, ground beef mixture and cheese in 4-quart casserole. Bake at 350 degrees for 10 minutes or until cheese melts. Yield: 8 servings.

Scott Eric Holder, El Dorado, CA

GREEN CHILI ENCHILADAS

1 lb. ground beef
Garlic, salt and pepper to taste
1 can chopped green chilies
1 sm. package corn tortillas
1 carton French onion dip
1 sm. can evaporated milk
Monterey Jack cheese
Picante sauce

Sauté hamburger with seasonings in skillet until brown and crumbly. Stir in green chilies. Fill each tortilla with spoonful chili mixture; roll and place in casserole. Combine next 3 ingredients in saucepan. Cook over low heat until blended, stirring constantly. Pour over enchiladas. Top with picante sauce. Bake at 350 degrees for 20 minutes. Yield: 6 servings.

Jill Ritchie, Enid, OK

COMANCHE CHILI

2 lb. lean ground beef
4   15-oz. cans ranch-style beans
1 can Ro-Tel tomatoes and green chilies
1   10-oz. package chili seasoning
1 tsp. cayenne pepper
1½   15-oz. cans tomato juice

Brown ground beef in large saucepan, stirring until crumbly; drain. Stir in remaining ingredients. Simmer for 30 minutes. Yield: 8 servings.

Scott Jackson, Comanche, OK

MY BEST CHILI CON CARNE

1 lg. onion, chopped
1 clove of garlic, minced
4 tbsp. chopped green pepper
4 tbsp. oil
1 lb. lean ground beef
2 tbsp. chili powder
1   28-oz. can tomatoes, chopped
1   6-oz. can tomato paste
1 tbsp. sugar
3   15-oz. cans pinto beans

Sauté onion, garlic and green pepper in oil in skillet for 2 minutes. Add ground beef. Brown lightly, stirring until crumbly. Stir in chili powder. Add tomatoes with juice, tomato paste and sugar; mix well. Cook over medium heat for 20 minutes; stir occasionally. Add beans. Simmer for 20 minutes, stirring frequently. Yield: 8 servings.

Evelyn Martone, Kent County, MD

SPICY MICROWAVE BEEF CHILI

2 lb. ground beef, crumbled
1 lg. onion, chopped
1 lg. green pepper, chopped
1   29-oz. can tomatoes, chopped
2 to 3 tbsp. chili powder
1 tsp. salt
Dash each of cayenne pepper, paprika
1   15-oz. can kidney beans, drained
1   6-oz. can tomato sauce

Brown ground beef in glass baking dish in microwave for 7 minutes, stirring twice; drain. Microwave onion and green pepper in 2 tablespoons water in glass baking dish for 2 minutes. Combine with ground beef and remaining ingredients in large ovenproof serving bowl; mix well. Microwave, covered, for 12 minutes, stirring once. Let stand, covered, for 5 minutes before serving. Yield: 8 servings.

Jan Tuchscherer, Durango, CO

FIESTA RICE

1 lb. ground beef
¼ c. chopped celery
¾ c. chopped green pepper
1   7-oz. box minute rice
1   16-oz. can tomato sauce
¼ tsp. garlic powder
1 tbsp. salt
1 tsp. each sugar, chili powder
1 bay leaf

Brown hamburger with celery in skillet, stirring until crumbly. Combine hamburger mixture with remaining ingredients in large saucepan, mixing well; cover. Bring to a boil. Simmer for 15 to 20 minutes or until rice is tender. Yield: 6 servings.

Brenda Simmons, Dayton, TX

Tip: Buy ground beef in quantities. Microwave in colander in bowl to catch drippings. Freeze in measured portions for later use.

MICROWAVE ONE-STEP LASAGNA

1 lb. ground beef, crumbled
32 oz. spaghetti sauce
1 tsp. salt
8 oz. lasagna noodles
2 c. cottage cheese
3 c. shredded mozzarella cheese
½ c. Parmesan cheese

Microwave ground beef on High in 2-quart glass casserole for 5 to 6 minutes; drain. Stir in spaghetti sauce, ½ cup water and salt. Microwave, covered, on High for 5 to 6 minutes or until heated through. Layer ⅓ of the sauce, half the noodles, 1 cup cottage cheese and half the mozzarella cheese in 9x13-inch casserole. Repeat layers, ending with sauce. Sprinkle with Parmesan cheese. Microwave, tightly covered, on High for 30 to 35 minutes or until bubbly. Let stand for 5 minutes before serving. Yield: 6-8 servings.

Brenda Brandt, LaCrosse, WI

SWEET AND SOUR MEATBALLS

1½ lb. ground beef
3 tbsp. pickle relish
1 green onion top, chopped
1½ tsp. soy sauce
1½ tsp. monosodium glutamate
¾ tsp. salt
¼ tsp. pepper
1 tbsp. oil
1 tbsp. cornstarch
2 tbsp. sugar
¾ c. fresh tangerine juice
1 tbsp. fresh lemon juice
2 tsp. grated tangerine rind
1½ c. California tangerine sections

Combine ground beef, pickle relish, green onion top, soy sauce, monosodium glutamate, salt and pepper in bowl; mix well. Shape into 2-inch balls. Brown evenly in oil in skillet. Simmer, covered, for 5 minutes. Remove to warm plate. Drain skillet, reserving 2 table-spoons drippings. Combine cornstarch and sugar in bowl. Blend in ¼ cup tangerine juice. Add remaining tangerine juice, lemon juice and grated tangerine rind; mix well. Stir into hot reserved drippings in skillet. Cook until thickened, stirring constantly. Add tangerine sections. Heat for 1 minute. Arrange meatballs on bed of hot rice. Spoon tangerine sauce over top. Yield: 4 servings.

Photograph for this recipe below.

MINI MEAT LOAVES

1 lb. ground beef
1 egg, beaten
¼ c. soft bread crumbs
1   1-serving env. instant
    onion soup mix
1   1-serving env. instant
    tomato soup mix
1   8-count can refrigerator
    crescent dinner rolls

Combine ground beef, egg, bread crumbs and soup mixes in bowl; mix well. Shape into 4 loaves. Separate rolls into 4 rectangles, pressing perforations to seal. Place 1 dough rectangle on each meat loaf, shaping to cover top and sides; trim excess dough. Prick dough with fork; garnish with trimmings. Place loaves in shallow baking pan. Bake at 350 degrees for 30 minutes or until golden brown.
Yield: 2 servings.

Sonya Jones, Lexington, SC

CORNED BEEF HASH STACKS

1 round can corned beef hash, chilled
1 onion, sliced
1 tomato, sliced
4 to 6 slices sharp cheese

Open chilled hash can at both ends; push out of can. Cut into 4 to 6 slices. Place on broiler pan. Top each hash slice with 1 slice onion and 1 slice tomato. Broil until heated through. Place 1 slice cheese on top. Broil until cheese is melted.
Yield: 4-6 servings.

Georgia W. Magers, Baltimore, MD

MACARONI-CORNED BEEF BAKE

1 pkg. macaroni and cheese dinner
1 tbsp. butter
2 c. chopped corned beef

Combine macaroni and cheese and butter with 2½ cups boiling water in 2-quart casserole. Add corned beef; mix well. Bake, covered, at 375 degrees for 20 to 25 minutes. Yield: 4 servings.

Charlene Charles, Boone, NC

BRITTANY SKILLET

¼ c. oil
4 lg. potatoes, peeled, thinly sliced
1 onion, finely chopped
1   8-oz. ham steak,
    cut into 3x½-inch strips
Salt and pepper to taste
4 eggs, well beaten
4 oz. Cheddar cheese, shredded

Heat oil in 11-inch skillet. Layer half the potatoes, onion and ham in skillet. Repeat layers with remaining potatoes and onion. Season with salt and pepper. Simmer, covered, for 20 minutes or until potatoes are tender. Arrange remaining ham spoke fashion over top. Pour eggs over all. Cook, covered, for 10 minutes. Top with cheese. Cook for 2 minutes longer or until cheese is melted.
Yield: 4 servings.

Elaine T. Bovee, Lompoc, CA

HAM JAMBALAYA

1½ c. rice
1 med. onion, minced
1 med. green pepper, diced
1 clove of garlic, crushed
1   16-oz. can tomatoes
1   13¾-oz. can chicken broth
1 bay leaf
½ tsp. salt
½ tsp. thyme leaves
1 lb. cooked ham, cubed
½ lb. shrimp
3 or 4 drops of hot pepper sauce
5 slices crisp-cooked bacon, crumbled

Sauté rice, onion, green pepper and garlic in bacon drippings in skillet until rice is lightly browned. Stir in tomatoes, broth, bay leaf, salt and thyme. Simmer, covered, for 15 minutes. Add ham, shrimp and hot pepper sauce. Cook, covered, for 15 to 20 minutes or until rice is tender, stirring occasionally. Spoon onto serving platter. Sprinkle with bacon.
Yield: 6 servings.

Joyce Dixon, Hendersonville, NC

Tip: Bake meat loaf in greased muffin cups for a quick meal.

HAM-BROCCOLI ROLLS

2   10-oz. packages frozen
     broccoli spears, cooked
16 thin slices cooked ham
2 cans cream of shrimp soup
½ c. dry white wine

Wrap each broccoli spear in ham slice. Arrange in 6x10-inch casserole. Blend soup and wine in bowl. Pour over ham rolls. Bake at 350 degrees for 20 to 25 minutes or until bubbly. Yield: 8 servings.

Jerome Melton, Raleigh, NC

MICROWAVE HAM-POTATO BAKE

1 can cream of chicken soup
½ c. milk
Dash of pepper
4 c. sliced potatoes
1 c. diced cooked ham
1 sm. onion, sliced
1 tbsp. butter
Paprika to taste

Combine soup, milk and pepper in small mixing bowl; mix well. Layer potatoes, ham, onion and soup mixture in 8x8x2-inch glass baking dish. Dot with butter. Sprinkle with paprika. Microwave on High for 15 minutes. Yield: 4 servings.

Tammy Winslow, Huntsville, AL

STIR-FRY DINNER

1 c. chopped onions
2 tbsp. low-fat margarine
½ c. chopped green pepper
1 c. chopped celery
1 c. chopped cabbage
1 c. sliced squash
1 c. chopped broccoli
1 c. sliced mushrooms
1 c. snow peas
1 c. chopped ham
3 tbsp. soy sauce
1 tsp. ginger

Stir-fry onions in margarine in wok for 3 minutes. Add remaining vegetables 1 at a time in order given. Stir-fry each for 1 to 2 minutes; push each to side before adding next vegetable. Add ham; sprinkle with soy sauce and ginger. Combine all ingredients. Heat to serving temperature. Serve over rice. Yield: 4 servings.

Alice Brooks, Des Moines, IA

QUICHE LORRAINE

½ c. mayonnaise
½ c. milk
2 eggs
1 tbsp. cornstarch
1½ c. cubed cooked ham
1½ c. chopped Swiss cheese
⅓ c. sliced green onions
Dash of pepper
1 unbaked 9-in. pie shell

Combine mayonnaise, milk, eggs and cornstarch; beat until smooth. Add ham, cheese, onions and pepper; mix well. Pour into pie shell. Bake at 350 degrees for 35 to 40 minutes or until knife blade inserted near center comes out clean. Yield: 6 servings.

Dorothy N. Ball, Somerset, NJ

YAM-HAM CASSEROLE

2   16-oz. cans Louisiana yams,
     drained, mashed
1   8-oz. jar sweetened applesauce
2 tbsp. melted butter
½ tsp. ginger
¼ tsp. salt
1   1½-lb. slice cooked ham
¼ c. chopped walnuts
2 tbsp. melted butter

Beat yams in mixer bowl until light and fluffy. Blend in applesauce, 2 tablespoons butter and seasonings. Place ham in baking dish. Spoon yams around ham. Sprinkle walnuts over yams. Drizzle 2 tablespoons butter over ham. Bake at 325 degrees for 35 minutes. Broil until lightly browned if desired. Garnish with parsley. Yield: 6 servings.

Lisa Jewitt, Tyler, TX

MICROWAVE LAMB WITH ORANGE MINT SAUCE

1   6-oz. can frozen orange juice
¼ c. lemon juice
¼ c. butter or margarine
½ tsp. salt
1   4-lb. lamb shoulder
½ c. finely chopped celery
½ c. blanched almonds, slivered
1 tbsp. mint flakes

Combine orange juice, lemon juice, butter and salt in 1-quart glass casserole. Microwave on High for 3 minutes. Place shoulder in 9-inch glass cake dish; brush with small amount of orange juice mixture. Microwave on High for 35 minutes or until of desired doneness, brushing with orange juice mixture and rotating dish frequently. Add celery, almonds and mint flakes to remaining orange juice mixture. Microwave on High for 5 minutes. Garnish lamb with orange slices and parsley. Serve with orange-mint sauce. Yield: 8 servings.

Carolyn Tucker, Winchester, KY

MICROWAVE PORK AND CABBAGE

1 to 1½-lb. boneless pork,
    cut into 1-inch cubes
1 can Cheddar cheese soup
4 med. carrots, shredded
2 tsp. brown sugar
1 tsp. salt
¼ tsp. caraway seed
Dash of pepper
1 tsp. vinegar
5 c. shredded cabbage

Place pork in 2½-quart glass casserole. Cover. Microwave on High for 8 to 10 minutes or until meat is no longer pink. Stir in soup, carrots, brown sugar, salt, caraway seed, pepper and vinegar. Cover. Microwave on High for 5 to 6 minutes or until mixture boils. Add cabbage. Cover. Microwave on High for 12 to 15 minutes or until pork and cabbage are tender, stirring every 5 minutes. Yield: 6 servings.

Myra Phelps, Greg Bull, WY

CRANBERRY PORK CHOPS

6 pork chops
1 can whole berry cranberry sauce
1 can cream of mushroom soup

Brown pork chops in a small amount of shortening in Dutch oven. Pour cranberry sauce over chops. Cover with soup. Bake, covered, at 350 degrees for 45 minutes or until chops are tender. Yield: 6 servings.

Connie Y. Crouch, Palatka, FL

FORTY-FIVE MINUTE PORK CHOP DINNER

6 pork chops
1 tbsp. shortening
4 potatoes, sliced
4 sm. onions, sliced
6 carrots, sliced
1 can peas, drained

Brown pork chops in shortening in large skillet. Remove three pork chops; add half the sliced vegetables in layers. Add remaining pork chops and sliced vegetables. Pour in peas. Add ½ cup hot water; cover. Simmer for 30 minutes. Yield: 6 servings.

Sandy Nease, Atchison, KS

MICROWAVE ITALIANO CHOPS

1   8-oz. can mushrooms, drained
1 c. chopped green pepper
1 med. onion, sliced
1   16-oz. can tomatoes, drained
1 tsp. each oregano, salt
¼ tsp. pepper
½ tsp. garlic powder
4 pork chops

Combine all ingredients except pork chops in 3-quart glass casserole; mix well. Arrange pork chops on top; cover. Microwave on Roast for 20 to 25 minutes, turning pork chops halfway through cooking cycle. Yield: 4 servings.

Carla Dodge, Prescott, AZ

MICROWAVE SMOKED PORK CHOPS

2 c. drained sauerkraut
1 sm. onion, chopped
2 med. apples, chopped
1 tbsp. sugar
4 smoked pork chops

Combine sauerkraut, onion, apples and sugar in bowl; mix well. Spread half the sauerkraut mixture in 2-quart glass baking dish. Place pork chops over sauerkraut mixture. Cover with remaining sauerkraut mixture. Pour ½ cup water over top. Cover. Microwave on High for 5 minutes. Microwave on Defrost for 6 to 8 minutes or until apples are tender.
Yield: 4 servings.

Sue Hepburn, San Diego, CA

BREAKFAST SCHNITZEL

2 breakfast pork chops, pounded thin
½ c. flour
½ c. milk
1 egg, well beaten
1 c. crushed saltine crackers
½ tsp. salt
Shortening for frying

Coat pork chops with flour. Dip in milk, then egg; coat with cracker crumbs. Sprinkle with salt. Fry in ½-inch deep shortening in skillet for 3 to 4 minutes on each side or until tender.
Yield: 2 servings.

Sabrina Brooking, Comanche, OK

MICROWAVE SPANISH PORK CHOPS

1   15½-oz. jar spaghetti sauce
¾ c. long-grain rice
1½ tsp. instant chicken bouillon
¾ tsp. salt
Dash of pepper
½ c. sliced black olives
1 med. onion, sliced
6 pork loin chops

Combine spaghetti sauce, rice, bouillon, salt, pepper, olives, onion and 1⅔ cups water in 2-quart glass baking dish; mix well. Cover.

Microwave on High for 5 minutes. Arrange pork chops on top; cover loosely. Microwave on High for 15 minutes. Turn and rearrange chops; stir rice. Cover tightly. Microwave on High for 10 to 15 minutes longer or until chops and rice are tender. Yield: 6 servings.

Cindy Longworth, Cedar Rapids, IA

BREAKFAST CASSEROLE

1 lb. sausage
4 slices bread, torn
1 c. grated sharp Cheddar cheese
6 eggs, beaten
2 c. milk
1 tsp. dry mustard
1 tsp. salt
Dash of pepper

Brown sausage in skillet; drain. Layer bread, sausage and cheese in 9 x 13-inch baking dish. Combine remaining ingredients in bowl; beat well. Pour over layers. Bake at 350 degrees for 35 to 40 minutes. Yield: 6-8 servings.

Eleanore Walsh, Worcester County, MD

BREAKFAST PIZZA

1 lb. hot pork sausage
1 pkg. refrigerator crescent rolls
1½ c. frozen hashed brown potatoes, thawed
1 c. shredded sharp Cheddar cheese
1 c. shredded Swiss cheese
5 eggs
¼ c. milk
½ tsp. salt
¼ tsp. pepper
2 tbsp. Parmesan cheese

Brown sausage in skillet, stirring until crumbly; drain. Separate rolls into 8 triangles; press over bottom and side of 12-inch pizza pan, sealing edges. Layer sausage, potatoes and Cheddar and Swiss cheese over top. Combine eggs, milk, salt and pepper in bowl; mix well. Pour over cheese. Sprinkle with Parmesan cheese. Bake at 375 degrees for 25 to 30 minutes or until set. Yield: 4-8 servings.

Mona L. Butler, Charlotte, NC

SAUSAGE JAMBOREE

½ lb. fresh mushrooms, sliced
¼ c. butter
1   1-lb. can French-style green beans,
     drained
½ c. minute rice
1   1-lb. can stewed tomatoes
¼ tsp. salt
½ lb. brown-and-serve sausage
½ c. shredded sharp Cheddar cheese

Sauté mushrooms in butter in skillet until tender. Add green beans; sprinkle rice over beans. Cover with tomatoes; season with salt. Cover. Simmer for 20 minutes or until rice is tender. Cook sausage in skillet until brown; drain. Place sausage on tomatoes; sprinkle cheese over sausage. Heat for 5 minutes or until cheese is melted. Yield: 6 servings.

Susan Carothers, Murrysville, PA

SAUSAGE QUICHE

1   9-in. pastry shell
½ lb. sausage
1 c. chopped fresh mushrooms
¼ c. chopped onion
2 to 3 tbsp. chopped green pepper
4 oz. Gruyère cheese, chopped
1 c. cream
3 eggs, well beaten
¼ tsp. salt

Bake pastry shell at 350 degrees for 10 to 12 minutes; set aside. Brown sausage in skillet, stirring until crumbly. Remove sausage; reserve drippings. Sauté mushrooms, onion and green pepper in reserved drippings for 5 minutes. Combine sausage, mushroom mixture, cheese, cream, eggs and salt in bowl; mix well. Pour into pastry shell. Bake at 350 degrees for 45 minutes or until quiche tests done.
Yield: 6 servings.

Kathy O'Brien, Baton Rouge, LA

VEAL PICCATA

1 lb. veal, thinly sliced
1 egg, beaten
Flour

Oil
8 oz. broth
1 tbsp. cornstarch
¼ to ½ c. white wine
2 tsp. parsley
⅛ tsp. garlic powder
2 tbsp. lemon juice
Salt and pepper to taste

Dip veal into egg then into flour to coat. Brown in oil in skillet; remove and keep warm. Add broth to pan juices, stirring to blend in meat particles. Combine cornstarch and wine and stir into broth with remaining ingredients. Cook until thickened, stirring constantly. Pour over veal and garnish with lemon slices.
Yield: 4 servings.

Kathleen O'Malley, North Arlington, NJ

SAUTÉED VEAL SCALLOPINI

2 tbsp. oil
¼ c. butter
1 lb. veal, thinly sliced
¾ c. flour
Salt and pepper to taste
1 tbsp. lemon juice
1 tsp. capers
2 tbsp. parsley flakes
½ lemon, sliced

Heat oil and 2 tablespoons butter in skillet over medium heat. Coat veal with flour; add to skillet. Brown on both sides. Transfer to warm platter; season with salt and pepper. Remove skillet from heat. Add lemon juice, capers, parsley and remaining butter; mix well with pan drippings. Warm sauce over medium heat; do not boil. Pour sauce over veal. Garnish with lemon slices. Yield: 4 servings.

Velma Simpson, Marshall, TX

Tip: When comparing the cost of different cuts of meat, consider cost per serving rather than cost per pound. A boneless roast may yield more servings than a cheaper cut with bone.

LIVER DINNER

1 lb. calves liver
¼ c. flour
¼ c. butter
1 med. onion, sliced
1   19-oz. can tomatoes
1 tsp. sugar
1 tsp. salt
⅛ tsp. pepper
1 tsp. Worcestershire sauce
¼ tsp. basil
1½ c. grated cheese

Cut liver into thin strips. Coat with flour. Brown in butter in skillet over low heat. Add onion. Sauté for several minutes. Add tomatoes and seasonings. Simmer, covered, for 15 minutes. Add cheese. Cook until melted, stirring constantly. Yield: 4-6 servings.

Doris Decker, Kingston, Ontario, Canada

FRIED LIVER STRIPS

8 slices bacon
1 lb. calves liver
1 bottle of French salad dressing
Flour
1 can French-fried onion rings

Fry bacon in skillet until crisp. Drain, reserving drippings. Cut liver into 1-inch strips. Dip in salad dressing; coat with flour. Brown in reserved bacon drippings. Garnish with bacon slices and onion rings.

Betty Rose Griffin, Bedford, IN

ONE-POT MACARONI DINNER

1½ lb. ground beef
1 med. onion, chopped
1 green pepper, chopped
2 c. uncooked macaroni
2   8-oz. cans tomato sauce
1 tsp. salt
¼ tsp. pepper
1 tbsp. Worcestershire sauce

Brown ground beef, onion and green pepper in large skillet, stirring until crumbly; drain. Stir in macaroni, remaining ingredients and 1½

cups water. Simmer, covered, for 25 minutes or until macaroni is tender, stirring occasionally and adding a small amount of water if necessary. Yield: 4-6 servings.

POLYNESIAN WIKI-WIKI

1   16-oz. can lunch meat
1 tbsp. cornstarch
⅓ c. pineapple juice
1 tbsp. vinegar
½ tsp. Worcestershire sauce
¼ tsp. prepared mustard
1 tsp. soy sauce
1   16-oz. can pineapple tidbits
1 tomato, chopped
½ green pepper, sliced
½ c. chopped celery
3 c. cooked rice

Chop lunch meat into ¾-inch cubes. Brown lightly in skillet. Blend cornstarch, pineapple juice, vinegar, Worcestershire sauce, mustard, soy sauce and 1 cup water in bowl. Stir into skillet. Cook until thickened, stirring constantly. Add next 4 ingredients. Simmer for 5 minutes. Serve over rice. Yield: 4 servings.

Lela Green, Tacoma, WA

HOT DOG SKILLET

1½ lb. hot dogs
¼ lb. sliced bacon, chopped
1 med. onion, chopped
1   16-oz. can whole kernel corn, drained
1   16-oz. can kidney beans, drained
Salt and pepper to taste

Slice hot dogs thinly. Sauté with bacon and onion in skillet until bacon is crisp; drain. Add remaining ingredients. Cook over medium heat for 15 minutes. Serve over rice or corn bread. Yield: 6 servings.

Barbara Cormier, Sulphur, LA

Tip: Salt sprinkled in the pan before browning meat will keep it from sticking.

Poultry

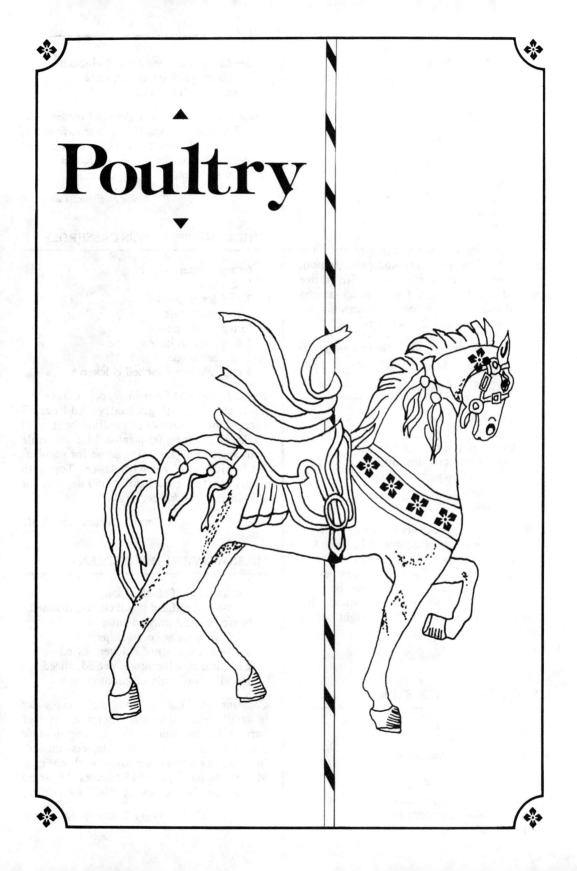

ARROZ CON POLLO

6 chicken thighs
Salt and pepper
2 tbsp. olive oil
1 or 2 cloves of garlic, minced
1 sm. onion, chopped
¼ green pepper, chopped
1 c. yellow rice mix
1 tsp. ground cumin
1 can peas
Pimentos

Season chicken with salt and pepper. Brown in olive oil in heavy skillet. Add garlic, onion, green pepper and water to cover. Stir in rice mix and cumin. Cook, covered, for 25 minutes or until tender. Stir in peas and pimentos just before serving. Yield: 2-4 servings.

Kathy S. Noble, Somerset County, MD

BARBECUED CHICKEN

2 c. vinegar
1 c. sugar
¼ to ½ tsp. red pepper
2 tbsp. Worcestershire sauce
1 to 2 tbsp. margarine
Tomato sauce
1 chicken, cut up

Combine first 5 ingredients and enough tomato sauce to color in saucepan; mix well. Bring to a boil; remove from heat. Arrange chicken in 9 x 13-inch casserole. Bake at 350 degrees for 25 minutes. Pour sauce over chicken. Broil for 10 minutes on each side or until browned. May marinate chicken in sauce overnight before baking. Yield: 4 servings.

Carolyn Evans Rose, Buxton, NC

QUICK BRUNSWICK STEW

1 c. sliced onions
3 tbsp. oil
2   16-oz. cans tomatoes
½ c. Sherry
1 env. beef stew seasoning mix
1   10-oz. package frozen lima beans
1 tbsp. Worcestershire sauce
½ tsp. salt

3½ to 4 c. chopped cooked chicken
1   10-oz. package frozen okra
1 sm. zucchini, sliced

Sauté onions in oil in skillet until tender. Add next 7 ingredients and ½ cup water. Simmer, covered, for 15 minutes. Add chicken, okra and zucchini. Simmer for 10 minutes longer. Yield: 6 servings.

Helen Eagleton, Tulsa, OK

CHICKEN-ASPARAGUS CASSEROLE

6 tbsp. butter
½ c. flour
2 c. chicken broth
1 c. mayonnaise
½ tsp. curry powder
1 tbsp. lemon juice
1 can asparagus
4 cups chopped cooked chicken

Blend butter and flour in saucepan over low heat; stir in broth gradually. Add next 3 ingredients. Cook over medium heat until thickened, stirring frequently. Line casserole with asparagus, reserving some for garnish. Add chicken; cover with sauce. Top with reserved asparagus. Bake at 350 degrees for 30 minutes. Yield: 8 servings.

Patricia Morgan, Laurel, MT

MICROWAVE CHILI CHICKEN

1 can cream of chicken soup
1   4-oz. can diced green chilies, drained
¼ tsp. instant minced onion
1   6-oz. package corn chips
2   5-oz. cans boned chicken, diced
2 lg. firm ripe tomatoes, peeled, sliced
1 c. shredded mild Cheddar cheese

Combine soup, chilies, onion and ½ cup water in small bowl; mix well. Alternate layers of corn chips, chicken, tomatoes, soup mixture and cheese in 2-quart glass baking dish until all ingredients are used ending with cheese. Microwave on High for 15 minutes. Let stand for 5 minutes before serving. Yield: 6 servings.

Peggy O. Munter, Moore, OK

CHICKEN AND ARTICHOKE HEARTS SUPREME

4 chicken breast filets
2 tbsp. oil
½ tsp. garlic powder
1 1-lb. can artichoke hearts, drained
2 1-lb. cans peeled whole tomatoes, drained
½ c. pitted ripe olives
½ c. white wine

Sauté chicken breasts in oil in skillet until tender. Place chicken on warm serving platter. Add garlic powder and artichoke hearts to pan drippings. Sauté for several minutes. Add tomatoes, olives and wine. Cook until heated through. Serve with chicken. Yield: 4 servings.

Patricia Tengel, Potomac, MD

EASY CHICKEN AND RICE

1¾ c. minute rice
½ stick margarine, melted
1 can cream of mushroom soup
1 can cream of chicken soup
1 can cream of celery soup
6 chicken breast filets

Combine first 5 ingredients and ½ soup can water; mix well. Pour into 9 x 12-inch baking pan. Arrange chicken over rice mixture; cover with aluminum foil. Bake at 400 degrees for 30 minutes; remove foil. Bake for 40 minutes longer or until rice is browned. Let stand for 10 minutes. Yield: 6 servings.

Helen McCubbins, Salisbury, MO

CHICKEN PICCATA

1 egg
1 tbsp. lemon juice
¼ c. flour
⅛ tsp. each garlic powder, paprika
4 to 6 chicken breast filets
¼ c. margarine
2 tsp. instant chicken bouillon
2 tbsp. lemon juice

Beat egg with 1 tablespoon lemon juice in bowl. Combine flour with garlic powder and paprika. Dip chicken in egg mixture; coat with seasoned flour. Brown in margarine in skillet. Dissolve bouillon in ½ cup boiling water. Stir in 2 tablespoons lemon juice. Pour over chicken. Simmer for 20 minutes.
Yield: 4 servings.

Noreen Mehrtens, Sarasota, FL

CHICKEN SPECTACULAR

3 c. chopped cooked chicken
1 pkg. long grain and wild rice
1 can cream of celery soup
1 med. onion, chopped
1 c. mayonnaise
1 can water chestnuts, drained, chopped
1 med. jar chopped pimentos
1 can French-style green beans
Salt and pepper to taste

Combine all ingredients in large bowl; mix well. Spoon into 9 x 13-inch baking dish. Bake at 350 degrees for 25 to 30 minutes or until bubbly. May prepare casserole and freeze to bake later. Yield: 6 servings.

Doris Sanders, Johnson City, TN

CURRIED CHICKEN

6 frozen breaded chicken breast
  filets, thawed
1 stick butter
1 tbsp. curry powder
1½ c. white wine
1 c. cream
3 c. chopped celery
2 lg. apples, chopped
2 c. minute rice, cooked

Cut chicken into bite-sized pieces. Brown in butter in skillet. Stir in curry powder. Add wine. Bring to a boil. Stir in cream. Sprinkle celery over chicken; reduce heat. Simmer, covered, for several minutes. Add apples. Simmer, covered, until apples are just tender. Place rice on serving platter. Spoon chicken over rice. Yield: 6-8 servings.

Mary Holcomb, Rusk, TX

CHICKEN ROLLS IN WINE

4 chicken breast filets
4 slices boiled ham
4 slices Swiss cheese
1 egg
Bread crumbs
¼ c. oil
2 tbsp. flour
Salt and pepper to taste
¾ c. chicken broth
½ c. white wine

Pound chicken breasts with meat mallet until thin. Cover each with 1 slice ham and 1 slice cheese; roll up. Fasten with toothpicks. Beat egg with 2 tablespoons water. Dip chicken rolls in egg mixture. Coat with bread crumbs. Brown in hot oil in skillet. Remove to platter; keep warm. Stir flour, salt and pepper into oil. Cook until brown. Add broth and wine. Cook until thick, stirring constantly. Pour over chicken. Yield: 4 servings.

Betty A. Armacost, Carroll County, MD

GREEN CHILIES WITH CHICKEN

2   10-oz. cans Old El Paso
    green chili enchilada sauce
1   7½-oz. can Old El Paso
    taco sauce
12 Old El Paso tortillas
2 tbsp. shortening
3 c. chopped cooked chicken
2 c. shredded Cheddar cheese
1 c. chopped onion
1 c. sour cream

Bring enchilada sauce and taco sauce to a simmer in saucepan. Fry tortillas 1 at a time in hot shortening in skillet for several seconds; drain. Dip tortillas in hot sauce mixture. Place 4 tortillas in large shallow baking dish. Sprinkle each tortilla with chicken, cheese, onion, sour cream and 1 tablespoon sauce mixture. Repeat layers. Top with remaining tortillas. Pour remaining sauce over stacks. Bake at 325 degrees for 30 minutes. Serve with guacamole and tortilla chips. Yield: 4 servings.

Photograph for this recipe below.

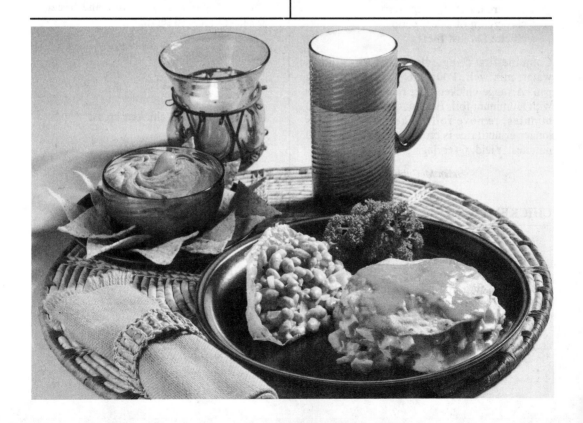

CHICKEN TETRAZZINI

1 green pepper, finely chopped
½ stick margarine
5 tbsp. flour
1 c. milk
1 can cream of chicken soup
1 can cream of mushroom soup
4 cups chopped cooked chicken
1 lg. can mushrooms, drained
2 tsp. soy sauce
½ lb. Cheddar cheese, grated
¼ lb. spaghetti, cooked
Garlic salt to taste

Sauté green pepper in margarine in skillet until tender. Blend in flour. Stir in milk. Cook until thick, stirring constantly. Mix in soups and chicken. Add remaining ingredients; mix well. Spoon into baking dish. Top with additional cheese. Bake at 325 degrees for 30 minutes. Yield: 6-8 servings.

Betty L. Warrenfeltz, Washington County, MD

CITRUS POACHED CHICKEN BREASTS

1 c. Florida orange juice
¾ c. chicken broth
2 scallions, chopped
2   6-oz. chicken breast filets
1½ tbsp. flour
1 bunch watercress
1 Florida orange peeled, sectioned

Combine orange juice, broth and scallions in saucepan. Simmer for 2 minutes. Add chicken breasts; cover with waxed paper. Simmer for 20 to 30 minutes or until tender. Place chicken on heated plate; cover with waxed paper. Combine ½ cup poaching liquid with flour; mix well. Bring remaining poaching liquid to a boil. Stir in flour mixture. Cook until sauce is thickened, stirring constantly. Blanch watercress in boiling water for 15 seconds; drain. Arrange watercress on serving plate. Place chicken breasts on watercress. Spoon a portion of sauce over chicken. Garnish with orange sections. Serve immediately with remaining sauce. Yield: 2 servings.

MICROWAVE CORDON BLEU

4 chicken breast filets
4 slices boiled ham
4 slices mozzarella cheese
1 egg white, beaten
1 c. fresh bread crumbs
1 stick butter, melted
1 tsp. salt
¼ tsp. paprika

Pound chicken breasts with meat mallet until thin. Place 1 slice ham and cheese on each chicken breast. Roll up; secure with toothpicks. Dip in egg white; roll in crumbs. Place in buttered glass baking dish. Pour butter over top. Sprinkle with remaining crumbs, salt and paprika. Microwave on Medium for 10 minutes. Microwave on High for 5 minutes, turning dish 1 time. Yield: 4 servings.

Sandi Jenkins, Elk City, OK

MICROWAVE CHICKEN DIVAN

2   10-oz. packages frozen
      chopped broccoli
1 chicken, cooked, chopped
1 can cream of chicken soup
2 c. grated Cheddar cheese
1 can French-fried onion rings

Place broccoli in 9 x 13-inch glass baking dish. Microwave on High for 3 minutes. Arrange chicken on top. Sprinkle with cheese. Cover with soup. Microwave, covered, on High for 7 minutes. Turn dish 180 degrees. Microwave for 8 minutes longer. Top with onion rings. Microwave for 1 minute longer. Yield: 4-6 servings.

Juli Hadfield, Noble, OK

Tip: For quick chicken and dumplings, tear flour tortillas. Place in canned chicken broth and cook until tender. Add canned chunk chicken.

MICROWAVE CHICKEN WITH WILD RICE

- 1   6-oz. package brown
  and wild rice mix
- ¼ lb. mushrooms, sliced
- ¼ c. dry Sherry
- 2 lb. chicken breasts and thighs
- Paprika

Reserve 1 tablespoon rice seasoning mix. Combine remaining seasoning with rice, mushrooms, Sherry and 1⅓ cups hot water in 7x11-inch glass baking dish. Cover. Microwave on High for 15 minutes; stir rice. Season chicken pieces with reserved seasoning mix. Arrange chicken skin side up over rice. Sprinkle with paprika; cover. Microwave on High for 12 to 15 minutes or until chicken is no longer pink near bone, turning dish every 5 minutes. Let stand for 5 minutes.
Yield: 4 servings.

Rochelle Vinson, Caldwell, MT

EASY MICROWAVE ORANGE CHICKEN

- 1   2½ to 3-lb. chicken, cut up, skinned
- ¼ c. chopped onion
- ¼ c. chopped green pepper
- ⅓ c. orange juice
- ⅓ c. catsup
- 2 tbsp. flour
- 2 tbsp. soy sauce
- 1 tsp. prepared mustard
- ½ tsp. salt
- ½ tsp. garlic powder
- ¼ tsp. pepper

Arrange chicken in 2-quart glass casserole with larger pieces around edge. Top with onion and green pepper. Mix remaining ingredients in bowl. Pour over chicken. Microwave, covered, on High for 20 to 24 minutes or until tender. Let stand for 5 minutes before serving. Garnish with orange slices. Yield: 6 servings.

Carolyn Jackson, Newton, KS

MOZZARELLA CHICKEN

- 1 c. bread crumbs
- 3 tbsp. Parmesan cheese
- 2 tbsp. chopped parsley
- 4 chicken breast filets
- 1 c. flour
- 1 tsp. salt
- ½ tsp. pepper
- 1 egg, beaten
- ¼ c. margarine
- 4 oz. Italian cooking sauce
- 4 slices mozzarella cheese

Combine bread crumbs, Parmesan cheese and parsley in bowl; mix well. Dredge chicken in flour seasoned with salt and pepper. Dip into egg; coat with crumb mixture. Brown chicken in margarine in skillet. Place in 8x8-inch baking dish. Pour cooking sauce over chicken. Top with cheese slices. Bake at 350 degrees for 15 minutes or until cheese melts.
Yield: 4 servings.

Karen Gattis, Friendswood, TX

MICROWAVE APRICOT CHICKEN

- 8 chicken pieces
- ¼ c. mayonnaise
- 1 pkg. dry onion soup mix
- ½ c. Russian dressing
- 1 c. apricot preserves

Arrange chicken in 9x13-inch glass baking dish with largest pieces around edges. Combine remaining ingredients in bowl; mix well. Spread over chicken. Microwave, covered, on High for 10 minutes. Turn dish 180 degrees. Microwave for 8 to 12 minutes longer. Let stand for 5 to 10 minutes. Yield: 8 servings.

Traci Foshee, McLoud, OK

OVEN-FRIED CHICKEN

- 2 tbsp. mustard
- Tabasco sauce, Worcestershire
  sauce and vinegar to taste
- 1 c. evaporated milk
- 2 broiler-fryers, cut up
- 1½ c. cornflake crumbs
- 2 tsp. salt
- 1 tbsp. paprika

Combine first 5 ingredients in bowl; mix well. Dip chicken in mixture. Coat with mixture of cornflake crumbs, salt and paprika. Place skin side up in foil-lined baking dish. Bake at 400 degrees for 45 minutes or until tender. Yield: 8 servings.

Sharron Coker, Knoxville, TN

PECAN-BREADED CHICKEN BREASTS

    4 chicken breast filets
    12 tbsp. butter
    4 tbsp. Dijon mustard
    6 oz. pecans, finely ground
    2 tbsp. safflower oil
    ⅔ c. sour cream
    ½ tsp. salt
    ¼ tsp. freshly ground pepper

Flatten chicken breasts between 2 pieces of waxed paper with meat mallet. Melt 8 tablespoons butter in saucepan; remove from heat. Whisk in 3 tablespoons mustard. Dip chicken pieces into butter mixture; coat generously with pecans. Melt remaining 4 tablespoons butter with oil in heavy skillet. Sauté chicken for 3 minutes on each side. Place in baking dish. Bake in preheated 200-degree oven for about 20 minutes. Drain excess drippings and pecans from skillet; deglaze with sour cream. Whisk in remaining 1 tablespoon mustard, salt and pepper. Place a small portion of sauce on warmed plate; cover completely with a serving of chicken. Yield: 4 servings.

Betty Dunn, Nashville, TN

CHICKEN AND BROCCOLI POTPIES

    1   10-oz. can refrigerator flaky biscuits
    ⅔ c. shredded Cheddar cheese
    ⅔ c. crisp rice cereal
    2 tbsp. butter (opt.)
    1 c. chopped cooked chicken
    1 can cream of chicken soup
    1   10-oz. package frozen chopped
        broccoli, cooked, well drained
    ⅓ c. slivered almonds
    1 recipe cheese sauce

Press each biscuit into ungreased muffin cup to cover bottom and side form ¼-inch rim. Spoon 1 tablespoon each cheese and cereal into each cup; dot with butter. Combine chicken, soup and broccoli in bowl; mix well. Spoon ⅓ cup chicken mixture over cereal; sprinkle with almonds. Bake at 375 degrees for 20 to 25 minutes or until biscuit cups are golden brown. Serve with cheese sauce. May be refrigerated up to 2 hours before baking or loosely wrapped in foil, for 18 to 20 minutes. Yield: 10 potpies.

Marian Miles, Nashville, TN

CHICKEN-IN-A-GARDEN

    1½ c. chopped cooked chicken
    1 can cream of chicken soup
    1 can Veg-All, drained
    1 can French-fried onions
    1 baked 9-in. pie shell

Combine chicken, soup, Veg-All and half the onions in bowl; mix well. Pour into pie shell. Bake at 350 degrees for 30 minutes. Sprinkle remaining onions over pie. Bake until onions are toasted. Yield: 6 servings.

Martha Tyra, Booneville, MS

CHICKEN PIE WITH VEGETABLES

    1 can refrigerator biscuits, separated
    1 can cream of mushroom soup
    2 c. chopped cooked chicken
    1 c. carrots, cooked
    1 can sweet peas
    ½ c. chopped celery

Roll biscuits thin. Line casserole, reserving several biscuits for top crust. Combine remaining ingredients in bowl; mix well. Spoon over biscuits. Top with reserved biscuits to form crust. Bake in moderate oven until golden brown. Yield: 4 servings.

Karen Conder, Monroe, NC

Tip: Buy chicken in quantities and bake or stew. Store meal-sized portions of chopped chicken in plastic bags in freezer—ready for a busy-day meal.

QUICK CHICKEN BREASTS

6 thin slices ham
6 chicken breast filets
1 can cream of chicken soup
½ cup Durkee Famous Sauce

Place 1 slice ham on each chicken breast. Roll to enclose ham; secure with toothpick. Place in shallow baking dish. Spread with mixture of soup and Durkee Sauce. Bake, covered, at 350 degrees until tender. Yield: 6 servings.

Phyllis McDuffie, Mesquite, TX

SAUCY CHICKEN

2 chicken breasts, skinned, boned
½ c. chopped onion
½ c. chopped green pepper
1 clove of garlic, minced
1 tbsp. oregano
1   4-oz. jar mushrooms
1   8-oz. can tomato sauce
¼ c. white wine
½ tbsp. chopped parsley

Cut chicken into bite-sized pieces. Brown, covered, in a small amount of oil in skillet for 5 to 10 minutes. Remove and drain. Sauté onion, green pepper and garlic in oil in skillet. Add chicken and remaining ingredients. Simmer, covered, for 15 to 20 minutes or until tender. Serve over spaghetti. Yield: 2 servings.

Sharon Mastrocco, Oklahoma City, OK

CHINESE ALMOND CHICKEN

2 chicken breast filets
1 egg, slightly beaten
½ c. flour
Salt and pepper to taste
3 tbsp. corn oil
3 c. chicken stock
1 tbsp. soy sauce
¼ c. slivered almonds, finely chopped
1 tbsp. cornstarch
⅓ head cabbage, shredded
½ tsp. sugar
1 bunch green onions, finely chopped
¼ c. slivered almonds

Dip chicken breast into beaten egg; coat with seasoned flour. Sauté in 2 tablespoons oil in skillet for 10 minutes. Slice into ½-inch strips; set aside. Bring chicken stock to boiling point in saucepan. Add soy sauce, finely chopped almonds and cornstarch. Cook until thickened, stirring constantly; set aside. Stir-fry cabbage with sugar in remaining oil in skillet for 3 minutes. Arrange on serving dish. Place chicken over cabbage; pour sauce over top. Sprinkle green onions and slivered almonds over all. Yield: 2 servings.

Larry Lee, Nashville, TN

STIR-FRY CHICKEN AND BROCCOLI

8 chicken breast filets
¼ tsp. ginger
¼ tsp. pepper
1 bunch fresh broccoli
1 c. chopped scallions
⅔ c. chicken broth
1 tsp. salt
½ tsp. sugar
1 tbsp. cornstarch
¼ c. chicken broth
¼ c. Parmesan cheese

Cut chicken into bite-sized pieces. Sprinkle with ginger and pepper. Slice broccoli thinly crosswise. Stir-fry chicken in hot oil in wok for 3 minutes or until golden brown; push to side. Add broccoli and scallions. Stir-fry for 3 minutes. Add mixture of ⅔ cup broth, salt and sugar. Simmer, covered, for 2 minutes. Blend cornstarch with ¼ cup broth. Stir into skillet. Cook for 1 minute, stirring constantly. Stir in Parmesan cheese. Serve over rice. Yield: 6 servings.

Adeline Smith, Harvey, LA

Tip: Baked or roasted chicken has fewer calories than stewed chicken. Remove skin to further reduce calories.

FRUITED STIR-FRY

1 lb. chicken breast filets
2 tbsp. safflower oil
1 c. fresh pear wedges
1 c. red apple chunks
¼ c. green grapes
¼ c. chopped walnuts
¼ c. Port
¾ c. apple juice
1 tbsp. cornstarch
1 tsp. salt
1 tsp. sugar
1 tsp. paprika
½ tsp. cinnamon

Partially freeze the chicken for easier slicing if desired. Cut into ½-inch strips. Stir-fry in hot oil in wok for 2 minutes. Add fruit and walnuts. Stir-fry for 1 to 2 minutes. Add mixture of remaining ingredients. Cook for 1 minute, stirring constantly. Serve over steamed brown rice. Yield: 4 servings.

WEST COAST CHICKEN SAUTÉ

4 chicken breast filets
Flour
2 tbsp. oil
2 tbsp. butter, melted
¾ c. orange juice
¼ c. dry white wine
1 c. sliced fresh mushrooms
2 tbsp. chopped parsley
½ tsp. rosemary

Pound chicken breasts with meat mallet. Coat lightly with flour. Brown in mixture of oil and butter in skillet. Add remaining ingredients. Simmer for about 5 minutes or until chicken is tender; remove chicken to warm serving platter. Cook pan drippings until slightly thickened. Pour over chicken. Garnish with orange sections and avocado slices. Yield: 4 servings.

Betsy Koonce, San Diego, CA

GAME HENS WITH MUSTARD

6 tbsp. melted butter
2 tbsp. oil
3 Rock Cornish game hens, split, trimmed
Salt and pepper to taste
6 tbsp. Dijon mustard
3 tbsp. minced green onions
½ tsp. (or more) thyme
½ tsp. basil
2 c. fresh white bread crumbs

Combine butter and oil in small bowl. Brush over game hens; arrange skin side down, on greased broiler rack. Broil 5 to 6 inches from heat source for about 10 minutes on each side, basting if necessary. Drain excess drippings; reserve. Sprinkle with salt and pepper. Mix mustard, green onions and herbs in small bowl. Beat in half the reserved drippings until creamy. Brush over game hens; coat with crumbs. Arrange skin side down, on broiler rack; drizzle with half the remaining drippings. Broil slowly until golden brown, turning once and basting with remaining drippings. Yield: 3 servings.

Valerie Meyer, Ann Arbor, MI

GOURMET CORNISH HEN

¼ c. chopped onion
1 clove of garlic, chopped
½ c. shredded zucchini
½ tsp. tarragon
Pinch of salt
2 tbsp. Parmesan cheese
2 tsp. lemon juice
1 22-oz. Cornish game hen

Sauté onion and garlic in a small amount of oil in skillet. Add zucchini, tarragon and salt; cool. Stir in cheese and lemon juice. Cut hen through breast and remove keel bone. Stuff vegetable mixture carefully under skin. Place skin side up in shallow baking pan. Bake at 375 degrees for 45 minutes or until tender and brown. Yield: 2 servings.

Rosanna Fahl, Oroville, CA

CRUNCHY TURKEY STRATA

1½ cans chow mein noodles
1 can water chestnuts, sliced
3 or 4 stalks celery, sliced thin
2 c. chopped cooked turkey
2 cans cream of mushroom soup
1 med. onion, minced
½ c. broken cashews

Spread half the noodles in buttered 2-quart casserole. Combine next 5 ingredients in bowl with ½ soup can water; mix well. Spread over noodles. Sprinkle remaining noodles over top. Bake at 350 degrees for 40 minutes. Top with cashews. Bake for 20 minutes longer.
Yield: 6 servings.

Karin Bargar, Lansing, MI

TURKEY-ALMOND CASSEROLE

1   8-oz. package frozen mixed
     vegetables in onion sauce
Milk
1   6-oz. package noodles
     with chicken-almond mix
2 c. cubed cooked turkey
2 tbsp. butter
½ c. crushed potato chips

Prepare vegetables according to package directions, substituting milk for water. Combine with noodles, sauce mix, turkey and butter in bowl. Stir in 2⅓ cups boiling water; mix well. Pour into 1½-quart casserole. Bake, covered, at 375 degrees for 25 minutes. Mix well. Sprinkle with chips and almonds from noodle mix. Bake for 5 to 10 minutes longer. Let stand for 5 minutes before serving.
Yield: 4 servings.

Rita Brown, Salem, MA

TURKEY-NOODLE BAKE

1½ c. milk
1 can cream of mushroom soup
3 eggs, beaten
3 oz. noodles, cooked
2 c. chopped cooked turkey
1 c. bread crumbs
1 c. shredded cheese

¼ c. chopped green pepper
¼ c. melted butter
2 tbsp. chopped pimento

Blend milk and soup in bowl. Stir in eggs. Add noodles, turkey, bread crumbs, cheese, green pepper, butter and pimento; mix well. Spoon into 7 x 12-inch baking dish. Bake at 350 degrees for 30 to 40 minutes.
Yield: 6-8 servings.

Debbie Barnhill, Worland, WY

QUICK TURKEY CASSEROLE

2 c. chopped cooked turkey
1 c. peas
1 c. chopped celery
1   10-oz. can mushrooms, drained
½ c. (or more) gravy
½ onion, chopped
Salt and pepper to taste
Bread crumbs

Combine turkey, peas, celery, mushrooms, gravy, onion and seasonings in 2-quart casserole; mix well. Cover with bread crumbs. Bake at 425 degrees for 35 minutes.
Yield: 6 servings.

Ruth Mowat, Manitoba, Canada

TURKEY CHEESEBURGER PIE

1 pkg. refrigerator crescent dinner rolls
1 lb. ground fresh turkey
Onion flakes to taste
1   8-oz. can tomato sauce
Italian seasoning to taste
4 oz. mozzarella cheese, shredded

Separate roll dough. Arrange triangles in pie plate; press to seal edges. Brown ground turkey with onion flakes in heavy nonstick skillet, stirring until crumbly. Stir in tomato sauce and Italian seasoning. Spoon into prepared plate. Top with cheese. Bake at 375 degrees for 12 minutes or until crust is golden brown. Cut into wedges. Yield: 4 servings.

Carol Cronister, Cantrall, IL

Seafood

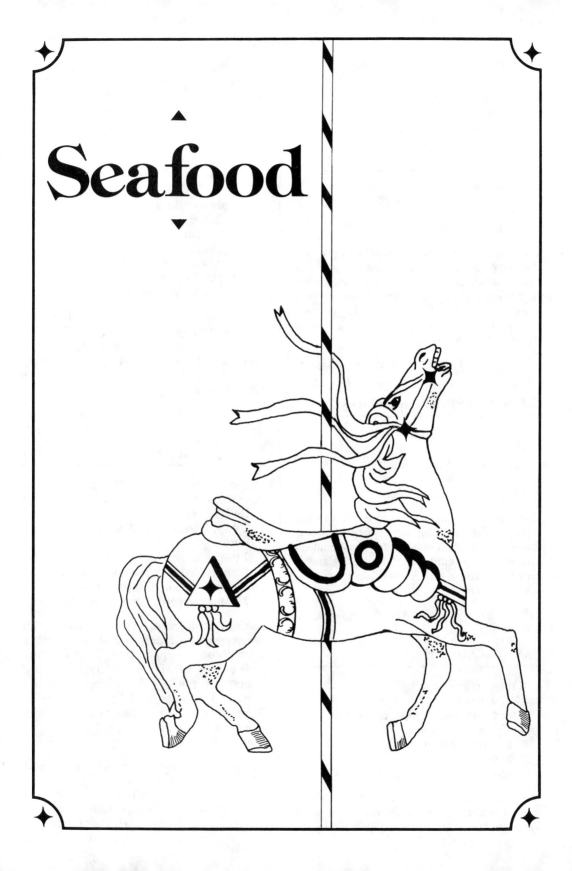

BAKED FISH WITH TOMATO SAUCE

2 pkg. frozen fish fillets,
  partially thawed
2 tbsp. minced onion
1 clove of garlic, minced
1 tbsp. butter
2 8-oz. cans tomato sauce
1 tsp. sugar
½ tsp. Worcestershire sauce
2 tbsp. lemon juice
Chopped parsley (opt.)

Cut fish into 6 portions. Arrange in greased shallow baking dish. Sauté onion and garlic in butter in skillet until tender. Add remaining ingredients except parsley. Simmer for 5 minutes. Pour over fish. Bake at 400 degrees for 20 to 25 minutes. Sprinkle with chopped parsley. Yield: 6 servings.

Eva Jane Schwartz, Gettysburg, PA

COUNTRY-FRIED FISH FILLETS

2 eggs
¼ c. mustard
½ tsp. seafood seasoning
1½ lb. fish fillets
Country-style mashed potato flakes

Combine first 3 ingredients in bowl, beating well. Dip fish in egg mixture. Coat with potato flakes. Fry in hot oil in skillet for 3 to 4 minutes on each side or until fish flakes easily and is browned. Garnish with parsley flakes.
Yield: 6 servings.

Anne Wilson, Morganton, NC

EASY BAKED FISH

2 tbsp. Italian dressing
¼ c. lemon juice
1 med. bag potato chips, crushed
¼ c. Parmesan cheese
1 tbsp. dried parsley
1 lb. fish
2 tbsp. oil

Blend dressing with lemon juice in shallow dish. Combine crushed potato chips with Parmesan cheese and parsley. Dip fish in lemon juice mixture. Coat with potato chip mixture. Arrange fish on baking sheet; drizzle with oil. Bake at 500 degrees for 10 to 15 minutes or until fish tests done. Yield: 4 servings.

Rachel Palmer, Knoxville, TN

FISH BAKED IN ONION SAUCE

3 c. sliced onions
⅓ c. butter
4 tbsp. flour
1 tsp. salt
2 c. milk
1 lb. fish fillets
½ c. dry buttered bread crumbs

Sauté onions in butter in skillet until golden. Blend in flour and salt. Stir in milk. Cook until thickened, stirring constantly. Place fish in greased 6 x 10-inch baking dish. Cover with sauce. Top with crumbs. Bake at 375 degrees for 30 minutes. Yield: 4 servings.

Donna Bingaman, Mifflinburg, PA

SUNNY CITRUS FILLETS

1 lb. frozen fish fillets, thawed
½ tsp. salt
Dash of pepper
2 tbsp. finely chopped onion
Butter
2 tbsp. orange or lemon juice
1 tsp. grated orange or lemon rind
1 orange, lemon or lime, thinly sliced
2 tbsp. chopped or slivered almonds

Place fillets in greased 8 x 8-inch baking dish. Sprinkle with sallt, pepper and onion. Combine 2 tablespoons melted butter, juice and rind; pour over fillets. Bake at 450 degrees for 5 minutes. Top with citrus slices. Bake for 5 minutes longer or until fish flakes easily. Brown almonds in 1 tablespoon butter in small saucepan. Sprinkle over fillets.
Yield: 3-4 servings.

Dorothy Bilton, Brampton, Ontario, Canada

Tip: Grill fish fillets for a quick dinner. Wrap fillets in bacon to retain their shape and prevent sticking to grill.

FASTER FLOUNDER

2 lb. flounder fillets, skinned
2 tbsp. grated onion
1½ tsp. salt
⅛ tsp. pepper
2 lg. tomatoes, chopped
½ c. margarine, melted
1 c. shredded Swiss cheese

Place flounder fillets in greased baking dish. Sprinkle with onion, salt and pepper. Top with tomatoes. Drizzle with margarine. Broil 4 inches from heat for 10 to 12 minutes or until fish flakes easily. Sprinkle with cheese. Broil for 2 or 3 minutes longer or until cheese melts. Yield: 6 servings.

Nelda K. Howell, Pickens, SC

CREOLE HADDOCK

2 lb. haddock fillets
1½ c. chopped fresh tomatoes
½ c. chopped green pepper
⅓ c. lemon juice
1 tbsp. safflower oil
2 tsp. salt
2 tsp. instant minced onion
1 tsp. crushed basil leaves
¼ tsp. coarse black pepper
4 drops of hot sauce

Place fillets in 13½ x 9-inch baking dish. Combine remaining ingredients; spoon over fillets. Bake at 500 degrees for 5 to 8 minutes. Yield: 6 servings.

Avis Henning, Miltonvale, KS

KING SALMON PIE

1   6½-oz. can Alaska salmon, drained
1 c. shredded sharp American cheese
1   3-oz. package cream cheese, softened
¼ c. sliced green onions
1   2-oz. jar chopped pimento, drained (opt.)
2 c. milk
1 c. Bisquick
4 eggs
¾ tsp. salt

Combine salmon, cheese, cream cheese, onions and pimento in bowl; mix well. Spoon into greased 10-inch pie plate. Place remaining 4 ingredients in blender container. Process for 15 seconds. Pour over salmon mixture. Bake at 400 degrees for 35 to 40 minutes or until knife inserted halfway between center and edge comes out clean. Let stand for 5 minutes before serving. Yield: 6-8 servings.

Elizabeth Wagner, Fairbanks, AK

CURRIED SALMON WITH CHEESE PINWHEELS

1   10-oz. package frozen mixed vegetables, cooked
1   1-lb. can salmon, drained
1 can cream of mushroom soup
¼ tsp. each salt, pepper, curry powder
Milk
2 c. prepared biscuit mix
½ c. shredded sharp cheese

Mix first 6 ingredients in bowl with ¼ cup milk. Pour into 6 x 12-inch baking dish. Combine biscuit mix and ⅔ cup milk in bowl. Roll out ⅛-inch thick on floured surface. Sprinkle with cheese. Roll as for jelly roll. Cut into 1-inch slices. Arrange over salmon mixture. Bake at 375 degrees for 30 minutes or until biscuits are golden brown. Yield: 6 servings.

Laura Hill, Spartanburg, SC

MICROWAVE SALMON DUMPLINGS

1   7½-oz. package refrigerator biscuits
1   7¾-oz. can salmon
1 can Cheddar cheese soup
1 c. milk
2 tbsp. flour
2 tbsp. chopped green pepper
1 tbsp. parsley

Arrange biscuits over bottom of 1½-quart microwave casserole. Combine remaining ingredients in bowl, blending well. Spoon over biscuits. Microwave on High for 12 minutes, spooning sauce over biscuits after 6 minutes. Yield: 4 servings.

Marilyn L. Burrows, Oklahoma City, OK

BAKED SOLE

¼ lb. mushrooms, chopped
1 sm. green onion, chopped
4 sprigs of parsley, chopped
¾ lb. sole, cut into 1-in. strips
1¼ c. white wine
2 tbsp. flour
½ stick margarine or butter, softened
1 c. hot cooked white rice

Layer mushrooms, green onion and parsley in 1½-quart casserole. Fold sole strips in half; layer over vegetables in herringbone pattern. Sprinkle with additional green onion. Cover with wine. Place over Low heat; heat until mixture bubbles. Bake at 350 degrees for 20 minutes. Drain, reserving liquid. Pour reserved liquid into saucepan; cook until liquid measures 1 cup. Combine flour and butter; add to hot liquid, stirring until thickened. Place sole over rice; cover with hot sauce. Yield: 2 servings.

Laura R. Heye, Olympia, WA

SOLE-BROCCOLI BAKE

2   10-oz. packages frozen
    broccoli spears
2 tbsp. butter
2 lb. sole fillets
1 c. chicken broth
2 tbsp. butter
2 tbsp. flour
½ tsp. salt
⅛ tsp. pepper
1 c. light cream
½ c. chicken broth
¾ c. shredded Swiss cheese
¼ c. toasted almonds
¼ c. shredded Swiss cheese

Cook broccoli according to package directions; drain well. Sauté in 2 tablespoons butter in skillet until butter is absorbed; set aside. Roll fish fillets; secure with wooden picks. Place in skillet. Add 1 cup chicken broth. Simmer, covered, for 12 minutes or until fish flakes easily. Place alternate rows of fish and broccoli in buttered shallow 2-quart baking dish. Melt 2 tablespoons butter in medium saucepan. Blend in flour and seasonings. Stir in cream and ½ cup chicken broth gradually. Cook until thickened, stirring constantly; remove from heat. Add ¾ cup cheese; stir until cheese is melted. Pour over fish. Sprinkle with almonds. Bake at 400 degrees for 10 minutes or until bubbly. Sprinkle with remaining ¼ cup cheese. Bake for 3 minutes or until cheese melts. Yield: 6 servings.

Photograph for this recipe below.

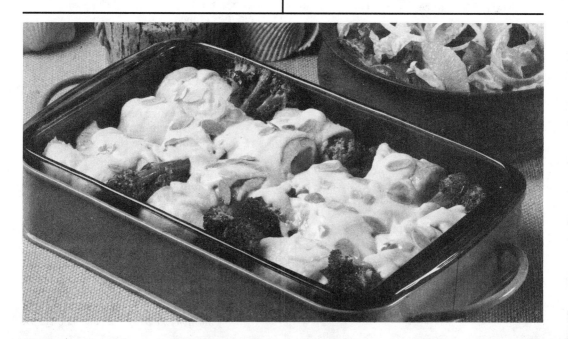

COMPANY TUNA BAKE

1 c. elbow macaroni
1 3-oz. package cream cheese,
    softened
1 can cream of mushroom soup
1 can tuna, drained, flaked
1 tbsp. each chopped pimento, onion
1 tsp. prepared mustard
⅓ c. milk
½ c. bread crumbs
2 tbsp. butter, melted

Cook macaroni using package directions. Beat cream cheese and soup in bowl until smooth. Add next 5 ingredients and macaroni; mix well. Pour into 1½-quart casserole. Combine bread crumbs and butter in bowl. Sprinkle over tuna mixture. Bake at 375 degrees for 20 minutes. Yield: 4 servings.

Margaret Brown, Wilkesboro, NC

SPAGHETTI WITH TUNA SAUCE

2 tbsp. flour
½ tsp. salt
2 tbsp. butter, melted
2 c. milk
¼ c. prepared mustard
2 7-oz. cans tuna, drained
8 oz. spaghetti, cooked
2 tbsp. grated Parmesan cheese

Blend flour and salt into butter in saucepan. Stir in milk. Bring to a boil, stirring constantly. Cook until thick, stirring occasionally. Add mustard and tuna. Pour over spaghetti. Top with cheese. Yield: 4 servings.

Faye Wills, Fort Wayne, IN

MICROWAVE TUNA NEWBURG

3 c. cooked elbow macaroni, drained
1 6½-oz. can tuna, drained, flaked
1 tbsp. instant minced onion
1 4-oz. jar pimento, drained, diced
Salt
3 eggs
2 c. half and half
¼ c. butter
¼ c. flour

2 tbsp. dry Sherry
1 c. chicken broth
Pepper to taste
Cooked peas, green beans or carrots

Combine macaroni, tuna, onion and pimento in bowl. Pour into greased glass ring mold. Mix 1 teaspoon salt, eggs and 1 cup half and half in bowl until smooth and well blended. Pour over macaroni. Microwave on Defrost for 22 to 24 minutes or until ring is firm, turning dish occasionally during cooking. Melt butter in saucepan; stir in flour. Stir in remaining half and half, Sherry and chicken broth gradually. Cook over medium heat until sauce bubbles and thickens, stirring constantly. Season with salt to taste and pepper. Loosen edges of ring; unmold on large plate. Fill center with hot vegetables; spoon sauce over ring. Yield: 4 servings.

Sue Brett, San Francisco, CA

TUNA QUICHE

2 c. tuna
½ c. grated cheese
½ c. chopped onion
1 unbaked 9-in. pie shell
1 c. evaporated milk
4 eggs, beaten
¼ tsp. salt
Pepper to taste

Layer tuna, cheese and onion in pie shell. Combine evaporated milk, eggs, salt and pepper in bowl; mix well. Pour over layers. Bake at 450 degrees for 15 minutes. Reduce temperature to 300 degrees. Bake for 30 minutes. Yield: 6 servings.

Angela White, Calhoun, SC

Tip: Tuna varies in color and oil content. The range from lighter and less oily to darker and more oily is Albacore, Yellowfin, Skipjack and Bluefin tuna.

TUNA CAKES

2 tbsp. butter
3 tbsp. flour
1 c. milk
2 egg yolks, beaten
1   12½-oz. can flaked tuna
¼ tsp. celery seed
¼ tsp. onion powder
⅛ tsp. cayenne pepper
½ c. soft bread cubes
¾ c. dry bread crumbs
Cooking oil
2 tbsp. chopped pickle
1 tbsp. minced onion
1 tbsp. parsley
2 tbsp. lemon juice
1 c. mayonnaise

Melt butter; add flour, stirring constantly. Add milk. Cook over low heat, stirring until smooth and thickened. Stir a small amount of hot mixture into egg yolks; stir egg yolks into hot mixture. Stir until thickened. Add tuna, celery seed, onion powder, cayenne pepper and bread cubes; mix well. Shape into eight 2½-inch patties; roll in dry crumbs. Fry in hot oil, turning once. Combine pickle, onion, parsley, lemon juice and mayonnaise; mix well. Serve with tuna cakes. Yield: 4 servings.

Patricia Bowman, British Columbia, Canada

CHEESY TUNA PUFF

3 eggs, separated
¾ c. milk
2 cans tuna, drained
1 c. soft bread crumbs
1 c. shredded Cheddar cheese
1 tsp. instant minced onion
½ tsp. salt
⅛ tsp. pepper
2 tsp. lemon juice

Beat egg yolks with milk in bowl. Add tuna and remaining ingredients except egg whites; mix lightly. Beat egg whites until stiff but not dry; fold into tuna mixture. Turn into shallow 1-quart baking dish. Bake at 350 degrees for 30 minutes or until knife inserted in center comes out clean. Serve with Parsley Sauce. Yield: 6 servings.

Parsley Sauce

3 tbsp. butter
3 tbsp. flour
¾ tsp. salt
1½ c. milk
1 tbsp. lemon juice
1½ tbsp. chopped parsley

Melt butter in saucepan; stir in flour and salt. Stir in milk gradually. Cook over medium heat until thickened, stirring constantly. Stir in lemon juice and parsley just before serving over Tuna Puff.

Agnes Huffman, Modesto, CA

TUNA-RICE CURRY SKILLET

2   6½-oz. cans tuna in vegetable oil
1 med. apple, chopped
1 med. onion, chopped
1 can cream of celery soup
1 to 2 tsp. curry powder
½ tsp. salt
1½ c. minute rice
⅓ c. each chopped peanuts,
   chopped green pepper, coconut
   and raisins

Drain tuna, reserving oil. Sauté apple and onion in reserved oil in skillet over low heat for 10 minutes or until apples are tender. Add 1⅓ cups water, soup, curry powder and salt; mix well. Stir in rice. Place tuna in center of skillet. Bring mixture to a boil; remove from heat. Let stand, covered, for 5 minutes. Fluff rice with fork. Sprinkle with remaining ingredients. Serve with chutney. Yield: 4 servings.

Wilma Evans, Akron, OH

BARBECUED WHITEFISH IN FOIL

2 lb. frozen whitefish fillets, thawed
2 green peppers, sliced
2 onions, sliced
2 tbsp. lemon juice
¼ c. butter or margarine, melted
2 tsp. salt
1 tsp. paprika
Pepper and lemon pepper to taste

Cut fillets into serving pieces. Cut six 12x12-inch pieces of heavy-duty aluminum foil; grease lightly. Place portion of fillets, skin side down, on each aluminum foil square. Top with green pepper and onion. Combine remaining ingredients; mix well. Pour sauce over fillets. Seal squares tightly. Cook on grill for 30 to 45 minutes or until fish flakes easily.
Yield: 6 servings.

Bonnie Reed, Saskatchewan, Canada

WHITE CLAM SAUCE

1 med. onion, chopped
2 cloves of garlic, minced
½ c. butter
½ c. oil
¼ c. parsley
½ lb. mushrooms, sliced
Juice of 1 lemon
½ c. white wine
2 10-oz. cans baby clams with broth
1 lb. thin spaghetti, cooked
Parmesan cheese

Sauté onion and garlic in butter and oil in skillet. Add parsley and mushrooms. Cook until vegetables are tender. Add lemon juice and wine. Stir clams into sauce. Pour sauce over hot spaghetti. Sprinkle with Parmesan cheese. Yield: 4 servings.

Sue L. Fry, Delray Beach, FL

CRAB PIE

4 eggs
2 tbsp. flour
1 c. each mayonnaise, milk
1 lb. crab meat
8 oz. Cheddar cheese, diced
1 tbsp. each minced onion, green pepper
8 oz. Swiss cheese, diced
2 9-in. deep dish pie shells

Combine eggs, flour, mayonnaise and milk in bowl; mix well. Stir in next 5 ingredients. Bake pie shells at 350 degrees for 5 minutes; cool. Spoon crab mixture into pie shells. Bake at 350 degrees for 50 minutes or until knife inserted in center comes out clean. Yield: 12 servings.

Sis LeGates, Talbot County, MD

DEVILED CRAB

1 med. onion
2 tbsp. butter
2 tbsp. flour
1 tbsp. lemon juice
Dash of cayenne pepper
1 tbsp. Worcestershire sauce
1 sm. can evaporated milk
1 egg, beaten
1 can crab meat, flaked
Fine bread crumbs
5 crab shells
1 c. buttered bread crumbs

Sauté onion in butter in skillet. Blend in flour, lemon juice, cayenne pepper and Worcestershire sauce. Stir in evaporated milk gradually. Cook until thickened, stirring constantly; remove from heat. Stir in egg, crab meat and enough crumbs to make of desired consistency. Spoon into crab shells. Sprinkle with buttered crumbs; smooth tops. Bake at 350 degrees until brown and bubbly. Serve with tartar sauce and lemon slices. Yield: 5 servings.

Barbie Ray, Alta Loma, TX

HOT CRAB MEAT ROSÉ

1 lb. crab meat
¼ c. rosé
½ c. sour cream
½ tsp. dry mustard
½ tsp. salt
Dash of cayenne pepper
Pinch of thyme
1 c. sliced celery
2 hard-boiled eggs, chopped
½ c. slivered almonds
¼ c. grated Parmesan cheese
¼ c. melted butter

Marinate crab meat in wine in bowl for 30 minutes. Combine sour cream, mustard, salt, cayenne and thyme in bowl, blending well. Toss crab meat and wine with sour cream mixture. Stir in celery and eggs. Pour into buttered casserole. Combine almonds, cheese and butter, sprinkling over top. Bake at 325 degrees for 25 minutes. Brown under broiler if necessary. Yield: 4 servings.

Gerald A. Hils, Keene, NH

MICROWAVE CRAB IMPERIAL

1 lb. crab meat
2 saltine crackers, crushed
2 to 4 tsp. chopped green pepper
2 tsp. pimento
1 tsp. mustard
2 tbsp. mayonnaise
Dash of red pepper
2 to 3 tsp. Sherry
Salt and pepper to taste
1 tsp. Worcestershire sauce
1 egg
½ c. medium white sauce

Combine all ingredients in bowl; mix well. Spoon into buttered glass casserole. Microwave for 10 minutes, turning once. Yield: 4 servings.

Mary Massey, Kent County, MD

STRAY CRAB STRUT

6 slices whole wheat bread, toasted
1 med. bunch broccoli, cooked
1 lb. crab meat, drained
⅓ c. low-calorie mayonnaise
1 sm. onion, finely chopped
Salt and pepper to taste
2 tsp. parsley flakes
1 to 3 slices low-fat cheese, grated
Paprika

Arrange toast slices on baking sheet. Arrange broccoli flowerets on toast. Mix crab meat with mayonnaise, onion, salt, pepper and parsley in bowl. Spoon mixture evenly over broccoli. Top with cheese; sprinkle with paprika. Bake at 375 degrees for 10 minutes or until cheese melts. Serve immediately. Yield: 6 servings.

Susan O'Connor, Miami, FL

OYSTERS BOTANY BAY

4 doz. oysters
4 tbsp. dry Sherry
3 oz. butter
1 lg. clove of garlic, crushed
1⅓ c. fresh white bread crumbs
1½ tbsp. freshly chopped parsley
2 tsp. finely grated lemon rind
Salt and pepper to taste

Arrange oysters on 4 oyster plates; drizzle with Sherry. Heat butter in heavy skillet until foamy; add garlic. Sauté until golden. Add remaining ingredients. Sauté until bread crumbs are golden. Spoon over oysters. Bake at 400 degrees for 5 minutes or until heated through. Serve at once garnished with decorated lemon half. Yield: 4 servings.

Sissy Sledge, Hopkinsville, KY

COQUILLE ST. JACQUES

⅓ c. chopped onion
½ tbsp. chopped shallots
1 clove of garlic, minced
Butter
½ lb. scallops
Flour
Salt and pepper
Olive oil
½ c. dry vermouth
½ bay leaf
⅛ tsp. thyme
Grated Swiss cheese

Sauté onion, shallots and garlic in a small amount of butter in skillet until tender; set aside. Coat scallops with flour seasoned with salt and pepper; shake off excess. Brown in small amount of butter and olive oil in skillet. Add vermouth, 3 tablespoons water, bay leaf, thyme and sautéed onion mixture. Simmer, covered, for 5 minutes. Discard bay leaf; spoon into shells on baking sheet. Top with cheese; dot with butter. Broil until cheese is brown. Yield: 4 servings.

Susan Greene, Little Rock, AR

SCALLOPS VERMICELLI

1 lb. mushrooms, quartered
6 oz. unsalted butter
Salt and pepper to taste
4 shallots, minced
2 cloves of garlic, minced
6 scallions, minced
1 lb. bay scallops
6 tbsp. vermouth
1 tbsp. minced parsley
1 lb. vermicelli

Sauté mushrooms in half the butter in skillet. Season with salt and pepper; remove mushrooms. Add remaining butter to skillet. Sauté shallots, garlic and scallions lightly. Add scallops and vermouth. Cook until heated through. Add parsley and mushrooms. Cook vermicelli in boiling salted water in saucepan for about 5 minutes; drain. Add to scallop mixture. Cook for 3 or 4 minutes or until most liquid is absorbed, stirring constantly. Serve with Parmesan cheese and hot pepper flakes. Yield: 4 servings.

Janet B. Stratton, Cecil County, MD

SHRIMP CREOLE ORLEANS

¾ c. chopped onions
1 clove of garlic, minced
1 c. chopped green pepper
3 c. sliced celery
¼ c. butter
1 29-oz. can tomatoes
3 tbsp. brown sugar
1½ tsp. salt
⅛ tsp. pepper
1 tsp. thyme
2 bay leaves, crumbled
2 lb. fresh cleaned shrimp
2 tbsp. lemon juice
3 c. hot cooked rice

Sauté onions, garlic, green pepper and celery in butter in skillet until tender. Add next 6 ingredients; mix well. Simmer for 15 minutes. Stir in shrimp and lemon juice. Simmer for 6 to 8 minutes longer. Stir in rice. Yield: 6 servings.

Caroline Bode, San Antonio, TX

SHRIMP JAMBALAYA

1 c. rice
¼ c. onion flakes
1½ tsp. salt
¾ tsp. crushed thyme leaves
¼ tsp. instant minced garlic
Pinch of ground red pepper
1 bay leaf
1 28-oz. can whole tomatoes, crushed
1 lb cooked ham, cut into 1-in. cubes
1 10-oz. package frozen peas, thawed
2½ lb. uncooked shrimp, peeled, deveined

Combine first 8 ingredients with 1¼ cups water in large soup pot. Bring to a boil; reduce heat. Simmer, covered, for 15 minutes. Add ham and peas. Simmer for 5 minutes. Add shrimp. Simmer, covered, for 5 minutes or until seafood is just cooked. Yield: 6-8 servings.

Provi Worley, Atlanta, GA

SHRIMP ROCKEFELLER

1 c. chopped onion
3 tbsp. margarine
24 oz. frozen shrimp
1 can cream of mushroom soup
2 c. grated Swiss cheese
½ c. dry Sherry
½ c. Parmesan cheese
4½ c. cooked rice
2 10-oz. packages frozen chopped spinach, cooked, drained
2 cans sliced water chestnuts
2 tbsp. lemon juice
1 tsp. each salt, pepper

Sauté onion in margarine in skillet. Add shrimp. Cook for several minutes, stirring frequently. Stir in soup, Swiss cheese and Sherry. Cook until cheese is melted, stirring frequently. Add ¼ cup Parmesan cheese and remaining ingredients; mix gently. Pour into 3-quart casserole. Sprinkle remaining ¼ cup Parmesan cheese over top. Bake at 350 degrees for 25 minutes. Yield: 8 servings.

Michael Shoup, San Joaquin, CA

SHRIMP SAVANNAH

1 lb. shrimp, peeled
1 stick butter, melted
1 can mushroom soup
1 8-oz. carton sour cream
Garlic salt and catsup to taste
1 tbsp. Worcestershire sauce
1 sm. can mushrooms, drained (opt.)

Sauté shrimp in butter in skillet until shrimp turn pink. Add remaining ingredients; mix well. Simmer until heated through. Serve with rice or in pastry shells. Yield: 4 servings.

Jenell R. Griffith, Savannah, GA

EASY JAMBALAYA

¼ c. chopped bacon
3 tbsp. each chopped onion, green pepper
1 clove of garlic, minced
1 tbsp. flour
½ tsp. salt
Cayenne pepper and paprika to taste
½ tsp. Worcestershire sauce
1   16-oz. can tomatoes
1½ c. pitted California ripe olive halves
12 oz. shrimp, cooked
2 c. cooked rice

Fry bacon in skillet until almost crisp. Add onion, green pepper and garlic. Cook until tender. Add flour, seasonings and tomatoes. Cook until thickened, stirring constantly. Add olives, shrimp and rice. Heat to serving temperature, stirring frequently.
Yield: 6 servings.

FISH AND SHRIMP PARMESAN

2 lb. white fish filets
½ lb. small cooked shrimp
2 tbsp. flour
3 tbsp. butter, melted
½ tsp. salt
1 c. milk
¼ c. Parmesan cheese

Layer fish and shrimp in buttered 2-quart baking dish. Blend flour into butter in saucepan. Cook until bubbly. Add salt and milk. Cook until thickened, stirring constantly. Spread over shrimp. Sprinkle with Parmesan cheese. Bake at 325 degrees for 20 minutes or until fish flakes easily. Yield: 4 servings.

Connie Bolle, Cleveland, TN

SHRIMP BOURGUIGNON

4 slices bacon, chopped
¼ c. butter
1 lb. shrimp, cleaned
1 c. canned small white onions, drained
8 sm. mushrooms, sliced
½ tsp. salt
2 tbsp. chopped parsley

⅛ tsp. pepper
2 c. Burgundy
1 tbsp. butter, melted
2 tsp. flour

Cook bacon in ¼ cup butter in skillet until brown. Remove bacon; add shrimp. Sauté until lightly browned; remove shrimp. Add onions and mushrooms. Sauté until browned. Add bacon, salt, parsley, pepper and Burgundy. Simmer for 15 minutes. Stir in mixture of melted butter and flour. Add shrimp. Simmer for 5 minutes. Serve over hot noodles.
Yield: 4 servings.

Laura Jeans, Baton Rouge, LA

SHRIMP TIPSY

1   12-oz. can beer
1 sm. onion, chopped
Juice of ¼ lemon
½ tsp. Worcestershire sauce
½ tsp. oregano
¼ c. chopped celery leaves
1 bay leaf
1½ tsp. salt
1 lb. unpeeled shrimp

Combine first 8 ingredients in saucepan; mix well. Add shrimp. Bring to a boil; reduce heat. Simmer for 8 minutes or until shrimp are cooked through, turning once. Serve shrimp with melted butter. Yield: 4 servings.

Teri Fleming, Santa Maria, CA

SEAFOOD CASSEROLE

1 lb. mushooms, sliced
1¼ c. wild rice, cooked
1 c. each chopped celery, onion,
    and green pepper
2   7-oz. cans each shrimp, crab meat
1½ c. mayonnaise
1 tsp. Worcestershire sauce
Curry powder, salt and pepper to taste

Sauté mushrooms in skillet. Combine with rice, vegetables, seafood, mayonnaise and seasonings in greased casserole. Bake, covered, at 350 degrees for 45 minutes. Yield: 8 servings.

Holly Loy, Johnson City, TN

Vegetables
& Side Dishes

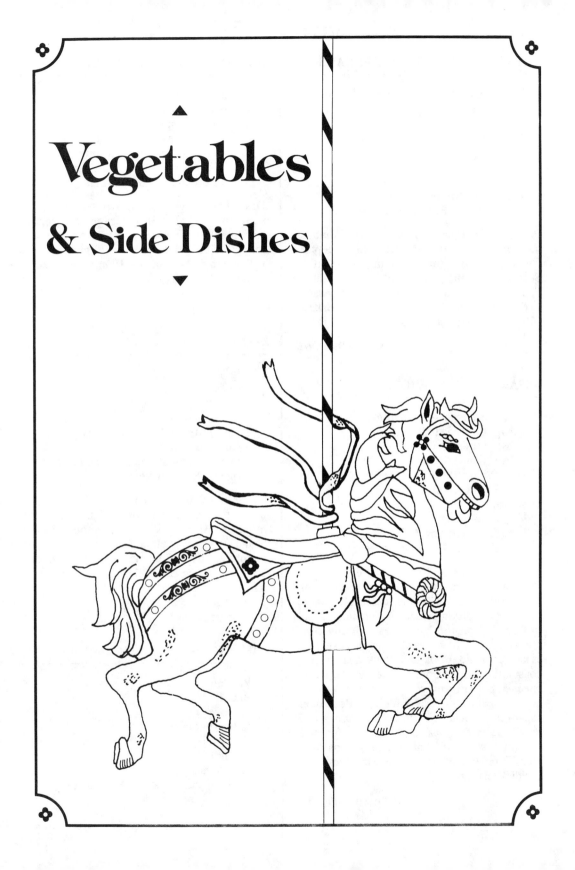

ARTICHOKE HEARTS AND PECANS

2 No. 2 cans artichoke hearts, drained
1 c. half and half
2 tbsp. butter
2 tbsp. flour
Salt and pepper to taste
Tabasco sauce to taste
½ c. broken pecans
¼ c. bread crumbs
2 tbsp. grated Parmesan cheese

Place artichoke hearts in casserole. Combine half and half, butter and flour in saucepan. Cook until thickened, stirring constantly. Season with salt, pepper and Tabasco sauce. Pour sauce over artichoke hearts; add pecans. Sprinkle with bread crumbs and cheese. Bake at 300 degrees until bubbly. Yield: 6 servings.

Selma Sailors, Diller, NE

ASPARAGUS CASSEROLE

2 lb. fresh asparagus, trimmed
2 tbsp. minced shallots
2 tbsp. butter
2 tbsp. flour
⅓ c. shredded Fontina cheese
¼ c. Parmesan cheese
⅛ tsp. pepper
¼ tsp. rosemary
¼ c. bread crumbs
⅓ c. shredded Provalone cheese

Cook asparagus in 2 quarts salted water in saucepan for 10 minutes. Drain, reserving 1 cup liquid. Place in 9 x 13-inch casserole. Sauté shallots in butter in skillet for 1 minute. Blend in flour. Cook for 2 minutes, stirring constantly. Do not brown. Stir in reserved asparagus liquid. Cook until thickened, stirring constantly. Stir in Fontina cheese, Parmesan cheese, pepper and rosemary. Cook for 1 minute or until cheese is melted. Pour over asparagus. Sprinkle with bread crumbs and Provalone cheese. Bake at 375 degrees for 15 to 20 minutes or until bubbly. May substitute broccoli or Brussels sprouts for asparagus. Yield: 4 servings.

Linda McKray, Colville, WA

ASPARAGUS AND WATER CHESTNUTS

1 can sliced water chestnuts
1 8-oz. can sliced mushrooms
1 sm. jar chopped pimentos
4 hard-boiled eggs, chopped
1 can cream of mushroom soup
2 cans asparagus spears, drained
1 can French-fried onion rings

Drain first 3 ingredients. Mix with eggs and soup in bowl. Layer asparagus in greased casserole. Spoon water chestnut mixture over top. Bake at 350 degrees for 20 minutes. Top with onion rings. Bake for 10 minutes longer. Yield: 6-8 servings.

Mary Ada Parks, Anna, IL

GREEN BEANS DELICIOUS

1 lg. onion, sliced
2 tbsp. margarine
1 can chopped pimentos
1 can mushroom pieces
1 jar Old English cheese
1 can mushroom soup
1 can French-cut green beans, drained
Crushed Ritz crackers

Sauté onion in margarine in skillet. Stir in pimentos and mushrooms. Simmer for 10 minutes. Blend in cheese and soup. Stir in beans. Pour into buttered casserole. Top with crumbs and a small amount of additional butter. Bake at 350 degrees until brown. Yield: 4 servings.

Julie Boone, Pawhuska, OK

NIPPY GREEN BEAN CASSEROLE

¼ c. butter, melted
¼ c. flour
½ tsp. pepper
½ tsp. paprika
1 tsp. salt
2 c. milk
½ c. horseradish
2 1-lb. cans seasoned French-style
  green beans, drained

Blend butter, flour and seasonings in skillet; stir in milk. Cook until thickened, stirring constantly. Add horseradish and beans. Pour into greased 2-quart baking dish. Bake at 350 degrees for 20 minutes or until bubbly. Yield: 8 servings.

Becky Talbot, Nashville, TN

ITALIAN GREEN BEANS

1 2-lb. package frozen green beans
¼ c. bacon bits
1 c. Italian salad dressing

Cook green beans using package directions; drain. Stir in bacon bits and salad dressing; toss to coat well. Spoon into serving dish. Yield: 6 servings.

Kathleen J. Shafer, Julesburg, CO

LIMA BEAN CASSEROLE

2 pkg. frozen lima beans
1 c. white sauce
1 c. grated Cheddar cheese
¼ c. catsup
1 sm. can sliced pimento
Salt and pepper to taste
Buttered bread crumbs

Cook lima beans using package directions; drain. Combine with white sauce, cheese, catsup, pimento, salt and pepper in bowl; mix well. Pour into 8x8-inch baking dish. Top with crumbs. Bake at 350 degrees for about ½ hour. Yield: 8 servings.

Mrs. Harold Coggin, Knoxville, TN

MICROWAVE CALICO BEAN POT

8 slices bacon
1 c. chopped onion
1 1-lb. can each green beans,
   kidney beans, butter beans,
   and lima beans, drained
1 1-lb. can pork and beans
½ tsp. garlic salt
½ tsp. dry mustard

Place bacon in 3-quart microwave dish. Microwave for 4 to 5 minutes or until crisp. Remove bacon and add onion. Sauté onion in bacon drippings for 3 minutes. Combine remaining ingredients with onion; mix lightly. Microwave, covered, at half power for ½ hour, stirring after 15 minutes. Let stand for 5 to 10 minutes before serving. Crumble bacon over top. Yield: 12 servings.

Ruth Demins, Longwood, FL

STOVE-TOP BAKED BEANS

2 slices bacon, chopped
1 onion, chopped
¾ c. packed brown sugar
1 c. catsup
2 tsp. vinegar
2 tbsp. liquid smoke
1 tsp. salt
1 tsp. chili powder
1 2-lb. can pork and beans

Sauté bacon and onion in skillet until brown. Add remaining ingredients; mix well. Simmer for 30 to 60 minutes. Yield: 6 servings.

Tonna Coffey, Hinton, OK

BEETS WITH PINEAPPLE

1 8-oz. can pineapple tidbits
2 tbsp. brown sugar
1 tbsp. cornstarch
1 tbsp. butter
1 tbsp. lemon juice
2 c. small cooked beets

Drain pineapple and reserve juice. Combine juice, sugar and cornstarch in heavy saucepan. Cook over medium heat until thickened and bubbly, stirring constantly. Remove from heat. Add butter and lemon juice. Stir until butter melts. Add beets and pineapple; stir gently to coat. Cook over medium heat, stirring constantly, for 5 minutes or until heated through. Yield: 4 servings.

Beverly Walton, Knoxville, TN

JUST BEET IT!

1½ tbsp. cornstarch
½ tsp. salt
3 tbsp. vinegar
⅓ c. honey
2 tbsp. melted butter
2 c. sliced cooked beets

Blend first 5 ingredients with 2 tablespoons water in saucepan. Cook over medium heat until thickened, stirring constantly. Add beets. Cook until heated through, stirring constantly. Yield: 4 servings.

Hassie Hunter Rogers, Goshen, AL

MICROWAVE CHEEZY BROCCOLI

2   10-oz. packages frozen
    chopped broccoli
2 c. minute rice
2 cans cream of chicken soup
1 c. milk
1   16-oz. jar Cheez Whiz
1 tbsp. salt
½ tsp. pepper
½ c. chopped onion
1 c. chopped celery
1 can sliced water chestnuts

Cook unopened broccoli in microwave for 4 to 5 minutes, turning over after 2 minutes. Drain broccoli, separate stalks and set aside. Combine next 6 ingredients in large microwave dish. Cook for 2 to 4 minutes or until cheese melts. Add ¾ cup water, onion, celery, drained water chestnuts and broccoli; mix well. Spoon into 2 lightly greased 10x6-inch microwave dishes. Microwave on High 1 at a time, for 12 to 14 minutes, rotating after 5 minutes. Let stand for 5 minutes before serving. Yield: 12 servings.

Janet Mayer, LeRoy, MN

BROCCOLI WITH SOUR CREAM SAUCE

2 pkg. frozen broccoli, cooked
½ c. sour cream
½ tsp. horseradish
¼ tsp. mustard
Salt and pepper to taste

Arrange broccoli on serving plate. Combine remaining ingredients in saucepan. Heat to serving temperature. Do not boil. Spoon over broccoli. Yield: 6 servings.

C. A. Zaiser, Kent County, MD

SPECIAL BROCCOLI CASSEROLE

2 boxes frozen chopped broccoli,
   thawed
1 c. mayonnaise
2 eggs, beaten
1 sm. onion, chopped
1 can cream of mushroom soup
1 c. grated sharp cheese
2 c. herb-seasoned stuffing mix
1 tbsp. oil (opt.)

Combine broccoli, mayonnaise, eggs, onion, soup and cheese in bowl; mix well. Pour into greased casserole. Combine stuffing mix and oil in bowl. Sprinkle over casserole. Bake at 350 degrees for 45 to 50 minutes or until brown and bubbly. Yield: 6 servings.

Mattie Lou Robinson, Knoxville, TN

STIR-FRY BROCCOLI

1 head broccoli, trimmed, separated
¼ c. butter, melted
12 to 16 almonds, slivered
Lemon juice (opt.)

Cut broccoli into flowerets; chop stems. Stir-fry in butter over medium-high heat in skillet for 8 to 10 minutes or until tender-crisp. Add almonds. Cook for several minutes longer. Serve with lemon juice. Yield: 4-5 servings.

Marion R. Hull, Shillington, PA

RED CABBAGE WITH APPLES

1   2½-lb. red cabbage, shredded
3 lg. apples, pared and sliced
3 tbsp. melted butter
¼ c. vinegar
1½ tsp. flour
¼ c. packed brown sugar
2 tsp. salt
Dash of pepper

Bring ¾ cup water to a boil. Add cabbage; cover. Cook for 10 minutes or until cabbage is tender. Add apples; cover. Cook for 10 minutes or until apples are tender. Combine butter, vinegar, flour, brown sugar, salt and pepper; mix well. Add to cabbage mixture; mix well. Cook until flavors blend. Yield: 4-6 servings.

Pauline Klepper, East Brunswick, NJ

MARINATED BRUSSELS SPROUTS

1   10-oz. package Brussels sprouts
½ c. Italian dressing
1½ tsp. dried dillweed
3 tbsp. sliced green onion

Prepare Brussels sprouts according to package directions; drain. Combine remaining ingredients; mix well. Pour over warm Brussels sprouts. Yield: 4 servings.

Jackie Meade, Oxon Hill, MD

GINGER CARROTS

3 to 4 c. diagonally sliced carrots
1 c. orange juice
½ c. chicken broth
3 whole cloves
¾ tsp. ginger
1½ tsp. grated lemon rind
3 tbsp. sugar

Combine all ingredients except sugar in saucepan. Bring to a boil. Stir in sugar. Simmer, covered, for 20 minutes or until carrots are tender. Yield: 6 servings.

Theresa Moore, Keystone, NE

ORANGE AND CARROT TIMBALES

1 egg, lightly beaten
¾ c. light cream, at room temperature
½ tsp. grated orange rind
2 drops of hot pepper sauce
⅛ tsp. hot pepper sauce
Pinch of cinnamon
1 Florida orange, peeled, chopped
½ c. finely grated carrots

Combine egg, cream, orange rind and seasonings in bowl; beat well. Add orange and carrots. Pour into 2 well-greased ½-cup molds. Place molds in deep baking dish. Add enough hot water to reach almost to tops of molds. Bake in 325-degree oven for 20 to 25 minutes or until set. Remove from water. Unmold onto serving plate. Yield: 2 servings.

MICROWAVE CHEDDAR CARROTS

½ c. chopped onion
2 tbsp. butter
½ tsp. dry mustard
⅛ tsp. pepper
1 can cream of celery soup
¼ c. milk
1 c. shredded sharp Cheddar cheese
1 lb. carrots, cooked, cut into strips
2 tbsp. fine dry bread crumbs

Combine onion, butter and seasonings in 1-quart glass casserole. Microwave for 2 minutes. Stir in soup, milk and cheese. Layer carrots and sauce in 8x12-inch glass casserole. Microwave, loosely covered, for 5 minutes, turning twice; stir. Sprinkle with bread crumbs. Microwave, uncovered, for 2 minutes. Yield: 6 servings.

Sandra Wall, Rockingham, NC

MICROWAVE
MUSTARD CAULIFLOWER

½ med. head cauliflower
¼ c. mayonnaise
Salt and pepper to taste
½ tsp. onion, chopped
½ tsp. mustard
½ tsp. lemon juice
¼ c. shredded Cheddar cheese

Place cauliflower in 1½-quart glass casserole with 1 tablespoon water. Microwave, covered, on High for 4 to 5 minutes or until tender. Combine remaining ingredients except cheese in small bowl, blending well. Pour over cauliflower. Top with cheese. Microwave on Medium for 1½ to 2 minutes. Let stand for 2 minutes. Yield: 5-6 servings.

Peggy Haynes, El Reno, OK

CORN PUDDING

1 can golden cream-style corn
1 can whole kernel corn, drained (opt.)
1 c. milk
1 tbsp. butter, melted
1 tbsp. sugar
3 lg. eggs, separated

Combine corn and milk in saucepan. Boil for 10 minutes. Stir in butter, sugar and beaten egg yolks. Fold stiffly beaten egg whites into corn mixture. Pour into lightly greased 2-quart casserole. Bake at 350 degrees for 35 minutes. Do not peek while baking. Yield: 8 servings.

Ann Weakley, Nashville, TN

MEXICAN CORN

1   8-oz. package cream cheese, softened
½ c. milk
2 cans whole kernel corn
1 tsp. salt
½ tsp. red pepper
1   2-oz. can chopped green chilies

Blend cream cheese with milk in bowl. Stir in remaining ingredients. Pour into greased baking dish. Bake at 350 degrees for 30 minutes. Yield: 6-8 servings.

Jeannie Laubach, Okeene, OK

MICROWAVE EGGPLANT CASSEROLE

1 med. eggplant, peeled, cubed
2 eggs, beaten
¼ c. margarine, melted
1 c. bread crumbs
¼ c. chopped pimentos
1 onion, chopped
2 c. cream-style corn
1 c. grated Colby cheese
Salt and pepper to taste
½ c. grated sharp Cheddar cheese

Cook eggplant in a small amount of boiling water in saucepan for 10 minutes; drain. Combine with next 7 ingredients and seasonings in greased 2-quart glass casserole; mix well. Microwave, covered, on High for 4 to 5 minutes. Turn casserole ¼ turn. Microwave on

High for 3 to 4 minutes. Top with Cheddar cheese. Microwave on High for 1 minute longer or until cheese melts. May bake at 350 degrees for 1 hour. Yield: 6 servings.

Marcy Carrick, Cleveland, OK

POTATO PANCAKES

3 eggs, separated
1 tsp. salt
1 tbsp. sugar
3 c. milk
2½ c. sifted flour
1 tbsp. melted shortening
3 c. grated potatoes
Finely grated onions (opt.)

Combine beaten egg yolks, salt, sugar and milk in bowl; mix well. Stir in flour and shortening gradually. Stir in potatoes. Fold in stiffly beaten egg whites. Pour desired amount of batter onto hot greased griddle. Sprinkle with onions. Cook until lightly browned on both sides. Yield: 12 pancakes.

Marge Swift, Hopkinsville, KY

MICROWAVE SCALLOPED POTATOES

4 c. sliced potatoes
¼ c. chopped onion
¾ tsp. salt
⅛ tsp. pepper
1 can cream of celery soup
½ c. milk
Paprika

Alternate layers of potatoes and onion in greased 2-quart casserole until all ingredients are used. Blend next 4 ingredients in bowl. Pour over potatoes. Cover. Microwave on High for 20 minutes, stirring every 5 minutes. Sprinkle with paprika. Let stand for 5 minutes before serving. Yield: 6 servings.

Pamela Vaughn, Clarksville, TX

HASHED BROWN CASSEROLE

32 oz. frozen hashed brown potatoes, thawed
2 c. grated Cheddar cheese

1   8-oz. carton sour cream
½ c. chopped onion
1 tsp. salt
¼ tsp. pepper
1 can cream of chicken soup
1 c. melted margarine
½ c. cracker crumbs

Combine first 7 ingredients and ½ cup margarine in bowl; mix well. Spoon into 2-quart greased casserole. Sprinkle cracker crumbs over top. Drizzle remaining margarine over crumbs. Bake at 350 degrees for 45 minutes. Yield: 8-10 servings.

Jeannie R. Atwell, Asheboro, NC

BAKED SPINACH WITH SOUR CREAM

3   10-oz. packages frozen chopped
     spinach
1 pkg. dry onion soup mix
1 pt. sour cream

Cook spinach using package directions; drain well. Combine onion soup mix and sour cream; mix well. Stir sour cream mixture into spinach. Place in baking dish. Bake, covered, at 350 degrees for 30 minutes or until bubbly. Yield: 8 servings.

Mable Wallmark, Mead, WA

SPINACH SQUARES

¼ c. butter
3 eggs, beaten
1 c. milk
1 c. flour
½ tsp. each salt, baking powder
2   10-oz. packages frozen chopped
     spinach, cooked, drained
1 lb. Monterey Jack cheese, grated
½ c. chopped onion

Melt butter in 9 x 13-inch baking dish. Beat eggs with milk. Add flour, salt and baking powder; mix well. Stir in remaining ingredients. Pour into prepared baking dish. Bake at 350 degrees for 35 minutes or until light brown. Cut into squares or small triangles. Yield: 12 servings.

Valerie Buchanan, Clayton, IN

YELLOW SQUASH CASSEROLE

4 green onions, chopped
½ onion, chopped
3 stalks celery, chopped
½ stick butter
8 yellow squash, sliced, cooked, drained
2 cans cream of chicken soup
1 pkg. green onion dip mix
2 c. grated Cheddar cheese
½ tsp. salt
Pepper to taste

Sauté onions and celery in butter in large skillet. Add squash, soup, dip mix, 1 cup cheese, salt and pepper; mix well. Pour into greased 9 x 13-inch casserole. Bake at 350 degrees for 30 minutes. Top with remaining cheese. Yield: 4 servings.

Shan Allen, Cedar Hill, TX

STIR-FRY SQUASH

¼ c. oil
3 or 4 squash, cut into 1-inch strips
1 lg. onion, sliced
1 lg. green pepper, cut into strips
¼ c. (about) soy sauce
Garlic salt (opt.)
Salt and pepper to taste

Heat oil in skillet until very hot. Add squash, onion, green pepper, soy sauce and seasonings. Stir-fry until tender. Yield: 4-6 servings.

Rachel Palmer, Knoxville, TN

SWEET POTATO BAKE

6 to 7 c. sliced cooked sweet potatoes
½ orange, thinly sliced
1   9-oz. can crushed pineapple
½ c. packed brown sugar
½ c. melted butter
½ tsp. salt

Alternate layers of sweet potatoes and orange slices in casserole, ending with sweet potatoes. Combine remaining 4 ingredients in bowl; mix well. Pour over sweet potatoes. Bake at 350 degrees for 30 minutes. Yield: 12 servings.

Eleanor Jensen, San Diego, CA

MICROWAVE SWEET POTATOES

3 c. mashed sweet potatoes
1 c. sugar
¼ c. evaporated milk
2 eggs, beaten
1 tsp. vanilla extract
½ c. coconut
1½ sticks margarine, softened
1 c. chopped nuts
1 c. packed brown sugar
½ c. flour

Combine first 6 ingredients with ½ stick margarine in bowl; mix well. Spread in 9x13-inch glass baking pan. Combine 1 stick margarine and remaining ingredients in bowl; mix well. Sprinkle over sweet potato mixture. Microwave on High for 7 minutes or bake at 325 degrees for 15 to 20 minutes. Yield: 6 servings.

Diane Stephens, Guymon, OK

ZUCCHINI IN CREAM

6 sm. zucchini, cut into ½-inch slices
⅔ c. sour cream
1 tbsp. butter
½ tsp. seasoned salt
6 tbsp. grated sharp Cheddar cheese
3 tbsp. fresh bread crumbs

Simmer zucchini in water to cover for 10 minutes; drain. Spread in 8-inch baking dish. Heat sour cream, butter, seasoned salt and 4 tablespoons cheese in small saucepan. Pour over zucchini. Top with bread crumbs and remaining cheese. Bake at 375 degrees for 10 minutes. Let stand for 5 minutes before serving. Yield: 4-6 servings.

Ardis East, El Paso, TX

VEGETABLE MEDLEY CASSEROLE

2 c. cut fresh green beans
2 c. sliced celery
2 c. coarsely shredded cabbage
¼ c. butter, melted
¼ c. flour
2 c. milk
1½ c. shredded Cheddar cheese
2 tomatoes, peeled, thickly sliced

Cook beans in a small amount of water in saucepan until tender-crisp. Add celery and cabbage. Cook for 2 to 3 minutes or until heated through; drain well. Blend butter and flour in saucepan over low heat. Stir in milk gradually. Cook until thickened, stirring constantly. Stir in 1 cup cheese and vegetables. Spoon into buttered baking dish. Top with tomato slices and remaining ½ cup cheese. Broil until cheese melts. Yield: 8 servings.

Photograph for this recipe below.

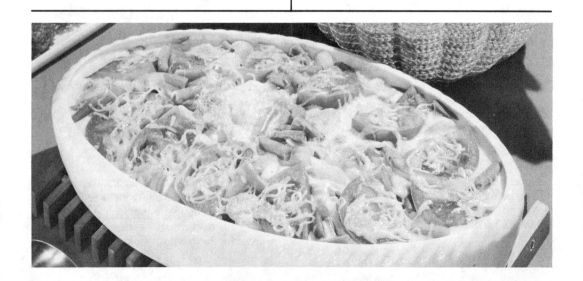

BULGUR-STUFFED WINTER SQUASH

4 sm. acorn squash
8 oz. brown and serve link sausages
½ c. chopped onion
2 tbsp. sausage drippings
¾ c. bulgur
1 tsp. sage
½ tsp. salt
1¼ c. Florida orange juice

Cook squash in boiling water in large saucepan for 20 minutes or until tender; drain. Brown sausages in skillet; drain and slice. Sauté onion in sausage drippings in skillet for 2 minutes. Add bulgur. Sauté for 5 minutes. Add sage, salt and orange juice. Simmer, covered, for 25 minutes or until liquid is absorbed. Stir in sausage. Cut tops from squash; scoop out seed. Spoon bulgur mixture into squash; place in baking dish. Bake at 375 degrees for 20 minutes or until heated through. Yield: 4 servings.

CREAMED VEGETABLE MEDLEY

1 pkg. frozen sliced carrots
1 pkg. frozen cauliflower
1 pkg. frozen green peas
1 can cream of chicken soup
¼ c. chopped parsley
1 tbsp. instant minced onion
½ tsp. salt
1 c. shredded sharp Cheddar cheese

Place vegetables in large bowl. Let stand until partially thawed. Combine soup, parsley, onion and salt in bowl; mix well. Stir in vegetables. Pour into 1½-quart casserole. Bake at 400 degrees for 35 minutes. Stir gently. Sprinkle cheese over top. Bake until cheese melts. Yield: 6-8 servings.

JoAnn J. Kresky, Lansing, MI

MIXED VEGETABLE CASSEROLE

1   20-oz. package frozen
       mixed vegetables
Cream
⅓ c. melted butter
¼ c. (heaping) flour

Pinch each of nutmeg, thyme
1½ tsp. salt
1 c. grated sharp cheese
2 tbsp. white wine
Bread cubes
3 to 6 tbsp. butter, melted

Pour 1¼ cups hot water over vegetables in bowl. Let stand for 5 minutes; drain, reserving liquid. Mix liquid with enough cream to measure 2 cups. Combine ⅓ cup butter and flour in saucepan. Stir in cream mixture and seasonings. Cook until mixture begins to thicken, stirring constantly. Stir in cheese. Cook until thickened, stirring constantly. Mix in wine. Pour over vegetables in 9 x 11-inch baking pan. Cover with bread cubes. Drizzle with 3 to 6 tablespoons butter. Bake at 350 degrees for 30 minutes or until hot and bubbly. Yield: 12 servings.

Reva J. Falk, Tucson, AZ

VEGETABLE HOT DISH

1   4-oz. can mushrooms, drained
1   8-oz. can green beans, drained
1   16-oz. can whole tomatoes
3 or 4 slices bacon, chopped
1 med. onion, chopped

Combine mushrooms, green beans and tomatoes in saucepan. Simmer for 15 minutes. Fry bacon with onion in skillet. Pour over vegetables in serving dish. Yield: 4-5 servings.

Irene Elter, Mandan, ND

VEGETABLE SKILLET

1 head cabbage, chopped
6 carrots, sliced
1 can each peas, whole kernel corn
1 head cauliflower, chopped
1 large onion, sliced
4 to 6 slices American cheese

Layer vegetables in skillet in order listed. Arrange cheese over top. Simmer over medium heat until vegetables are tender and cheese is melted, adding ¼ cup water if necessary. Yield: 10 servings.

Judy Williams, Noblesville, IN

FETTUCINI ALFREDO

1 pt. heavy cream
1 stick margarine
2 eggs, beaten
½ c. grated Italian cheese
½ c. parsley
Pinch of garlic powder
1 16-oz. package fettucini, cooked

Combine heavy cream and margarine in saucepan. Cook over low heat until margarine is melted. Do not boil. Stir a small amount of hot cream into eggs. Stir eggs, cheese, parsley and garlic powder into hot cream. Pour sauce over hot fettucini in serving dish; toss lightly. Yield: 6-8 servings.

Ida Damesimo, Fayetteville, NY

TOMATO AND BASIL FETTUCINI

¼ c. chopped onion
1 clove of garlic, minced
¼ c. olive oil
1 28-oz. can peeled tomatoes
1 tsp. salt
½ tsp. pepper
6 fresh basil leaves, chopped
1 12-oz. package fettucini, cooked

Sauté onion and garlic in oil in skillet until onion is tender. Chop tomatoes into small pieces; reserve liquid. Add tomatoes, tomato liquid, salt, pepper and basil to skillet. Bring to a boil over medium heat; reduce heat. Simmer for 15 minutes, stirring occasionally. Combine hot fettucini with tomato-basil sauce in large serving dish. Toss until coated. Garnish with Parmesan cheese. Yield: 4-6 servings.

Evelyn Apple, Clearwater, FL

MUSHROOM TETRAZZINI

½ lb. mushrooms, thickly sliced
1 med. onion, chopped
6 tbsp. butter
3 tbsp. flour
1½ tsp. salt
Pinch of pepper
2 c. milk
¼ c. Sherry

1 c. grated provolone cheese
½ c. chopped parsley
1 8-oz. package spaghetti, cooked
½ c. grated provolone cheese

Sauté mushrooms and onion in butter in saucepan. Add flour, salt and pepper; mix well. Stir in milk and Sherry gradually. Add 1 cup cheese and parsley. Cook until thickened, stirring constantly. Place hot spaghetti in greased 2-quart baking dish. Pour sauce over top. Sprinkle with ½ cup cheese. Bake at 350 degrees or until cheese melts. Yield: 8-12 servings.

Karen Perry, Castalia, OH

TORTELLINI WITH GARGONZOLA SAUCE

¾ c. dry white vermouth
1 c. heavy cream
Freshly ground pepper and nutmeg
⅓ to ½ lb. Gorgonzola cheese
1 tbsp. Parmesan cheese
8 oz. tortellini, cooked

Boil vermouth in saucepan until reduced by ½. Stir in cream, pepper and nutmeg. Simmer until reduced by ⅓. Remove from heat. Stir in cheeses until melted. Pour over drained tortellini in saucepan. Simmer for 5 minutes. Serve immediately. Yield: 4 servings.

Susan Michaelson, Fort Lauderdale, FL

FAST FOUR-WAY CASSEROLE

1 6-oz. package wide noodles, cooked
1 carton cottage cheese
1 carton sour cream
¼ c. milk
1 c. cubed Cheddar cheese
1 tbsp. chopped pimento
¼ tsp. Worcestershire sauce
¼ tsp. salt

Combine all ingredients in large bowl; toss to mix. Place in buttered casserole. Bake at 325 degrees for 20 to 30 minutes. Garnish with olives. Yield: 6 servings.

Patricia Johnson, Gadsden, AL

DILLED ZUCCHINI-RICE BAKE

4 med. zucchini, sliced
2 c. cooked brown rice
1   16-oz. carton cottage cheese
1 med. onion, chopped
2 eggs, beaten
Salt and pepper to taste
1 tbsp. dillweed
Parmesan cheese

Cook zucchini in water to cover in saucepan for 5 minutes or until tender-crisp; drain. Combine rice, next 3 ingredients and seasonings in bowl; mix well. Layer zucchini and rice mixture ½ at a time in buttered 2-quart casserole. Top with Parmesan cheese. Bake at 350 degrees for 45 minutes or until browned and bubbly. Yield: 4-6 servings.

Mary Helen Pope, McCall, IL

ELEGANT RICE

2 c. rice
4 c. chicken broth
½ lg. onion, minced
4 stalks celery, sliced diagonally
4 tbsp. butter
1 pkg. frozen tiny peas, cooked
3 tbsp. chopped fresh parsley

Combine rice and broth in large saucepan. Simmer for 20 minutes or until rice is fluffy. Sauté onion and celery in butter in skillet until tender. Add to rice with remaining ingredients; mix well. Press into ring mold. Invert on serving plate. Garnish with parsley sprigs and serve immediately. Yield: 8 servings.

Sally Bauman, Boone, NC

FAVORITE RICE CASSEROLE

2 med. onions, chopped
6 tbsp. butter
1 c. rice
1   6-oz. can mushroom sauce
1 can beef consommé
¼ tsp. oregano

Sauté onions in butter in skillet. Combine with remaining ingredients in baking dish; mix well.

Bake, covered, at 350 degrees for 45 minutes or until liquid is absorbed and rice is tender. Yield: 8 servings.

Sue Kent, Batavia, NY

RICE à la GOOD

¼ c. each chopped onions,
   green peppers and mushrooms
2 tbsp. butter
½ tsp. sweet basil
1 c. rice
Salt and pepper to taste

Sauté onions, green peppers and mushrooms in butter in skillet for 10 minutes. Add remaining ingredients with 2 cups water; mix well. Simmer, covered, for 15 minutes or until rice is tender. Yield: 6-8 servings.

Cecilia Kilbride, Miami, FL

CALIFORNIA RICE

1 c. canned tomatoes
5 slices bacon, diced
½ c. diced celery
4 oz. mushrooms, sliced
¾ c. grated Cheddar cheese
1 env. onion soup mix
1⅓ c. instant rice

Drain tomatoes, reserving juice. Add enough water to juice to measure 1⅓ cups. Fry bacon until crisp; drain, reserving 2 tablespoons bacon drippings. Sauté celery and mushrooms in drippings until tender. Stir in ½ cup cheese, tomato juice and remaining ingredients. Pour into 1½-quart baking dish. Top with remaining cheese. Bake, covered, at 375 degrees for 20 minutes. Yield: 4 servings.

Lila Zobac, Cornell, WI

Tip: For easier cleanup, fill cooking pans immediately with hot water to soak. Fill pans with cold water for cereal, egg and milk dishes.

SPECIAL RICE PILAF

1 c. rice
¼ c. slivered almonds
¼ c. margarine
⅛ tsp. saffron
1 teaspoon salt
2 c. chicken broth
¼ c. chopped green pepper
¼ c. chopped green onions
½ c. sliced mushrooms

Brown rice and almonds lightly in margarine in skillet. Add seasonings and broth; mix well. Bring to a boil. Cook, covered, over low heat for 15 minutes. Add green pepper, onions and mushrooms. Cook for 5 to 10 minutes longer or until rice is tender. Yield: 4-6 servings.

Tinka Piper, Honolulu, HI

INFALLIBLE RICE

1 med. onion, chopped
2 tbsp. margarine
1 c. rice
2 c. hot chicken broth

Sauté onion in margarine in Dutch oven until tender. Stir in rice. Add hot chicken broth. Bring to a boil; cover. Bake in preheated 325 degree oven for 20 minutes. Yield: 8 servings.

Ladye Corbin, Cedar Hill, TN

CAJUN CHEESE GRITS

1½ c. grits
1½ tbsp. seasoned salt
¾ c. margarine
¾ lb. Velveeta cheese, grated
½ tsp. garlic powder
3 eggs, beaten
2 or 3 jalapeño peppers,
    finely chopped

Stir grits into 6 cups boiling salted water. Cook until water is absorbed, stirring frequently. Stir in remaining ingredients. Pour into greased casserole. Bake at 350 degrees for 30 to 35 minutes or until set. Yield: 6 servings.

Margareta J. Miles, Azle, TX

MICROWAVE CRANBERRY RELISH

¼ c. orange juice
1½ c. sugar
1   12-oz. package cranberries
2 tsp. lemon juice
2   1-in. pieces orange rind
½ c. nuts

Combine orange juice, sugar, cranberries, lemon juice and orange rind in 3-quart glass bowl. Microwave, covered, on High for 7 minutes or until cranberries burst, stirring several times. Serve warm or cool.
Yield: 2 cups.

Linda Metz, Hendersonville, TN

CURRIED FRUIT

1 lg. can peach halves
1 lg. can pear halves
1 lg. can pineapple chunks
⅓ c. margarine
1 c. packed brown sugar
½ tsp. curry powder

Drain peaches, pears and pineapple well. Arrange in large baking dish. Melt margarine and sugar in saucepan. Stir in curry powder. Drizzle over fruit. Bake at 325 degrees for 45 minutes or until bubbly. Yield: 8-10 servings.

Agnes Moore, Knoxville, TN

PINEAPPLE SCALLOP

1 c. melted margarine
2 c. sugar
3 eggs
4 c. bread cubes
1   29-oz. can crushed pineapple
¼ c. milk

Combine margarine, sugar and eggs in baking dish; mix well. Top with bread cubes, pineapple and milk. Bake at 325 degrees for 1 hour.

Carol Glaeser, Gladstone, MO

Eggs
& Cheese

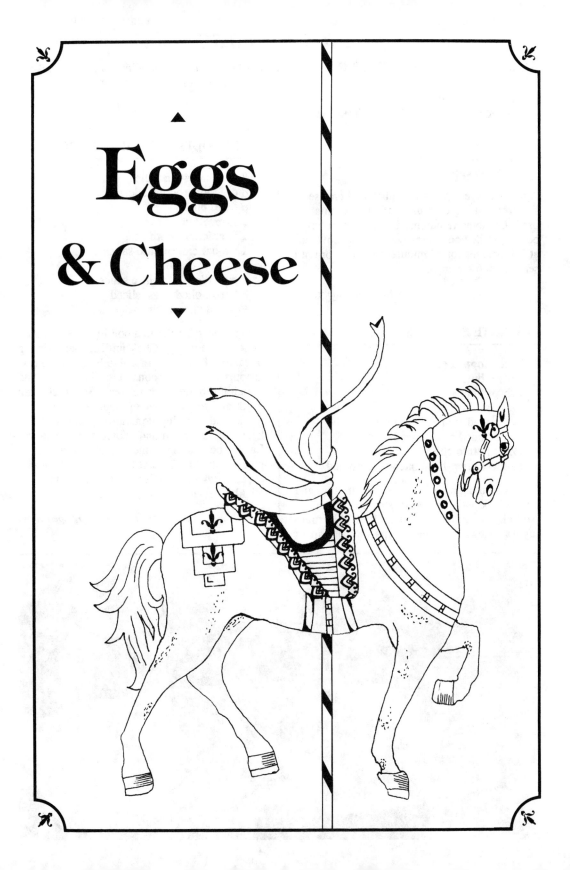

BAKED EGG AND CHEESE DISH

5 slices bread, buttered, cubed
4 oz. sharp Cheddar cheese, shredded
4 eggs
2 c. milk
1 tsp. each salt, dry mustard
Dash of pepper

Alternate layers of bread cubes and cheese in buttered baking dish until all ingredients are used. Combine remaining ingredients in bowl, beating well. Pour over layers. Bake, covered, at 350 degrees for 45 minutes to 1 hour or until set. Yield: 6 servings.

Jennifer Harmon, Moore, OK

FAVORITE EGG CASSEROLE

½ c. chopped onion
1 tbsp. butter
2 tbsp. flour
1¼ c. milk
1 c. grated sharp cheese
6 to 8 boiled eggs, sliced
1½ c. potato chips
10 slices crisp-fried bacon, crumbled

Sauté onion in butter in skillet. Stir in flour and milk. Cook until thickened, stirring constantly. Add cheese and stir until melted. Alternate layers of eggs, sauce, chips and bacon in casserole until all ingredients are used. Bake at 350 degrees for ½ hour. Yield: 6-8 servings.

Salli Cline, Knoxville, TN

EGG NOODLE SUPPER CASSEROLE

8 oz. fine egg noodles
8 oz. mushrooms, sliced
6 tbsp. butter
3 tbsp. flour
1 c. chicken broth
1   8-oz. can tomato sauce
1 c. light cream
1 tsp. Worcestershire sauce
8 hard-boiled eggs, sliced
⅓ c. Parmesan cheese

Bring 3 quarts water to a boil in saucepan. Add noodles gradually. Cook until tender, stirring occasionally; drain in colander. Sauté mushrooms in 2 tablespoons butter in skillet. Add remaining butter. Stir in flour. Stir in chicken broth and tomato sauce gradually. Cook until thickened, stirring constantly; remove from heat. Stir in cream and Worcestershire sauce. Layer noodles, eggs and sauce ½ at a time in greased shallow 2-quart baking dish. Top with cheese. Bake at 450 degrees for 15 minutes. Yield: 6 servings.

Photograph for this recipe below.

CHEESE AND EGG WEDGES

1 box instant hashed brown
  potatoes with onions
Butter, melted
6 eggs
6 tbsp. milk
2 oz. Cheddar cheese, shredded

Prepare potatoes using package directions. Brown in butter in skillet; turn. Mix remaining 3 ingredients in bowl. Pour over potatoes. Cook, tightly covered, for several minutes or until egg mixture is set. Cut into pie-shaped wedges. Yield: 6 servings.

Robyn Mosher, Port Huron, MI

CHILIES AND CHEESE

¼ lb. longhorn cheese, shredded
¼ lb. Monterey Jack cheese, shredded
1 c. half and half
⅓ c. flour
3 eggs
1 lg. can chilies
1 8-oz. can tomato sauce

Combine the cheeses and mix lightly. Mix half and half, flour and eggs in bowl. Alternate layers of chilies, cheeses and cream mixture in casserole until all ingredients are used, ending with cheeses. Pour tomato sauce over layers. Bake at 350 degrees for 30 to 35 minutes or until set. Yield: 6 servings.

Roberta Walker, Knoxville, TN

CHILI-CHEESE EGGS

2 8-oz. cans green chilies
½ lb. sharp Cheddar cheese, grated
9 eggs
1 pkg. taco seasoning mix

Rinse chilies; drain. Place ½ the chilies in 8x8x2-inch baking dish. Sprinkle with ½ of the cheese. Cover with remaining chilies. Combine eggs and seasoning mix; beat well. Pour over chilies. Top with remaining cheese. Bake at 350 degrees for 30 minutes or until eggs are puffy and lightly browned. Yield: 6 servings.

Frances Dillman, Buena Park, CA

CHILIES RELLENOS CASSEROLE

3 7-oz. cans whole green chilies
1 lb. Monterey Jack cheese, shredded
4 corn tortillas, cut into wide strips
5 eggs, beaten
½ c. milk
½ tsp. each salt, pepper, ground
  cuminseed, garlic
¼ tsp. onion salt
Paprika to taste
1 lg. tomato, sliced

Layer chilies, cheese and tortilla strips in greased baking dish. Beat eggs, milk and seasonings except paprika together in bowl. Pour over layers. Sprinkle with paprika. Arrange tomato slices over top. Bake at 350 degrees for 40 minutes. Let stand for several minutes before serving. Yield: 8 servings.

Carol Purvine Sanchez, Seiling, OK

EGGS BAKED IN GREEN PEPPERS

3 green peppers
Buttered bread crumbs
Salt and pepper to taste
6 eggs
Grated Parmesan cheese

Cut green peppers in half lengthwise; remove seeds and ribs. Blanch peppers in boiling water. Combine bread crumbs and seasonings. Spoon into peppers to half full. Break 1 egg into each pepper; sprinkle with cheese. Bake at 350 degrees for 15 minutes or until eggs are set. Serve with Hollandaise sauce. Yield: 6 servings.

Ann Clayton, Nashville, TN

Tip: To poach or hard-cook an egg in the microwave, break it into a glass dish and pierce the yolk with a toothpick to allow steam to escape.

EGGS FLORENTINE

2 pkg. frozen spinach
2 tbsp. lemon juice
2 tbsp. minced onion
½ c. shredded Cheddar cheese
4 hard-boiled eggs, sliced
Butter or margarine
3 tbsp. flour
½ tsp. each salt, dry mustard
¼ tsp. pepper
2¼ c. milk
½ c. dry bread crumbs

Prepare spinach according to package directions; drain. Add lemon juice and onion; mix well. Spread spinach mixture in 8x8x2-inch baking dish. Sprinkle with cheese. Top with egg slices. Melt 3 tablespoons butter in saucepan over low heat. Blend in flour and seasonings. Cook over low heat until smooth and bubbly, stirring constantly. Remove from heat. Stir in milk. Bring to a boil, stirring constantly. Boil for 1 minute; stir. Pour over egg slices. Toss bread crumbs in 1 tablespoon melted butter. Sprinkle over sauce. Bake at 400 degrees for 20 minutes. Yield: 4-6 servings.

Diane E. Taylor, Spangdahlem, Germany

CHEESE AND PEPPER ENCHILADAS

1 onion, chopped
10 banana peppers, chopped
6 to 8 tortillas
1 can cream of mushroom soup
1 lb. Cheddar cheese, shredded
½ soup can milk

Sauté onion and peppers in small amount of margarine in skillet until tender. Soften tortillas over steam from vegetables. Place 1 spoonful soup, 1 spoonful vegetables and 2 spoonfuls cheese in each tortilla. Roll tortillas to enclose filling. Place seam side down in casserole. Top with remaining cheese and vegetables. Add milk to remaining soup, stirring to mix. Pour over enchiladas. Bake at 325 degrees for 15 to 20 minutes or until bubbly. Yield: 6 servings.

Durene French, Cameron, OK

CHEESE ENCHILADAS

12 corn tortillas
½ c. oil
¾ c. chopped onion
2 c. shredded Monterey Jack cheese
¼ c. butter
¼ c. flour
2 c. chicken broth
1 8-oz. carton sour cream
1 4-oz. can chopped green chilies

Soften tortillas in hot oil in skillet; drain. Place 1 tablespoon onion and 1 tablespoon cheese on each tortilla; roll to enclose filling. Place seam side down in baking dish. Blend butter and flour over low heat in saucepan. Stir in chicken broth. Cook until thick, stirring constantly. Stir in sour cream and green chilies. Cook until just warm. Pour over tortillas. Bake at 375 degrees for 10 to 15 minutes or until heated through. Sprinkle remaining cheese over top. Bake until cheese is melted. Yield: 6 servings.

RoLayne Gardner, Provo, UT

FRIED RICE

3 eggs, well beaten
4 tbsp. oil
4 c. cold cooked rice
¼ c. soy sauce
½ tsp. salt
½ c. chopped green onions
½ lb. bacon, crisp-fried, crumbled

Scramble eggs in 1 tablespoon oil in medium skillet until set. Sauté rice in 3 tablespoons hot oil in wok. Stir in soy sauce and salt. Add eggs, green onions and bacon; mix well.
Yield: 6-8 servings.

Marianne Allen, Spokane, WA

GERMAN FARMER'S BREAKFAST

½ lb. sliced bacon, cut into ½-inch strips
½ c. chopped cooked potatoes
2 tbsp. each chopped green pepper, onion
¾ tsp. salt
⅛ tsp. pepper

½ c. shredded Cheddar cheese
6 eggs

Cook bacon over medium heat in large skillet until crisp; drain, reserving 3 tablespoons drippings. Cook potatoes with bacon and next 4 ingredients in reserved drippings over medium heat until lightly browned, stirring frequently. Sprinkle with cheese; mix well. Break eggs into skillet. Cook over low heat until eggs are set, stirring constantly. Yield: 4 servings.

Audra Ogle, Caddo, OK

OVEN OMELET

6 spring onions, thinly sliced
1 tbsp. bacon drippings
9 eggs
1 c. milk
½ tsp. seasoned salt
8 slices crisp-fried bacon, crumbled
3 c. shredded Monterey Jack cheese

Sauté onions in bacon drippings in skillet until tender. Beat eggs with milk and seasoned salt in bowl. Stir in bacon, onions and 2¼ cups cheese. Pour into buttered 2-quart casserole. Bake at 350 degrees for 35 to 40 minutes or until mixture is set and top is lightly browned. Sprinkle with remaining cheese. Bake until cheese melts. Yield: 6 servings.

Janin Hale, Nashville, TN

OMELETS WITH SPANISH SAUCE

1 clove of garlic, minced
2 lg. onions, chopped
3 tbsp. butter
1 dried chili pepper, chopped
3½ c. chopped tomatoes
8 eggs
¼ tsp. each salt and pepper
¼ c. butter

Sauté garlic and onions in 3 tablespoons butter in skillet until tender. Add pepper and to-matoes. Simmer for 15 minutes. Combine eggs, salt, pepper and 3 tablespoons water in bowl; mix well. Melt 2 tablespoons butter in omelet pan. Pour in half the eggs. Cook until almost set, stirring several times with fork. Shake pan during cooking to loosen omelet. Fold in half; slide onto heated platter. Repeat with remaining eggs and butter. Spoon sauce over top.
Yield: 4 servings.

Sue Joyner, Panama City, FL

IMPOSSIBLE QUICHE

1 sm. onion, chopped
2 tbsp. butter
4 slices crisp-cooked bacon, crumbled
1½ c. milk
3 eggs, beaten
½ c. biscuit mix
1 c. grated cheese
¼ tsp. salt
½ tsp. dry mustard
Dash of red pepper
1 4-oz. can sliced mushrooms, drained

Sauté onion in butter in skillet until tender. Combine with remaining ingredients except mushrooms in mixer bowl. Beat until well mixed. Fold in mushrooms. Pour into greased pie plate. Bake at 375 degrees for 35 minutes or until knife inserted in center comes out clean. Let stand for 5 minutes before slicing.
Yield: 6-8 servings.

Marilyn Barfield, Ayden, NC

QUICK QUICHE LORRAINE

1 can crescent dinner rolls
1 egg, beaten
1 c. evaporated milk
½ tsp. salt
½ tsp. Worcestershire sauce
1 c. shredded Swiss cheese
1 can French-fried onions, crumbled
9 slices crisp-cooked bacon, crumbled

Separate roll dough into 8 triangles. Place in 9-inch pie plate, pressing together to form crust. Combine next 5 ingredients in bowl; mix well. Sprinkle half the onions over crust. Pour egg mixture over onions. Top with bacon and remaining onions. Bake at 325 degrees for 25 to 30 minutes until quiche tests done. Cool for 5 minutes before serving. Yield: 6 servings.

Barbara E. Smoot, Selma, IN

MUSHROOM-CHILI PEPPER PIE

Butter, melted
3 tbsp. flour
1 c. cream
1 lb. mushrooms, sliced
½ can green chili peppers, drained,
    diced
2 egg yolks, beaten
1 c. grated Cheddar cheese
2 tbsp. white wine
1 baked 9-in. pie shell

Blend 3 tablespoons butter, flour and cream in saucepan. Cook until thickened, stirring constantly; cool. Sauté mushrooms in butter in skillet. Stir into sauce with next 4 ingredients. Pour into pie shell. Bake at 350 degrees for 20 minutes. Yield: 4 servings.

Claudia Garrett, Pocatello, ID

VEGETARIAN LASAGNA

1 c. grated carrots
½ c. chopped onion
2 c. sliced mushrooms
1 tbsp. vegetable oil
1   15-oz. can tomato sauce
1   6-oz. can tomato paste
½ c. chopped pitted olives
1½ tsp. oregano
9 lasagna noodles, cooked
16 oz. cream-style cottage cheese
2   10-oz. packages frozen
    chopped spinach, cooked
16 oz. Monterey Jack cheese, sliced

Sauté carrots, onion and mushrooms in hot oil in medium saucepan. Stir in tomato sauce, tomato paste, olives and oregano. Layer ⅓ of the noodles, ⅓ of the cottage cheese, ⅓ of the spinach, ¼ of the Monterey Jack cheese and ⅓ of the sauce mixture in greased 9 x 13-inch baking dish. Repeat layers 3 times. Top with remaining cheese slices. Bake at 375 degrees for 30 minutes. Let stand for 10 minutes. Garnish with Parmesan cheese.
Yield: 10 servings.

Crystal Marschel, LaCrosse, WI

GOURMET MACARONI AND CHEESE

2 tbsp. butter
2 tbsp. each chopped onions, celery
2 tbsp. flour
2 c. milk
1 tsp. salt
¼ tsp. pepper
2 c. cooked macaroni
½ lb. sharp Cheddar cheese, grated
¼ lb. Swiss cheese, grated
½ can olives, drained

Melt butter in skillet. Add onions and celery; cook until tender. Add flour; mix well. Add milk, salt and pepper; stir until smooth. Cook for 2 minutes. Combine with remaining ingredients; mix well. Pour into buttered 1½-quart casserole. Sprinkle with additional cheese; cover. Bake at 350 degrees for 25 minutes. Bake, uncovered, for 5 minutes longer. Yield: 6 servings.

Helen M. Williams, Sebastopol, CA

LINGUINE WITH SALMON SAUCE

¼ c. diagonally sliced green onions
¼ c. olive oil
1 c. flaked smoked salmon
2 c. cream
Pepper to taste
¼ c. olive oil
2 lb. fresh linguine
½ c. Parmesan cheese
2 tbsp. diagonally sliced green onions
2 tbsp. minced parsley

Sauté ¼ cup green onions in ¼ cup olive oil in skillet for 1 minute. Add salmon, cream and pepper. Simmer until reduced by ⅓. Bring 4 quarts salted water and 2 tablespoons olive oil to a boil. Add linguine. Cook al dente; drain. Add remaining 2 tablespoons olive oil; toss to coat. Place on serving plates. Top with salmon sauce, Parmesan cheese, 2 tablespoons green onions and parsley. Yield: 6 servings.

Mary Helen Pope, McCall, ID

*Tip: Add 1 or 2 tablespoons oil to
    the cooking water to keep
    pasta separated.*

CHEESY MANICOTTI

1 8-oz. package manicotti
2 c. shredded mozzarella cheese
1 16-oz. carton ricotta cheese
12 2-in. crackers, crushed
2 eggs, beaten
¼ c. chopped chives
½ tsp. each basil, marjoram
¼ tsp. garlic salt
1 32-oz. jar thick spaghetti sauce

Cook manicotti in boiling water for 5 minutes; drain. Mix 1½ cups mozzarella cheese with remaining ingredients except spaghetti sauce. Stuff into manicotti. Arrange manicotti in half the sauce in 9x13-inch baking dish. Top with remaining sauce. Bake, covered, at 350 degrees for 25 minutes. Sprinkle with remaining mozzarella cheese. Bake for 5 minutes longer. Yield: 7 servings.

Hadena Roberts, Mercer, WV

MOSTACCIOLI WITH BROCCOLI

1 pt. ricotta cheese
1 c. butter, melted
1 tsp. salt
½ tsp. each pepper, garlic salt
2 10-oz. packages frozen broccoli, cooked
1 lb. mostaccioli, cooked
½ c. Parmesan cheese

Combine ricotta cheese, ½ cup butter and seasonings in bowl. Mix with broccoli. Add ½ cup butter to drained mostaccioli in saucepan. Sprinkle with Parmesan cheese. Stir in broccoli mixture. Yield: 8 servings.

Jeanette DeCarlo, Marion, WV

BAKED SPAGHETTI

1 med. onion, chopped
1 sm. green pepper, chopped
1 can tomatoes
1 sm. can mushrooms, drained
1 jar pizza sauce
½ pkg. spaghetti, cooked

Dash each of garlic salt, Italian seasoning
Salt and pepper to taste
1 c. grated cheese
8 slices crisp-cooked bacon, crumbled

Sauté onion and green pepper in skillet for 5 minutes. Combine tomatoes, mushrooms and pizza sauce in bowl. Add to spaghetti in casserole with sautéed vegetables and seasonings; mix well. Top with cheese and bacon. Bake at 350 degrees for ½ hour. Yield: 4 servings.

Sandie Shrum, Charlotte, NC

SCRAMBLED EGGS SUPREME

6 slices bacon, chopped
8 eggs, beaten
¼ c. sour cream
¼ c. process cheese spread
¾ tsp. salt
Dash of pepper

Fry bacon in large skillet until crisp; drain, reserving 3 tablespoons drippings. Mix eggs, sour cream, cheese spread, salt and pepper in bowl. Pour over bacon and reserved drippings in skillet. Cook over low heat until eggs are set, stirring gently. Yield: 6 servings.

Marsha Young, Alfalfa, OK

WELSH RAREBIT

¼ c. butter
½ tsp. salt
⅛ tsp. dry mustard
Dash of pepper
½ c. flour
2 c. milk
1 tsp. Worcestershire sauce
2 c. shredded sharp Cheddar cheese

Melt butter in saucepan over low heat. Blend in salt, mustard, pepper and flour; add milk and Worcestershire sauce. Cook until mixture thickens, stirring constantly. Add cheese gradually, stirring constantly until melted and blended. Serve hot over slices of toast or cheese bread. Yield: 4 servings.

Don Smith, McMinnville, TN

BRUNCH PUDDING

3 pkg. frozen cut corn in butter sauce
2 tbsp. flour
½ c. light cream, scalded
2 eggs, separated
½ tsp. each salt and pepper
¼ c. each chopped onion, green pepper
  and pimento

Heat corn pouches according to package directions. Strain corn in colander, reserving butter sauce. Blend butter sauce, flour and cream in saucepan. Add egg yolks, salt and pepper; mix well. Fold in stiffly beaten egg whites gently. Fold in mixture of corn, onion, green pepper and pimento. Pour into buttered baking dish. Bake at 350 degrees for 30 minutes. Serve with browned sausage links.

BLINTZ SOUFFLÉ

12 frozen cheese blintzes
6 eggs, beaten
6 tbsp. melted margarine
¼ c. sugar
1½ c. sour cream
1 tsp. vanilla extract
¼ tsp. salt
¼ c. orange juice

Arrange blintzes in single layer in buttered 9 x 13-inch baking dish. Combine remaining ingredients in bowl; beat well. Pour over blintzes. Bake at 350 degrees for 45 minutes or until set. Garnish with cherries, blueberries or strawberries. Yield: 12 servings.

Louisa Noble, Montgomery County, MD

HOT COTTAGE CHEESE SALAD

2 8-oz. cartons cottage cheese
1 stick margarine, sliced
6 eggs
6 tbsp. flour
20-oz. frozen chopped spinach, thawed
Bread crumbs
8 oz. sliced American cheese

Combine cottage cheese, margarine, eggs and flour in bowl; mix well. Stir in well-drained spinach. Spoon into greased 1½-quart baking dish. Top with bread crumbs and cheese. Bake at 350 degrees for 1¼ hours.
Yield: 8-12 servings.

Ruth E. Hughes, Mansfield, OH

THREE-CHEESE PASTA

4 oz. tofu, crumbled
1 c. each chopped mushrooms, onion
½ c. chopped celery
1 clove of garlic, chopped
2 tbsp. butter
1 tbsp. each chopped chives, parsley
½ tsp. basil
1 c. mozzarella cheese
½ c. Parmesan cheese
1 8-oz. can tomato sauce
2 c. canned tomatoes and juice
½ c. wine
1 8-oz. package pasta
2 tbsp. half and half
½ tsp. basil
1 tbsp. butter
½ c. Romano cheese

Sauté tofu, mushrooms, onion, celery and garlic in 2 tablespoons butter in skillet. Add next 8 ingredients; mix well. Simmer for 30 minutes. Cook pasta using package directions just until tender; drain. Add half and half, ½ teaspoon basil and 1 tablespoon butter; toss to coat well. Place on serving platter. Spoon sauce over top. Sprinkle with Romano cheese.
Yield: 6 servings.

Mary Foreman, Durango, CO

MICROWAVE EGG-CHEESE PUFF

1 tbsp. butter, melted
4 eggs, well beaten
¼ c. flour
1 c. milk
1 c. grated cheese
¼ tsp. each salt, pepper

Melt butter in 9-inch glass pie plate. Pour in mixture of remaining ingredients. Microwave tightly covered, on Medium-High until puffed.

Sharon Pangle, Rosman, NC

Breads

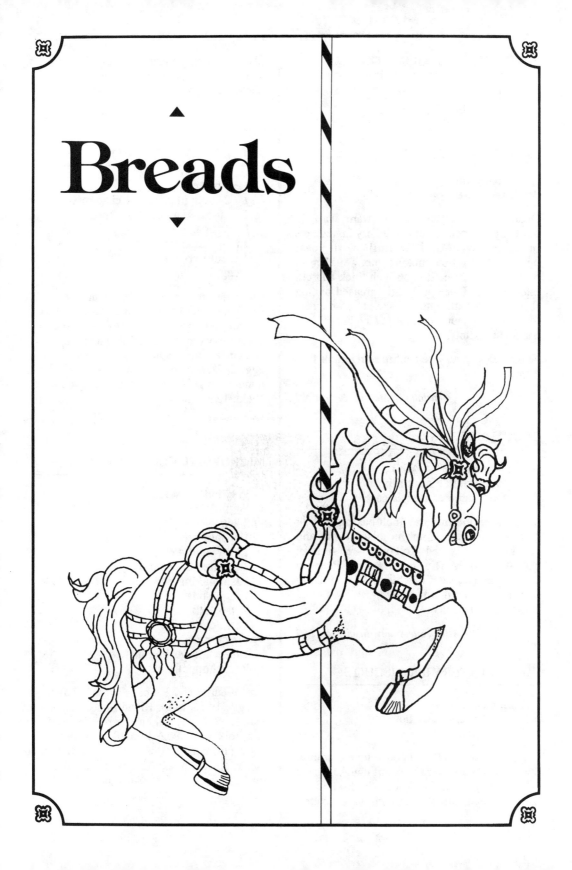

FAVORITE ANGEL BISCUITS

1 pkg. dry yeast
1 c. shortening
5 c. flour
1 tsp. each salt, soda
1 tbsp. baking powder
¼ c. sugar
2 c. buttermilk
Melted butter

Dissolve yeast in 2 tablespoons warm water in bowl. Cut shortening into sifted dry ingredients in large bowl. Mix buttermilk with yeast mixture. Add to flour mixture; mix well. Knead on floured surface. Roll ½ inch thick and cut into squares. Place on lightly greased baking sheet. Brush with butter. Bake at 375 degrees for 10 to 15 minutes or until golden brown. Yield: 48 biscuits.

NOTE: Dough may be kept in refrigerator for 2 weeks.

Charlotte L. McCall, Boone, NC

GOODY BISCUITS

¾ c. margarine
2 c. buttermilk biscuit mix
1   8-oz. can cream-style corn

Melt margarine in 9x13-inch baking dish in 350-degree oven. Combine biscuit mix and corn in bowl; mix well. Roll on floured surface; cut into squares. Dip in margarine. Place in baking pan with sides touching. Bake for 20 to 25 minutes or until brown. Yield: 12-15 biscuits.

Betty Sue Stuart, Brunswick, MO

QUICK BUTTERMILK BISCUITS

1 stick margarine
2 c. sifted self-rising flour
¾ c. buttermilk

Cut margarine into flour in bowl until crumbly. Stir in buttermilk to make a soft dough. Knead dough gently for about 30 seconds. Roll out on lightly floured surface. Cut with biscuit cutter; place on baking sheet. Bake at 375 degrees for about 12 minutes or until golden brown. Yield: 12 biscuits.

Jean Hicks, Knoxville, TN

APPLE KUCHEN COFFEE CAKE

½ c. butter
1   2-layer pkg. yellow cake mix
1   20-oz. can sliced pie apples
½ c. sugar
1 tsp. cinnamon
1 c. sour cream
1 egg, beaten

Cut butter into cake mix until crumbly. Pat into 9x13-inch baking pan, shaping rim. Bake at 350 degrees for 10 minutes. Arrange apple slices on warm crust. Sprinkle mixture of sugar and cinnamon on apples. Blend sour cream and egg. Drizzle over apples. Bake for 20 to 25 minutes longer or until edges are light brown. Yield: 12 servings.

Virginia Rankin, Florence, CO

MICROWAVE COFFEE CAKE

½ c. butter, softened
Sugar
2 eggs
1 c. sour cream
1 tsp. vanilla extract
2 c. sifted cake flour
1 tsp. baking powder
½ tsp. soda
¼ tsp. salt
1 tsp. cinnamon
¼ tsp. mace
1 tbsp. margarine, melted
½ c. chopped nuts

Cream butter and 1¼ cups sugar in bowl. Beat in eggs 1 at a time. Blend in sour cream and vanilla. Sift in flour, baking powder, soda and salt; mix well. Pour into 10-inch round glass baking dish. Top with mixture of 2 tablespoons sugar, spices, margarine and nuts. Microwave on High for 6 to 7 minutes or until cake tests done. Yield: 12 servings.

Eileen Nottingham, San Diego, CA

PLUCK-IT COFFEE CAKE

1 c. chopped nuts
1½ sticks margarine, melted
1½ c. packed light brown sugar
1 tsp. cinnamon
½ tsp. nutmeg
3 cans buttermilk refrigerator
   biscuits, quartered

Combine first 5 ingredients in bowl; mix well. Layer half the biscuits and sugar mixture in greased bundt pan. Repeat layers with remaining ingredients. Bake at 350 degrees for 25 to 30 minutes or until browned. Remove from pan while warm. Yield: 16 servings.

Mary Clare Turner, Charlotte, NC

YOGURT COFFEE CAKE

½   2-layer pkg. yellow cake mix
1 egg
½ c. raisins (opt.)
1 carton fruit-flavored yogurt
3 tbsp. sugar
½ tsp. cinnamon

Combine first 4 ingredients in bowl; mix well with wooden spoon. Pour into greased and floured 8-inch square cake pan. Sprinkle mixture of sugar and cinnamon over batter. Bake at 350 degrees for 25 minutes. Cool. Yield: 9 servings.

NOTE: May use strawberry cake mix with strawberry yogurt or lemon cake mix with lemon yogurt.

Colleen Slaughter, Las Vegas, NV

MICROWAVE CORN BREAD RING

1 c. each yellow cornmeal, flour
2 tbsp. sugar
4 tsp. baking powder
½ tsp. salt
1 egg
1 c. milk
½ c. oil
½ c. crushed French-fried onions
1 tbsp. Parmesan cheese

Combine first 5 ingredients in mixing bowl. Add egg, milk and oil. Beat for 1 minute or until smooth. Coat greased 8-inch glass tube pan with onion crumbs and cheese, reserving excess crumbs. Pour batter into prepared pan. Sprinkle with reserved crumbs. Microwave on Low for 6 minutes. Turn dish 180 degrees. Microwave on High for 3 to 5 minutes or until bread tests done. Invert on wire rack to cool. Yield: 8 servings.

Molly Arnold, Granville, OH

QUICK CORN BREAD

1   12-oz. package corn muffin mix
1   20-oz. can cream-style corn
1   8-oz. carton sour cream
½ c. oil
1 tsp. salt
3 eggs, beaten

Combine all ingredients in bowl; mix well. Pour into greased 9 x 13-inch baking pan. Bake at 375 degrees for ½ hour. Yield: 20 servings.

Ruth J. Waters, Olin, NC

SOUTHERN SPOON BREAD

2⅓ c. milk
¾ c. cornmeal
1½ tbsp. butter
½ tsp. salt
2 eggs, well beaten

Scald milk in saucepan. Add cornmeal. Cook until smooth, stirring constantly; remove from heat. Add butter and salt; mix well. Stir a small amount of hot mixture into eggs; stir eggs into hot mixture. Pour into buttered 9 x 13-inch baking dish. Bake at 350 degrees for 25 minutes. Yield: 8-12 servings.

Rosalie Floyd, Bowling Green, KY

Tip: Give variety to biscuits made with buttermilk baking mix by adding cheese, crumbled bacon, chives or other herbs.

BREWSKY BREAD

3 c. sifted self-rising flour
3 tbsp. sugar
1   12-oz. can beer

Combine all ingredients in bowl; mix well. Batter will be lumpy. Pour into greased loaf pan. Bake at 400 degrees for 40 minutes. Yield: 10 servings.

Virginia Chenault, Littleton, CO

CHEESE-ONION BREAD

1 c. chopped onion
¼ c. butter, melted
2 eggs, slightly beaten
1 c. milk
2½ c. Bisquick
1 c. grated Cheddar cheese
1 tbsp. poppy seed

Sauté onion in 2 tablespoons butter in skillet until tender. Combine eggs, milk, Bisquick and ⅔ cup cheese in bowl; mix well. Add onions, stirring to blend. Pour into greased 5x9-inch loaf pan. Mix remaining 2 tablespoons butter, ⅓ cup cheese and poppy seed. Sprinkle topping over batter. Bake at 400 degrees for 20 to 25 minutes or until loaf tests done. Yield: 12 servings.

Carolyn Cotton, Bristow, OK

CONFETTI BREAD

1 c. chopped green pepper
1 c. chopped onion
1 c. butter
3   8-count cans refrigerator biscuits, quartered
1 sm. jar bacon bits
½ c. Parmesan cheese

Sauté green pepper and onion in butter in skillet. Add biscuits with bacon bits and cheese; mix lightly. Spoon into bundt pan. Bake at 375 degrees for 30 minutes. Invert onto serving plate. Yield: 24 servings.

Sherrie Haub, Canton, OK

ONION-TOPPED BREAD

1½ c. biscuit mix
¾ tsp. salt
½ c. milk
1   3-oz. can French-fried onions
1 egg
1 c. sour cream

Combine biscuit mix, ¼ teaspoon salt and milk; mix well. Spread in greased 8-inch baking pan. Sprinkle with ½ of the onions. Combine egg, sour cream and ½ teaspoon salt; beat well. Spoon over onions. Top with remaining onions. Bake at 375 degrees for 25 minutes or until bread tests done. Yield: 6 servings.

Freda F. Pirtle, West Frankfort, IL

PARMESAN CHEESE BREAD

2 c. buttermilk baking mix
1 c. sugar
1 stick butter, softened
2 eggs, well beaten
1 c. milk
¾ c. Parmesan cheese

Combine baking mix and sugar in bowl; mix well. Cut in butter until crumbly. Stir in eggs and milk. Add cheese; mix well. Pour into greased 9x13-inch baking pan. Bake at 350 degrees for 45 minutes. Cut into squares. Yield: 12 servings.

Janet K. Wallace, Everett, WA

SALLY LUNN

½ c. butter, softened
Sugar
2 tsp. baking powder
2 c. cake flour
1 c. milk
1 egg, beaten

Cream butter and ¼ cup sugar together in bowl. Add baking powder, flour and milk. Add egg; mix well. Pour into greased 9-inch cake pan. Bake at 350 degrees for 30 minutes. Cut into wedges to serve. Sprinkle with additional sugar. Yield: 6 servings.

Lonny James, Biloxi, MS

BASIC SWEET MUFFINS

1 egg, beaten
½ c. milk
¼ c. oil
1½ c. flour
½ c. sugar
2 tsp. baking powder

Combine first 3 ingredients in bowl; mix well. Mix dry ingredients together. Add to liquid mixture, stirring until just moistened. Fill muffin cups ⅔ full. Bake for 20 minutes. Yield: 1 dozen muffins.

Marcy Poulton, Bountiful, UT

BEER MUFFINS

4½ c. biscuit mix
¾ c. sugar
1   12-oz. can beer

Combine all ingredients in bowl; mix well. Batter will be slightly lumpy. Spoon into 12 greased and floured muffin cups. Bake at 375 degrees for 20 to 30 minutes or until brown. Yield: 24-36 muffins.

Teresa Helton, Waynoka, OK

BLUEBERRY MUFFINS

1¾ c. self-rising flour
¾ c. sugar
1 egg, beaten
¾ c. milk
⅓ c. oil
½ tsp. vanilla extract (opt.)
¾ c. blueberries

Combine first 6 ingredients in bowl, mixing to blend. Fold in blueberries. Spoon into greased and floured muffin cups. Bake at 400 degrees for 25 minutes. Yield: 12 muffins.

Marcia F. Swanson, McDonough, GA

QUICK BRAN MUFFINS

1 c. golden pure bran
¾ c. unbleached flour
¾ tsp. salt

¼ c. packed brown sugar
½ c. sugar
½ tsp. soda
¾ c. buttermilk
¾ c. oil
1 egg, beaten

Combine first 6 ingredients in bowl. Make well in center. Mix buttermilk, oil and egg in small bowl. Pour into well; mix just until moistened. Fill greased muffin cups ⅔ full. Bake at 400 degrees for 20 minutes. Yield: 12 muffins.

Monnie Winingham, Knoxville, TN

COCOA-SPICE MUFFINS

¼ c. melted butter
¼ c. unsweetened cocoa
¾ c. applesauce
1¼ c. flour
1 c. sugar
¾ tsp. soda
½ tsp. cinnamon
¼ tsp. each nutmeg, salt
1 egg, slightly beaten
½ c. chopped nuts

Blend butter and cocoa in bowl. Add applesauce; mix well. Add egg and mixture of dry ingredients; mix just until moistened. Stir in nuts. Fill greased muffin cups ⅔ full. Bake at 350 degrees for 20 minutes. Yield: 12 muffins.

Photograph for this recipe on page 102.

POPPY SEED MUFFINS

1½ c. biscuit mix
½ c. sugar
1 tbsp. poppy seed
¾ c. raisins, chopped
1 egg, beaten
¾ c. sour cream
1 tsp. vanilla extract

Mix first 3 ingredients in bowl. Make well in center of mixture. Add remaining ingredients, stirring until just moistened. Fill greased muffin cups ½ full. Bake at 400 degrees for 20 minutes. Yield: 12 muffins.

Betty Lowrance, Paden, OK

SURPRISE MUFFINS

1½ c. flour
½ c. sugar
2 tsp. baking powder
½ tsp. salt
1 egg, slightly beaten
½ c. milk
¼ c. oil
½ c. miniature semisweet
    chocolate chips
¼ c. apricot or peach preserves

Combine flour, sugar, baking powder and salt in bowl. Add egg, milk and oil; stir just until blended. Fill greased muffin cups ¼ full. Place 1 teaspoon chocolate chips and ½ teaspoon preserves in center of batter. Fill muffin cups ⅔ full. Bake at 400 degrees for 25 to 30 minutes or until golden. Yield: 12 muffins.

Photograph for this recipe below.

OATMEAL MUFFINS

Toasted wheat germ
¼ c. creamy peanut butter
⅓ c. packed brown sugar
1 egg
¾ c. flour
⅓ c. quick-cooking oats
2 tbsp. toasted wheat germ
1 tsp. baking powder
¼ tsp. soda
⅛ tsp. salt
½ c. milk
½ c. miniature semisweet
    chocolate chips

Grease 8 muffin cups. Sprinkle lightly with toasted wheat germ. Cream peanut butter and brown sugar in mixer bowl until fluffy. Blend in egg. Add mixture of flour, oats, 2 tablespoons wheat germ, baking powder, soda and salt alternately with milk, beating at low speed just until mixed after each addition. Stir in chocolate chips. Fill prepared muffin cups ¾ full. Sprinkle with additional wheat germ. Bake at 400 degrees for 15 to 20 minutes or until golden. Serve warm. Yield: 8 muffins.

Photograph for this recipe below.

POPOVERS

3 eggs
1 c. milk
¾ c. sifted flour
1 tsp. salt

Combine all ingredients in bowl; mix well. Fill greased muffin cups ⅓ full. Place in cold oven. Bake at 450 degrees for 45 minutes.
Yield: 6 popovers.

Wilma Sanders, Atlanta, GA

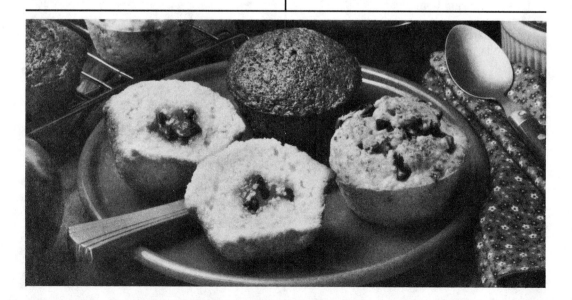

APPLE-CINNAMON DELIGHTS

2 tbsp. butter
½ c. each packed brown sugar, raisins
    and red cinnamon candies
1   20-oz. can apple pie slices
2 can refrigerator cinnamon rolls
½ c. chopped pecans

Melt butter at 200 degrees in electric skillet.
Sprinkle brown sugar, ¼ cup raisins and ¼ cup
cinnamon candies over butter. Add apple slices
and remaining candies. Arrange rolls over top.
Sprinkle with remaining raisins and pecans.
Cook, covered, at 300 degrees for 20 to 25
minutes or until cooked through.
Yield: 16 servings.

Troy Lozano, McKinney, TX

CINNAMON-SUGAR BOWKNOTS

1 can Hungry Jack Flaky biscuits
½ stick butter, melted
½ c. sugar
½ tsp. each cinnamon, nutmeg
¼ c. honey

Separate each biscuit into 2 thin biscuits. Pull
each into long strip; pinch in center and twist.
Dip 1 side in butter then in mixture of sugar,
cinnamon and nutmeg. Place sugared side up on
baking sheet. Bake at 425 degrees for 8 to 10
minutes or until brown. Mix remaining butter
with honey. Brush over bowknots.
Yield: 20 bowknots.

Kim Remington, Nowata, OK

QUICK CINNAMON ROLLS

2 c. flour
1 tbsp. baking powder
¾ tsp. salt
½ c. sugar
¼ c. shortening
1 egg, beaten
½ c. milk
2 tbsp. butter, melted
1 tsp. cinnamon

Sift flour, baking powder, salt and ¼ cup sugar
into bowl. Cut in shortening until crumbly. Mix

in egg and milk. Knead 5 or 6 times on lightly
floured surface. Roll ¼-inch thick. Spread with
mixture of butter, ¼ cup sugar and cinnamon.
Roll as for jelly roll. Cut into 1-inch slices.
Place on baking sheet. Bake at 450 degrees for
15 minutes. Yield: 12 rolls.

Lara Doyle, Kings, CA

BUSY-DAY YEAST ROLLS

1 pkg. dry yeast
¼ to ½ c. sugar
¾ c. oil
4 c. self-rising flour

Dissolve yeast in 2 cups very warm water. Stir
in sugar and oil until sugar is dissolved. Mix in
flour. Spoon into greased muffin cups. Bake at
350 degrees until browned. Yield: 24 rolls.

Teresa Aaron, Knoxville, TN

MYSTERY ROLLS

1 c. self-rising flour
2 tbsp. mayonnaise
½ c. milk

Combine all ingredients in bowl; mix well.
Drop by spoonfuls into small greased muffin
cups. Bake at 400 degrees for 15 minutes or
until brown. Yield: 6-8 rolls.

Betty Forsythe, Nashville, TN

QUICK HERB ROLLS

½ c. butter, softened
1½ tsp. parsley flakes
½ tsp. dillweed
1 tbsp. onion flakes
2 cans refrigerator biscuits
2 tbsp. Parmesan cheese

Spread butter over bottom of 9-inch pie pan.
Sprinkle with mixture of next 3 ingredients. Cut
biscuits into halves; place in pie pan. Sprinkle
Parmesan cheese on top. Bake at 425 degrees
for 12 to 15 minutes. Yield: 10 servings.

Andrea Gay Mitchell, Morrison, OK

QUICKIE YEAST ROLLS

1 pkg. dry yeast
2 tbsp. sugar
2 tbsp. oil
½ tsp. salt
1 egg
2½ to 2¾ c. flour
Butter, softened

Dissolve yeast in ¾ cup warm water in 2½-quart bowl. Add sugar, oil, salt and egg. Stir until sugar and salt dissolve. Add 1 cup flour; mix well. Cover. Place on rack over bowl of hot water. Let rise for 15 minutes. Stir batter. Add 1½ cups flour; mix well. Knead in remaining flour if necessary on floured cloth. Knead for 3 minutes. Shape into balls. Arrange in baking pan. Brush with butter. Let rise, covered, over hot water for 25 minutes. Bake at 425 degrees for 12 to 15 minutes or until light brown. Remove from pan to wire rack. Brush with butter. Yield: 15 rolls.

Bette L. Carraher, Ashtabula, OH

SIXTY-MINUTE ROLLS

3½ to 4½ c. flour
3 tbsp. sugar
1 tsp. salt
2 pkg. yeast
1 c. milk
¼ c. margarine

Combine 1½ cups flour with next 3 ingredients in mixer bowl; mix well. Mix milk and margarine with ½ cup water in saucepan. Heat to 120 to 130 degrees. Add to dry ingredients gradually. Beat at medium speed for 2 minutes. Add ½ cup flour. Beat at high speed for 2 minutes. Stir in enough remaining flour to make soft dough. Knead on lightly floured surface for about 5 minutes or until smooth and elastic. Place in greased bowl, turning to coat surface. Let rise in covered bowl in very warm water for 15 minutes. Roll on floured surface and cut into 24 rolls. Let rise, covered, on buttered pan over hot water for about 15 minutes. Bake at 425 degrees for 12 minutes. Yield:18-24 rolls.

Ann L. Bost, Newton, NC

SPOON ROLLS

1 pkg. dry yeast
1½ sticks margarine, melted
¼ c. sugar
1 egg, beaten
4 c. flour

Dissolve yeast in 2 cups warm water in bowl. Cream margarine with sugar in large bowl. Add beaten egg, dissolved yeast and flour. Spoon into greased muffin cups. Bake at 350 degrees until brown. Store any remaining mixture in airtight bowl in refrigerator for about 1 week. Yield: 24 rolls.

Ember O'Hara, Knoxville, TN

YORKSHIRE PUDDING

1 c. flour
½ tsp. salt
1 c. milk
2 eggs, separated
1 tbsp. melted butter
Roast beef drippings

Sift flour and salt into bowl. Add milk, beaten egg yolks and butter. Fold in stiffly beaten egg whites. Spoon drippings into muffin cups or baking dish. Pour batter over drippings. Bake at 400 degrees for 20 minutes. Baste with drippings after pudding is well risen.
Yield: 6-8 servings.

Mabel O. Walters, Baltimore, MD

YUMMY FRIED TOAST

6 slices bread
2 tbsp. butter, softened
¼ c. cinnamon-sugar
¼ c. maple syrup

Butter bread on both sides. Brown 1 side of bread in skillet over medium heat. Turn over. Sprinkle with cinnamon-sugar. Perforate several times with fork. Pour syrup over bread. Cook until brown on both sides.
Yield: 6 servings.

Peggy Hendricks, Chouteau, OK

HERB STICKS

4 hot dog buns, split
½ c. butter, melted
¼ tsp. each dried savory, paprika
½ tsp. each celery seed, thyme
Cayenne pepper to taste
1 clove of garlic, minced

Cut bun halves into 4 long strips each. Combine remaining ingredients in bowl. Let stand for several hours. Brush butter mixture on all sides of bread. Place on cookie sheet. Bake at 275 degrees for 45 minutes or until lightly browned. Store in airtight container. Yield: 2½ dozen.

Lynn MacIntyre, Des Plaines, IL

CREOLE BREAD

8 thin slices French bread
½ c. margarine, softened
2 tsp. garlic powder
1 tsp. pepper
2 tbsp. Romano cheese
Parsley flakes

Spread bread slices with margarine. Place on baking sheet. Sprinkle with garlic powder, pepper, cheese and parsley. Broil until lightly browned. Yield: 6-8 servings.

Alison McDonald, Tatum, TX

EASY HERBED BREAD

½ c. butter or margarine, softened
2 tsp. garlic powder
½ tsp. each savory, rosemary and thyme
1 tsp. each celery, salt and sage
½ tsp. each chervil, basil and oregano
1 tbsp. parsley
1 loaf French bread, sliced

Blend butter and seasonings in bowl. Spread on bread slices. Reassemble slices into loaf. Wrap in foil or plastic wrap. Bake foil-wrapped loaf at 350 degrees for 30 minutes or heat on grill. Microwave plastic-wrapped loaf for 1 to 3 minutes or until heated through.
Yield: 8-10 servings.

Kaye Lusk, Ontario, Canada

FRENCH BREAD MONTEREY

¼ c. butter or margarine, softened
1 long loaf French bread, split
1 c. mayonnaise
½ c. Parmesan cheese
½ c. grated onion
½ tsp. Worcestershire sauce

Spread butter on each French bread half. Place on baking sheet or wrap in foil. Bake at 350 degrees or until bread is heated through. Combine remaining ingredients in bowl; mix well. Spread on hot bread. Bake until light brown. Cut into serving pieces.
Yield: 4 servings.

Sharon Richter, MO

GARLIC BREAD

¼ c. mayonnaise
¼ c. margarine, softened
1 tbsp. Romano cheese
1 clove of garlic, minced
¼ tsp. Italian seasoning
⅛ tsp. paprika
⅛ tsp. poppy seed
1 loaf sourdough French bread

Combine mayonnaise, margarine, cheese, garlic, seasonings and poppy seed in bowl; mix well. Slice bread to but not through bottom. Spread slices with garlic mixture. Wrap in foil. Chill for several hours if desired. Bake over hot coals or at 400 degrees until heated through.
Yield: 4 servings.

Marve Handley, CA

PITA BREADSTICKS

1 pkg. pita-bread rounds
Margarine, softened
Krazy salt

Split pita-bread rounds open. Spread inside of each round with margarine. Sprinkle with salt. Cut each round into ½-inch strips. Place on baking sheet. Bake at 350 degrees for 15 minutes. Yield: 8 dozen.

Corrine Soper, Selinsgrove, PA

DOUGHNUTS

1 egg, beaten
1 c. sugar
2½ tsp. melted butter
3½ tsp. baking powder
1 tsp. salt
½ tsp. nutmeg
3½ c. flour
1 c. milk
Oil for deep frying

Combine egg, sugar and butter; beat well. Mix baking powder, salt, nutmeg and flour. Add flour mixture alternately with milk to creamed mixture, beating well after each addition. Pat dough to ½-inch thickness on floured surface; cut with well-floured doughnut cutter. Deep-fry until brown on both sides. Yield: 3 dozen.

Vera Jennings, Sparta, NJ

ORANGE-GINGER LOAF

1 c. sugar
½ c. unsalted butter, softened
2 eggs
2 c. sifted flour
2 tsp. baking powder
1 tsp. ginger
½ c. Florida orange juice
½ c. milk
1 tsp. grated orange rind
½ c. coarsely chopped blanched almonds

Cream sugar and butter in bowl until light and fluffy. Beat in eggs. Sift dry ingredients together. Add to creamed mixture alternately with mixture of orange juice and milk, mixing well after each addition. Stir in orange rind and almonds. Pour into greased 5x9-inch loaf pan. Bake at 350 degrees for 45 minutes or until loaf tests done. Remove to wire rack to cool. Yield: 12 servings.

HAWAIIAN TOAST
WITH CUSTARD SAUCE

2 eggs
½ c. milk
1 tbsp. honey
½ tsp. salt
¼ tsp. vanilla extract
6 slices bread
¾ c. fine cornflake crumbs
3 oranges, peeled, sliced

Combine eggs, milk, honey, salt and vanilla in bowl; beat lightly. Dip bread slices into egg mixture; coat on both sides with crumbs. Place in well-buttered 10x15-inch baking pan. Bake at 400 degrees for 5 minutes. Turn slices over. Bake for 5 to 7 minutes or until crisp. Top each slice with orange slices and ½ cup Custard Sauce. Yield: 6 servings.

Custard Sauce

⅓ c. honey
2 tbsp. flour
½ tsp. salt
2 c. milk
3 eggs
1 tsp. grated orange rind

Combine honey, flour and salt in saucepan; mix well. Stir in milk gradually. Cook over low heat until thickened, stirring constantly. Combine eggs and orange rind in mixing bowl; beat lightly. Stir a small amount of hot mixture into eggs; stir eggs into hot mixture. Cook for 2 minutes, stirring constantly. Yield: 3 cups.

Judy Myron, Greenville, TN

OVEN-BAKED FRENCH TOAST

French bread, sliced 1½ inches thick
8 eggs
1 tsp. vanilla extract
3 c. milk
1 tbsp. sugar
½ tsp. salt
Margarine, softened
Cinnamon

Arrange bread slices tightly in greased 9x13-inch baking dish. Combine eggs, vanilla, milk, sugar and salt in bowl; mix well. Pour over bread. Chill, tightly covered, overnight. Spread generously with margarine; sprinkle with cinnamon. Place in cold oven. Bake at 375 degrees for 45 minutes. Serve with confectioners' sugar and syrup. Yield: 8 servings.

Sally McFarland, Gresham, OR

Desserts

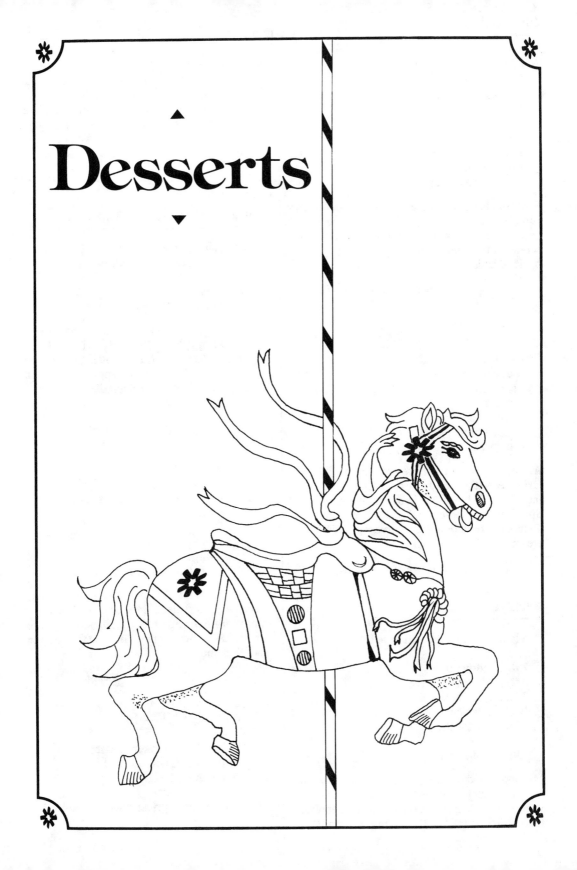

AMBROSIA YOGURT

2 bananas, sliced
1 apple, chopped
1 pear, chopped
¼ c. lemon juice
2 oranges, sectioned
1⅓ c. coconut
1 c. pineapple yogurt

Combine bananas, apple and pear with lemon juice in bowl; toss lightly. Combine with oranges in serving bowl; mix well. Chill until serving time. Fold in coconut and yogurt. Yield: 8 cups.

Paula Page, Cartersville, GA

APPLE BETTY

4 c. sliced tart apples
¼ c. orange juice
1 c. sugar
¾ c. flour
½ tsp. cinnamon
¼ tsp. nutmeg
½ c. butter

Arrange apples in buttered 9-inch pie plate. Drizzle with orange juice. Combine dry ingredients in bowl. Cut in butter until crumbly. Sprinkle over apples. Bake at 375 degrees for 45 minutes or until tender. Serve warm with ice cream. Yield: 6 servings.

Sally Haveman, Grand Rapids, MI

APPLE BURRITOS

6 lg. apples, peeled, chopped
½ c. sugar
2 tbsp. cornstarch
2 tbsp. dry white wine
2 tsp. cinnamon
¼ tsp. allspice
8 lg. flour tortillas
¼ c. butter
Cinnamon-sugar

Mix apples and sugar in saucepan. Add water to cover. Simmer until tender. Blend cornstarch, wine and spices in small bowl. Stir into apples. Cook until thickened, stirring constantly.

Soften tortillas 1 at a time in butter in skillet for several seconds on each side. Spoon ¼ cup apples on each; roll to enclose filling. Place seam side down on ovenproof serving plate. Sprinkle with cinnamon-sugar. Broil until light brown. Serve with sour cream or yogurt. Yield: 8 servings.

Wendy Milford, Corsicana, TX

MICROWAVE APPLE CRISP

3 c. sliced apples
1 3-oz. package red gelatin
1 c. flour
¾ c. sugar
½ c. butter, softened

Arrange apple slices in buttered 6x10-inch glass baking dish. Sprinkle with gelatin. Combine flour and sugar in bowl. Cut in butter until crumbly. Sprinkle over apples and gelatin. Microwave on Roast for 8 minutes. Yield: 4-6 servings.

Alice Brooks, Atlanta, GA

ORANGE-GLAZED APPLES

2 20-oz. cans sliced apples, drained
¼ c. butter, melted
¼ c. flour
1½ c. sugar
½ c. orange juice
2 tbsp. grated orange rind

Spread apples in 1½-quart baking dish. Blend remaining ingredients in saucepan. Cook over medium heat until thickened, stirring constantly. Pour over apples. Bake at 375 degrees for 30 minutes. Yield: 8 servings.

Nita Mayr, Troy, AL

APRICOT CRUMBLE

1¼ c. graham cracker crumbs
⅓ c. packed dark brown sugar
½ tsp. cinnamon
½ c. melted butter
1 30-oz. can apricot halves, drained

Combine cracker crumbs, brown sugar and cinnamon in bowl. Add butter; mix just until moistened. Reserve 2 tablespoons mixture. Sprinkle half the remaining crumb mixture in buttered shallow 1-quart baking dish. Arrange half the apricots over crumbs. Repeat layers. Sprinkle with reserved crumbs. Bake at 350 degrees for 30 minutes. Serve warm with whipped cream or sour cream. Yield: 6 servings.

Photograph for this recipe below.

BANANAS FOSTER

4 sm. ripe bananas
Lemon juice
⅔ c. packed brown sugar
6 tbsp. butter, melted
Cinnamon
3 tbsp. light rum

Slice bananas in half lengthwise; then crosswise. Brush with lemon juice. Blend brown sugar and butter in skillet. Add bananas. Cook for 3 to 4 minutes, turning once. Sprinkle with cinnamon. Heat rum to lukewarm in saucepan.

Ignite rum and pour over bananas in serving dish. Serve over ice cream. Yield: 8 servings.

Jeff Parker, Tomball, TX

BANANA SPLIT CAKE

2 c. graham cracker crumbs
1 stick margarine, melted
2½ c. confectioners' sugar
2 egg whites
1 stick margarine, softened
1 lg. can crushed pineapple, drained well
3 lg. bananas, sliced lengthwise
1 lg. carton Cool Whip

Combine graham cracker crumbs, melted margarine and ½ cup confectioners' sugar in bowl. Press into bottom of 9 x 13-inch pan. Beat egg whites, remaining 2 cups confectioners' sugar and softened margarine in mixing bowl for 10 minutes. Pour over crumb crust. Layer pineapple, bananas and Cool Whip over cream layer. Garnish with nuts and cherries. Chill for 15 minutes. Yield: 12 servings.

Zane Townsend, Pelahatchie, MS

FAST BLINTZES

4 oz. cream cheese, softened
½ c. confectioners' sugar
¼ tsp. vanilla extract
½ c. whipped topping
12 slices bread, trimmed
Margarine, melted
Cinnamon-sugar to taste

Combine first 4 ingredients in bowl; mix well. Flatten bread. Spread with cream cheese mixture; roll as for jelly roll. Dip in margarine; roll in cinnamon-sugar. Place on baking sheet. Bake at 425 degrees for 10 minutes. Serve warm with whipped cream, sour cream or fruit filling. Yield: 12 servings.

Dena Y. Bauer, Wadesville, IN

CREAM CHEESE QUICKIE

1 box chocolate cake mix
3 eggs
1 tsp. vanilla extract
1 stick butter
1 box confectioners' sugar
1   8-oz. package cream cheese, softened

Combine cake mix, 1 egg, ½ teaspoon vanilla and butter in bowl; mix well. Pat into greased 9 x 13-inch baking pan. Mix remaining ingredients in bowl. Pour over first mixture. Bake at 350 degrees for 30 minutes. Yield: 12 servings.

Debbie Orgain, Hammon, OK

BROWNIE FUDGE PUDDING

1   17-oz. package brownie mix
½ c. chopped pecans
¾ c. each packed brown sugar, sugar
⅓ c. cocoa
1¼ c. cold coffee

Prepare brownie mix using package directions for cake-type brownies. Stir in pecans. Pour into greased 9 x 13-inch baking pan. Mix brown sugar, sugar and cocoa together in bowl. Sprinkle over brownie mixture. Drizzle coffee over top. Bake using package directions. Serve warm with ice cream. Yield: 12 servings.

Michelle Epps, Cleveland, TX

FUDGE MARBLE PUDDING

1 sm. box white cake mix
½ c. sugar
5 tbsp. cocoa
⅛ tsp. salt

Prepare cake mix using package directions. Combine remaining ingredients with 1⅔ cup boiling water in bowl; mix well. Pour into 10x6-inch baking dish. Spoon batter over top. Bake at 350 degrees for 40 to 45 minutes. Yield: 6 servings.

Agnes Smithwich, Roanoke Rapids, VA

CHOCOLATE ANGEL FOOD DESSERT

12 oz. chocolate chips
4 eggs, separated
8 oz. whipping cream
½ c. sugar
2 c. chopped pecans
1 angel food cake

Melt chocolate chips in double boiler over hot water. Cool slightly. Combine with egg yolks in bowl; mix well. Fold in stiffly beaten egg whites. Whip cream with sugar in mixer bowl. Fold gently into chocolate mixture. Stir in pecans. Break cake into small pieces. Alternate cake and chocolate mixture ½ at a time in 9 x 13-inch dish. Chill in refrigerator. Yield: 12 servings.

Allison Evans, Broken Arrow, OK

MICROWAVE
CHERRY CHEESECAKE CUPS

1   8-oz. package cream cheese, softened
⅓ c. sugar
1 egg
1 tbsp. lemon juice
½ tsp. vanilla extract
6 vanilla wafers
1 can cherry pie filling

Beat cream cheese in bowl until fluffy. Add sugar, egg, lemon juice and vanilla, beating well. Line muffin cups with cupcake papers. Place 1 vanilla wafer in each cup. Fill cups ⅔ full with cheesecake mixture. Microwave on Medium for 4½ minutes or until almost set, turning once. Top with pie filling. Chill until serving time. Yield: 6 servings.

Deb Sundem, Dunning, NE

MICROWAVE CHERRY COBBLER

1 can cherry pie filling
1 tsp. lemon juice
½ c. butter, melted
1 c. flour
¼ tsp. allspice
⅓ c. packed brown sugar
¾ tsp. cinnamon
⅔ c. chopped nuts

Combine pie filling and lemon juice in shallow 1-quart glass casserole. Combine remaining ingredients in bowl; mix until crumbly. Sprinkle over cherries. Microwave on High for 5 to 6 minutes or until bubbly.
Yield: 6 servings.

Nancy Roop, Caldwell, KS

BRANDIED FRUIT FONDUE

½ c. orange juice
2 tbsp. sugar
¼ c. cornstarch
2 10-oz. packages frozen
   strawberries, thawed
6 oz. cream cheese, softened
¼ c. Brandy

Blend orange juice, sugar and cornstarch in saucepan. Crush strawberries; stir into orange juice mixture. Cook until thickened, stirring constantly. Add cream cheese. Heat over low heat until melted, stirring constantly. Stir in Brandy gradually. Pour into fondue pot. Serve with fresh fruit for dipping. Yield: 3 cups.

Tammy Naples, Wichita, KS

Tip: Create a quick dessert with fresh fruit slices, sour cream or yogurt and a sprinkle of brown sugar or coconut.

MICROWAVE CHOCOLATE FONDUE

1 can sweetened condensed milk
1 10-oz. jar marshmallow creme
½ c. milk
12 oz. chocolate chips
1 tsp. vanilla extract

Combine condensed milk, marshmallow creme, milk, chocolate chips and vanilla in medium glass bowl. Microwave on Medium for 4 to 6 minutes or until bubbly. Beat until smooth. Pour into fondue pot. Serve with assorted bite-sized pieces of cake and fresh fruit for dipping. Yield: 4 cups.

R. J. Noice, Naples, FL

FRESH FRUIT TORTE

1 10-oz. pound cake
2 bananas, sliced
¼ c. lemon juice
1 c. ricotta cheese
¼ c. confectioners' sugar
1 tsp. vanilla extract
1½ c. sliced fresh strawberries

Cut cake into 3 layers. Coat banana slices with lemon juice. Combine ricotta cheese, confectioners' sugar and vanilla in mixer bowl; beat until smooth. Alternate layers of cake, bananas, cheese mixture and strawberries on cake plate, ending with cheese mixture. Chill for 45 minutes. Garnish with additional banana slices and whole strawberries. Yield: 12 servings.

Sue Ellen Green, Pittsburgh, PA

QUICK FRUIT CASSEROLE

1 can cherry pie filling
2 sticks pie crust mix, crumbled
½ c. sugar
¼ tsp. each cinnamon, nutmeg

Pour pie filling into greased 8x8-inch baking dish. Mix remaining ingredients in small bowl. Spread over filling. Bake at 375 degrees for 20 minutes or until brown. Yield: 6 servings.

Helen Cade, Thomaston, AL

SAUTÉED RAINBOW FRUIT CUP

2 apples, sliced
2 tbsp. butter
2 oranges, sectioned
2 peaches, sliced
2 bananas, sliced
3 tbsp. honey
2 c. sliced strawberries
1 c. blueberries

Sauté apples in butter in skillet for 2 minutes. Add oranges and peaches. Sauté for 5 minutes. Add bananas and honey. Sauté for 2 minutes. Add strawberries and blueberries. Heat to serving temperature. Spoon into dessert dishes. Garnish with coconut and whipped cream. Yield: 8-10 servings.

Thelma Savale, Syracuse, NY

BUTTER BRICKLE ICE CREAM PIE

1 c. chopped pecans
1 c. crushed graham crackers
1 c. sugar
1 tsp. baking powder
3 egg whites, stiffly beaten
1 qt. butter brickle ice cream
1 Heath bar, crushed

Combine first 4 ingredients in bowl; mix well. Fold into egg whites. Spread over bottom and side of buttered pie pan. Bake at 325 degrees for 20 minutes. Cool. Fill with scoops of ice cream just before serving. Sprinkle Heath bar over top. Yield: 6 servings.

Vallie Jo Lung, Fort Cobb, OK

CHAMPIONCHIP

6 scoops chocolate chip ice cream
6 lg. chocolate chip cookies
Hot fudge sauce
Whipped topping

Place scoop of ice cream on each cookie in serving dish. Pour fudge sauce over top. Top with whipped topping. Yield: 6 servings.

Michelle M. Calzini, Natick, MA

FRENCH-FRIED ICE CREAM

6 lg. scoops vanilla ice cream
3 c. cornflakes, crushed
2 tsp. cinnamon
Oil for deep frying
1   9-oz. carton whipped topping
¼ c. honey
6 maraschino cherries

Roll ice cream in mixture of cornflakes and cinnamon, covering completely. Freeze until firm. Deep-fry in 375-degree oil for 2 to 4 seconds. Layer whipped topping, ice cream balls, honey, whipped topping and cherries in individual serving dishes. Serve immediately. Yield: 6 servings.

Lynn Boldt, Hampton, MN

INDIVIDUAL BAKED ALASKAS

6 individual sponge dessert shells
1   9-oz. can crushed pineapple, drained
6 scoops strawberry ice cream
6 egg whites
¾ c. sugar

Place shells on baking sheet. Place 1 tablespoon pineapple and 1 scoop ice cream in each shell. Freeze until firm. Beat egg whites in bowl until soft peaks form. Add sugar gradually, beating until stiff. Cover ice cream and shells completely with meringue. Bake at 500 degrees for 4 minutes. Serve immediately. Yield: 6 servings.

Evelyn Piper, Devils Lake, ND

ROCKY ROAD ICE CREAM

3 pts. chocolate ice cream, softened
1 c. each chocolate chips, chopped nuts
2 c. miniature marshmallows

Spread half the ice cream in 8-inch square dish. Mix chocolate chips, nuts and marshmallows. Sprinkle ⅔ of the mixture over ice cream. Spread remaining ice cream on top. Sprinkle with remaining nut mixture. Freeze, covered, until firm. Yield: 8 servings.

Treas Koyama, San Francisco, CA

MAPLE-GLAZED PEACHES

⅓ c. maple syrup
1 c. sour cream
6 c. sliced fresh peaches
1 tbsp. brown sugar

Blend maple syrup and cream in small bowl until smooth. Chill until serving time. Arrange peaches in serving dishes. Pour syrup mixture over peaches. Sprinkle with brown sugar. Yield: 6 servings.

Lois Cynewski, Portsmouth, NH

MICROWAVE PEACH CRISP

4 fresh peaches, peeled, sliced
½ c. quick-cooking oats
½ c. packed brown sugar
¾ c. buttermilk baking mix
3 tbsp. margarine, softened
½ tsp. cinnamon
¼ tsp. nutmeg

Place peaches into 8-inch square glass dish. Mix remaining ingredients in bowl until crumbly. Sprinkle over peaches. Microwave, uncovered, on High for 10 to 12 minutes or until peaches are tender, turning dish once. Let stand for 3 minutes. Spoon into dessert dishes. Serve with ice cream. Yield: 6 servings.

Dorothy Eckert, Columbus, OH

PEACHY CRUMB COBBLER

1 pkg. wild blueberry
   muffin mix
¾ c. sugar
1½ tsp. cinnamon
6 tbsp. butter
½ c. chopped pecans
2 cans peach pie filling
1 tbsp. almond extract

Drain blueberries; set aside. Combine dry muffin mix, ½ cup sugar and ½ teaspoon cinnamon in bowl. Cut in butter until crumbly; stir in pecans. Combine pie filling, almond extract, blueberries, remaining sugar and cinnamon in 9x13-inch baking dish. Spoon crumb topping over filling. Bake at 350 degrees for 30 minutes or until brown. Yield: 12 servings.

Nona Pratt, Portland, OR

PERSIAN PEACHES

4 c. sliced peaches
1 c. orange juice
6 tbsp. honey
1 tbsp. finely chopped candied ginger
Dash of salt

Combine all ingredients in bowl; mix gently. Chill, covered, in refrigerator. Spoon into chilled dessert glasses. Yield: 5 servings.

Phyllis Lovette, Durham, NC

HOT RASPBERRY SOUFFLÉ

2 tbsp. sugar
1   10-oz. package frozen raspberries
   in syrup, thawed
4 egg whites, at room temperature
½ c. sugar
1 c. chilled whipping cream
2 tbsp. Grand Marnier

Butter 6 individual soufflé dishes; sprinkle with 2 tablespoons sugar. Purée raspberries in food processor or blender. Beat egg whites until soft peaks form. Add ½ cup sugar 1 tablespoon at a time, beating constantly until stiff peaks form. Fold egg whites gently into raspberries. Spoon into prepared dishes. Bake in preheated 375-degree oven for 12 to 15 minutes or until puffed and light golden. Whip cream with Grand Marnier until soft peaks form. Serve soufflés hot with whipped cream. Yield: 6 servings.

Joan Dew, Nashville, TN

Tip: For easy but elegant desserts, spoon cream Sherry over a chilled grapefruit or Crème de Menthe over vanilla ice cream.

APPLE PIE CAKE

1 pkg. yellow cake mix
1 stick margarine, softened
1 c. coconut
1 can apple pie filling
½ c. sugar
1½ tsp. cinnamon
1 c. sour cream
1 egg, well beaten

Combine cake mix, margarine and coconut in bowl; mix well. Press over bottom of 9 x 13-inch baking pan. Bake at 350 degrees for 5 to 8 minutes or until golden. Mix pie filling, sugar and cinnamon in bowl. Spoon over baked layer. Top with mixture of sour cream and egg. Bake at 350 degrees for 20 minutes.
Yield: 12 servings.

Mitzi R. Neely, Longview, TX

CRUNCHY APRICOT CAKE

1 can apricot pie filling
1 sm. package white cake mix
1 egg
½ c. flaked coconut
½ c. chopped pecans
½ c. melted butter

Spread pie filling in 9 x 9-inch baking dish. Combine cake mix, egg and ⅓ cup water in mixer bowl; beat for 4 minutes. Pour over pie filling. Sprinkle with coconut and pecans. Drizzle butter over top. Bake at 350 degrees for 40 minutes. Yield: 9 servings.

Sandra J. Lau, Lockport, NY

CHERRY CHOCOLATE CAKE

1 box fudge cake mix
1 can cherry pie filling
2 eggs, beaten
1 tsp. almond extract

Combine all ingredients in bowl; mix well. Spread in greased and floured 9 x 13-inch baking pan. Bake at 350 degrees for 25 to 30 minutes or until cake tests done.
Yield: 12 servings.

Cynthia Kirby, Grinnell, IA

EASY CHOCOLATE ROLL-UP

¼ c. melted butter
1 c. chopped pecans
1⅓ c. coconut
1 can sweetened condensed milk
3 eggs
1 c. sugar
⅓ c. cocoa
⅔ c. flour
¼ tsp. each salt, soda
1 tsp. vanilla extract
1 c. confectioners' sugar

Layer butter, pecans, coconut and condensed milk in order given in foil-lined 10 x 15-inch cake pan. Beat eggs in mixer bowl at high speed for 2 minutes. Add sugar gradually, beating constantly. Beat for 2 minutes. Add mixture of cocoa, flour, salt and soda. Beat at low speed for 1 minute. Blend in vanilla. Pour into prepared pan. Bake at 350 degrees for 20 minutes or until cake tests done. Sprinkle with confectioners' sugar. Cover with towel and baking sheet. Invert cake; remove foil. Roll as for jelly roll from short side. Place on serving plate. Cool. Cut into slices. Yield: 12 servings.

Vicky Jo Hyek, Midland, TX

TURTLE CAKE

1 box German chocolate cake mix
1   14-oz. bag caramels
½ c. evaporated milk
¾ c. melted butter
2 c. nuts
1 c. chocolate chips

Prepare cake mix using package directions. Pour half the batter into greased 9 x 13-inch baking pan. Bake at 350 degrees for 15 minutes. Melt caramels with milk and butter in saucepan over low heat, stirring constantly. Pour over cake. Sprinkle with 1 cup nuts and chocolate chips. Pour remaining batter over filling. Sprinkle with remaining nuts. Bake for 20 minutes longer. Yield: 16 servings.

Nancy Conway, Washington, MO

Tip: Frozen nuts are easier to chop than fresh nuts.

SELF-FILLED CUPCAKES

⅓ c. sugar
8-oz. cream cheese, softened
1 egg
6-oz. semisweet chocolate chips
1 package chocolate cake mix

Cream sugar and cream cheese in mixer bowl. Beat in egg. Stir in chocolate chips. Prepare cake mix using package directions. Fill paper-lined muffin cups ⅔ full. Drop one rounded teaspoonful of the cheese mixture into each cupcake. Bake according to package directions. Yield: 30 cupcakes.

Carol Harding, Florence, TX

WACKY CAKE

3 c. flour
2 c. sugar
½ c. cocoa
1 tsp. salt
2 tsp. soda
¾ c. oil
2 tsp. vinegar
2 tsp. vanilla extract

Sift first 5 ingredients into prepared 9 x 13-inch baking dish. Make 3 wells in mixture. Mix remaining ingredients with 2 cups water. Pour over sifted ingredients. Stir with fork. Bake at 350 degrees for 35 minutes. Yield: 12 servings.

C. A. Zaiser, Kent County, MD

MICROWAVE LEMON BUNDT CAKE

1 pkg. lemon supreme cake mix
1 pkg. instant lemon pudding mix
2 tbsp. oil
4 lg. eggs
1 6-oz. can frozen lemonade, thawed
1 c. confectioners' sugar

Combine first 4 ingredients with ¾ cup water in bowl; mix well. Pour into microwave bundt pan. Let stand for 15 minutes. Microwave on Medium for 12 to 14 minutes or until completely risen, turning ¼ turn every 4 minutes. Microwave on High for 1 to 2 minutes or until cake tests done. Let stand for 5 minutes. Turn out onto plate. Blend lemonade and confectioners' sugar in glass bowl. Microwave on High for 2 minutes. Pour over hot cake. Yield: 20 servings.

Lucinda B. Helton, Orlando, FL

ORANGE JUICE CAKE

1 pkg. yellow cake mix
1 pkg. instant coconut pudding mix
½ c. coconut
¾ c. oil
4 eggs
2 c. confectioners' sugar
½ c. orange juice
2 tbsp. melted butter

Beat first 5 ingredients and ¾ cup water in mixing bowl for 8 minutes. Pour into 9 x 12-inch pan. Bake at 350 degrees for 30 to 40 minutes. Pierce with fork. Pour mixture of remaining ingredients over hot cake. Yield: 12 servings.

Christine Anders, New Haven, IN

STRAWBERRY SHORTCUT CAKE

2 c. sweetened strawberries
1 sm. package strawberry gelatin
½ c. shortening
1½ c. sugar
3 eggs
2¼ c. flour
½ tsp. salt
1 tbsp. baking powder
1 c. milk
1 tsp. vanilla extract
1 to 2 c. miniature marshmallows

Mix strawberries and gelatin in bowl. Let stand for several minutes. Cream shortening and sugar in mixer bowl until fluffy. Beat in eggs. Add mixture of dry ingredients alternately with milk and vanilla, mixing well after each addition. Sprinkle marshmallows in greased 9 x 13-inch cake pan. Pour batter over marshmallows. Spoon strawberry mixture over top. Bake at 350 degrees for 40 minutes or until golden. Cool. Cut into squares. Invert squares onto dessert plates. Yield: 12 servings.

Catherine Bradley, Huntington, WV

APRICOT BARS

½ c. margarine
1½ c. graham cracker crumbs
1   6-oz. package dried apricots,
    chopped
1 can sweetened condensed milk
1   3½-oz. can flaked coconut
½ c. coarsely chopped nuts

Melt margarine in 9 x 13-inch baking dish.
Spread crumbs and apricots in dish. Pour
condensed milk evenly over all. Top with
coconut and nuts, pressing gently. Bake at 350
degrees for 25 to 30 minutes or until lightly
browned. Cool in pan. Cut into bars.
Yield: 2 dozen.

Norita Adam, Okeene, OK

BLONDE BROWNIES

4 eggs
1 box brown sugar
2½ c. biscuit mix
1 tsp. vanilla extract
1 c. coconut
1 c. nuts

Combine all ingredients in bowl; mix well.
Pour into greased and floured 9 x 12-inch baking
pan. Bake at 350 degrees until browned. Cut
into squares while warm. Yield: 2 dozen.

Helen Vinson, Calypso, NC

CARAMEL BROWNIES

7 oz. caramels, melted
¼ c. evaporated milk
1 pkg. Duncan Hines Brownie Mix

Blend caramels and evaporated milk over hot
water until smooth. Prepare brownie mix using
package directions for chewy fudge. Spread
half the batter in greased 8-inch square pan.
Layer caramel mixture and remaining batter on
top. Bake at 350 degrees for 30 to 35 minutes.
Yield: 1 dozen.

Jeanie L. Taylor, Hinton, OK

CRUNCHY CARAMEL BARS

1   14-oz. bag caramels
4 c. Cheerios
3 c. crisp rice cereal
1   16-oz. package semisweet
    chocolate chips, melted

Melt caramels in ¼ cup water in saucepan over
low heat, stirring frequently until smooth. Pour
caramel mixture over combined cereals in
bowl, tossing until well coated. Press mixture
into greased 9 x 13-inch pan. Drizzle chocolate
over top. Cut into bars when cool.
Yield: 2 dozen.

Laura Clawson, Newland, NC

CHOCOLATE MACAROONS

1 can sweetened condensed milk
3 sq. unsweetened chocolate
¼ tsp. salt
2   4-oz. cans shredded coconut
1 tsp. vanilla extract

Combine first 3 ingredients in double boiler.
Cook until chocolate melts and mixture
thickens, stirring frequently. Remove from
heat. Add coconut and vanilla. Drop by
rounded tablespoonfuls 1 inch apart on greased
cookie sheet. Bake at 350 degrees for 10 to 12
minutes or until just set. Cool cookies on wire
rack. Yield: 2 dozen.

Beverly Barnes, Hudson, NC

HELLO DOLLIES

½ c. melted butter
1 c. graham cracker crumbs
1 sm. package chocolate chips
1 sm. package butterscotch chips
1 c. chopped pecans
1 can flaked coconut
1 can sweetened condensed milk

Combine butter and crumbs in bowl; mix well.
Press into baking dish. Layer next 4 ingredients. Drizzle milk over top. Bake at 350
degrees for 30 minutes or until brown.
Yield: 1 dozen.

Barbara J. Kiker, Wadesboro, NC

CRUNCHY PEANUT BUTTER BARS

1 sm. box yellow cake mix
1 egg
7 tsp. oil
¼ c. peanut butter
¼ c. chopped peanuts

Combine all ingredients except peanuts with 1 tablespoon water in bowl; mix well. Spread in 7½ x 11½-inch baking pan. Sprinkle peanuts evenly over top. Bake at 375 degrees for 13 to 15 minutes. Cool slightly and cut into bars. Yield: 2 dozen.

DeAnn Pence, Chandler, OK

EASY PEANUT BUTTER COOKIES

1 c. sugar
1 c. peanut butter
1 egg
1 tsp. vanilla extract

Blend all ingredients together in bowl. Drop by teaspoonfuls onto greased baking sheet. Bake at 350 degrees for 10 minutes. Yield: 2 dozen.

Sandra C. Owen, Lebanon, KY

STRAWBERRY COOKIES

1 box strawberry cake mix
1 4½-oz. container whipped topping
2 eggs
Confectioners' sugar

Beat cake mix, whipped topping and eggs in mixer bowl until well blended. Roll by teaspoonfuls in confectioners' sugar, shaping into balls. Place on greased cookie sheet. Bake at 350 degrees for 10 minutes. Yield: 3½ dozen.

Gloria Carrier, Fort Worth, TX

NO-BAKE FUDGE COOKIES

2 c. sugar
¼ c. cocoa
½ c. milk
1½ tbsp. margarine
1 tsp. vanilla extract

½ c. peanut butter
3 c. oats
1 c. chopped nuts (opt.)

Combine sugar and cocoa in medium saucepan. Add milk and margarine. Bring to a boil over medium heat. Cook for 1 minute. Add vanilla and peanut butter; mix well. Stir in oats and nuts. Drop by tablespoonfuls onto waxed paper. Cool completely before removing. Yield: 2 dozen.

Dee Williamson, Caroline County, MD

SUPER PIZZA COOKIE

1 stick butter, softened
⅓ c. packed brown sugar
¼ c. sugar
1 egg
1 tsp. vanilla extract
1⅓ c. flour
½ tsp. soda
¼ tsp. salt
1 6-oz. package semisweet
   chocolate chips
½ c. chopped nuts (opt.)

Cream butter and sugars in large mixer bowl until light and fluffy. Add egg and vanilla, beating well after each addition. Beat in flour, soda and salt gradually on low speed. Fold in chocolate chips and nuts. Spread evenly in greased 13-inch round baking pan. Bake at 350 degrees for 15 to 20 minutes or until golden brown. Cut into wedges. Yield: 16 servings.

Betty Woodall, Longview, TX

ORANGE-COCONUT BALLS

1 med. box vanilla wafers, crushed
1 sm. can flaked coconut
1 c. chopped nuts
1 sm. can orange juice
   concentrate, thawed
Confectioners' sugar

Combine first 4 ingredients in bowl; mix well. Shape into balls. Roll in confectioners' sugar. Yield: 2-2½ dozen.

Emily Jayne, Salisbury, NC

MICROWAVE PECAN BARS

½ c. butter, melted
1 lb. light brown sugar
2 eggs, beaten
2 tsp. vanilla extract
2 c. chopped pecans
1½ c. pancake mix
Confectioners' sugar

Combine first 4 ingredients in bowl; mix well. Blend in pecans and pancake mix. Pour into greased 8x12-inch glass baking dish. Microwave on High for 8 to 10 minutes, rotating dish every 3 minutes. Center will appear soft. Cut into bars when thoroughly cooled and set. Roll in confectioners' sugar. Yield: 3 dozen.

Bonnie L. Stover, Tampa, FL

PECAN DREAM BARS

1 pkg. pudding recipe yellow
  cake mix
⅓ c. margarine, softened
2 eggs
1 14-oz. can sweetened
  condensed milk
1 tsp. vanilla extract
1 c. chopped pecans
½ c. brickle baking chips

Combine cake mix, margarine and 1 egg in mixer bowl. Beat at high speed until crumbly. Press into greased 9x13-inch baking pan. Beat 1 egg, condensed milk and vanilla in bowl until blended. Stir in pecans and brickle chips. Spread evenly over top. Bake at 350 degrees for 25 to 35 minutes or until golden brown. Cut into bars when cool. Yield: 2 dozen.

Mrs. Earl Nicholson, Gilmer, WV

EASY CHEESECAKE PIE

2 8-oz. packages cream
  cheese, softened
¾ c. sugar
2 eggs
1 tbsp. lemon juice
1 tsp. vanilla extract
1 graham cracker crust

Combine first 5 ingredients in blender container. Process until smooth. Pour into crust. Bake at 375 degrees for 20 to 25 minutes. Yield: 7 servings.

Janice Jobson, Annapolis, MD

CHERRY-CHEESE PIE

1 8-oz. package cream cheese,
  softened
1 can sweetened condensed milk
⅓ c. lemon juice
1 tsp. vanilla extract
1 graham cracker pie crust
1 can cherry pie filling, chilled

Beat cream cheese in bowl until light and fluffy. Blend in condensed milk, lemon juice and vanilla. Pour into crust. Chill until serving time. Top with pie filling. Yield: 6 servings.

Mary Beth Talerico, Ravenna, OH

CHOCOLATE BROWNIE PIE

2 sq. unsweetened chocolate,
  melted
2 tbsp. butter, melted
3 eggs
½ c. sugar
¾ c. dark corn syrup
¾ c. chopped pecans
1 unbaked 9-in. pie shell

Combine first 5 ingredients in bowl, beating well. Mix in pecans. Pour into pie shell. Bake at 350 degrees for 30 minutes or until set. Yield: 6 servings.

Wanda Carol Belknap, Ryan, OK

COCONUT MAGIC PIE

1 stick butter, softened
2 c. milk
2 tsp. vanilla extract
1 c. sugar
4 eggs
½ c. flour
1 c. shredded coconut

Combine all ingredients in blender container. Process until smooth. Pour into greased and floured 10-inch pie plate. Bake at 350 degrees for 45 minutes or until brown and pie tests done. Yield: 8 servings.

Meg Kerr, Queen Anne's County, MD

CRUSTLESS FUDGE PIE

½ c. butter
2 sq. unsweetened chocolate
¼ c. flour
1 c. sugar
2 eggs, beaten
1 tsp. vanilla extract
¼ c. broken pecans

Melt butter and chocolate together in saucepan over low heat. Add flour, sugar, eggs, vanilla and pecans; mix well. Pour into greased and floured pie pan. Bake at 320 degrees for 20 to 25 minutes. Serve warm or cool. Top with vanilla ice cream. Yield: 8 servings.

Madeline Sawyer, Tampa, FL

LEMON PIE

½ pkg. vanilla wafers, crushed
¼ c. margarine, softened
1 6-oz. can frozen lemonade
   concentrate
1 can sweetened condensed milk
1 8-oz. carton whipped topping

Reserve ¼ to ½ cup wafer crumbs. Mix remaining crumbs and margarine in bowl. Press onto bottom and side of 9-inch pie plate. Mix lemonade and condensed milk in bowl. Fold in whipped topping. Spoon into pie shell. Sprinkle reserved crumbs in circle around edge of pie. Chill in refrigerator. Yield: 6 servings.

Elaine Bonino, San Martin, CA

FRUIT PIZZA

1 lg. package refrigerator
   sugar cookie dough, sliced
1 8-oz. package cream cheese,
   softened
⅓ c. sugar

Assorted bite-sized fresh fruit
1 6-oz. jar apricot preserves
¼ c. lemon juice

Place cookies ½ inch apart on large pizza pan. Bake using package directions. Cool. Beat cream cheese and sugar in bowl until smooth. Spread over cookie crust. Arrange fruit over cream cheese layer. Heat preserves and lemon juice in saucepan until melted, mixing well. Pour over fruit. Chill until serving time. Yield: 8-10 servings.

Linsae Snider, Baytown, TX

PEANUT BUTTER PIE

2 1¾-oz. packages instant
   vanilla pudding mix
2 c. cold milk
⅓ c. crunchy peanut butter
1 graham cracker crust
Cool Whip or whipped cream

Combine pudding mix, milk and peanut butter in mixer bowl; beat with electric mixer until thickened. Pour into graham cracker crust. Top with Cool Whip. Chill until set. Yield: 6-8 servings.

Marie Kuper, St. Joseph, MO

STRAWBERRY CREAM PIE

20 ladyfingers, split
1½ tbsp. cream Sherry
1 sm. package vanilla instant
   pudding mix
1½ c. milk
1 pt. California strawberries
6 tbsp. currant jelly, melted

Arrange enough ladyfingers soft side up to cover bottom of 9-inch pie plate. Cut remaining ladyfingers crosswise into halves; arrange around side of pie plate. Sprinkle with Sherry. Prepare pudding mix according to package directions using 1½ cups milk. Spoon into prepared pie plate. Arrange strawberries in rings around edge of pie. Spoon jelly over strawberries. Chill until serving time or serve immediately. Yield: 6-8 servings.

SUGAR PIE

2½ c. packed brown sugar
1 unbaked 9-in. pie shell
¼ c. whipping cream
2 tbsp. butter, softened

Sprinkle enough brown sugar in bottom of pie shell to measure ½ inch. Pour cream gradually over brown sugar. Dot with butter. Bake at 375 degrees for 15 to 20 minutes or until bubbly. Yield: 6 servings.

Wendy Smythe, Palm Beach Gardens, FL

SYRUP PIE

2 tbsp. flour
½ c. sugar
1 c. light corn syrup
3 eggs, beaten
1 tsp. vanilla extract
1 unbaked 9-inch pie shell

Combine flour and sugar in bowl; mix well. Stir in corn syrup, eggs and vanilla. Pour into pie shell. Bake at 300 degrees for 1 hour or until light brown and firm. Yield: 8 servings.

Patsy Moore, Beaver, IA

MINIATURE PECAN TARTS

½ c. margarine, softened
3 oz. cream cheese, softened
1 c. flour
1 egg, slightly beaten
⅔ c. packed brown sugar
1 tbsp. melted margarine
½ tsp. vanilla extract
⅛ tsp. salt
1 c. chopped pecans

Cut margarine and cream cheese into flour in bowl. Shape into ball or long roll. Divide into 24 small balls. Press over bottom and side of muffin cups to form tart shells. Combine egg, brown sugar, margarine, vanilla, salt and pecans in bowl. Pour into muffin cups. Bake for 20 to 25 minutes or until set. Yield: 24 tarts.

Mary Rodgers, New Market, AL

BUTTER TARTS

1 tbsp. (rounded) butter
1 c. slightly packed brown sugar
1 egg
½ c. (scant) raisins
¼ c. chopped pecans
½ tsp. vanilla extract
6 tart shells

Cream butter and brown sugar in mixer bowl until light and fluffy. Add egg; beat well. Stir in raisins, pecans and vanilla. Fill tart shells ¾ full. Bake at 350 degrees for 6 to 8 minutes. Reduce oven temperature to 300 degrees. Bake for 6 to 8 minutes longer. Yield: 6 tarts.

Trudie Wayman, Antioch, TN

CHEESECAKE TARTS

24 oz. cream cheese, softened
¾ c. sugar
3 eggs
1 tbsp. vanilla extract
24 vanilla wafers
1 can fruit pie filling

Combine first 4 ingredients in mixer bowl. Beat for 5 minutes. Place 1 vanilla wafer in bottom of paper-lined muffin cups. Fill ¾ full with batter. Bake at 350 degrees for 25 minutes or until tops crack. Cool. Spoon pie filling onto tarts. Store in refrigerator. Yield: 24 tarts.

Lisa Edgars, Larkspur, CA

WHITE MOUNTAIN TARTS

1 14-oz. can sweetened condensed milk
1 20-oz. can crushed pineapple, drained
½ c. coconut
½ c. chopped pecans
2 tbsp. lemon juice
16 oz. whipped topping
12 baked tart shells

Combine condensed milk, pineapple, coconut, pecans and lemon juice in bowl; mix well. Fold in whipped topping gently. Spoon into tart shells. Chill until serving time. Yield: 16 servings.

Brenda Sordelett, Midlothian, VA

Meal Makers

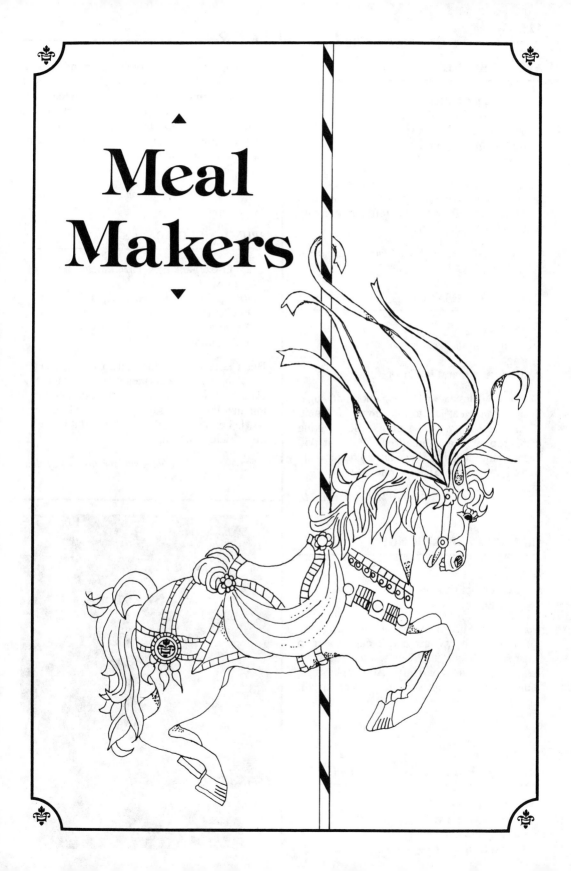

APPLE CHUTNEY

1 1/4 c. apple butter
1 3/4 c. prepared mincemeat
2/3 c. sweet pickle relish
Red pepper seasoning to taste
1 tsp. finely chopped onion

Combine apple butter, mincemeat, relish, red pepper and onion in bowl; mix well. Spoon into glass jars; seal tightly. Store in refrigerator for up to 2 weeks. Yield: 32 servings.

Maude Clary, Pasadena, CA

BAKED APPLESAUCE

Applesauce
- Cinnamon
Sugar
Miniature marshmallows

Combine applesauce with cinnamon and sugar in saucepan. Heat just to the simmering point, stirring constantly. Spoon into shallow baking dish. Top with marshmallows. Bake at 350 degrees until marshmallows are golden brown. Serve immediately. Yield: variable.

Lea Mullis, Boston, MA

CINNAMON APPLE RINGS

3 med. apples
1/2 c. red hot candies
1/4 c. sugar

Core apples. Slice crosswise into 1/2-inch rings. Combine candies, sugar and 2 cups water in large skillet. Cook until candies and sugar are dissolved, stirring constantly. Add apple rings. Simmer just until apples are translucent but still firm. Serve warm or cold. Yield: 6 servings.

Pat Stockford, Phoenix, AZ

MINTED GRAPEFRUIT SECTIONS

2 13 1/2 oz. cans frozen grapefruit
sections, thawed
1/8 tsp. mint extract
Green food coloring

Combine grapefruit sections and mint in large bowl; mix well. Add enough food coloring to tint a delicate mint green. Chill until serving time. May use 2 teaspoons crumbled dried mint or 2 tablespoons chopped fresh mint for mint extract. May also use frozen pineapple chunks instead of grapefruit or a combination of both.
Yield: 4 servings.

Photograph for this recipe below.

SPICED MELON BALLS

2 12-oz. packages frozen melon balls, thawed
1/4 c. packed light brown sugar
1/4 c. cider vinegar
5 whole cloves
1 cinnamon stick

Drain juice from melon balls. Combine melon juice, brown sugar, vinegar, cloves and cinnamon in saucepan; mix well. Simmer for 5 minutes. Pour hot syrup over melon balls in large bowl. Let stand until cool. Chill until serving time. Yield: 3 servings.

Photograph for this recipe below.

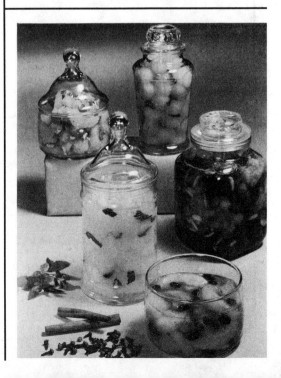

GINGER-PEACH CONSERVE

1   12-oz. package frozen sliced peaches,
 thawed
1/4 c. sugar
1/2 tsp. cinnamon
1/2 c. coarsely chopped walnuts
2 tbsp. finely chopped crystallized ginger
1/4 c. maraschino cherries

Drain juice from peaches into small bowl. Add
sugar and cinnamon, stirring until sugar is dissolved. Pour mixture over peaches in medium
bowl. Add walnuts, ginger and cherries; mix
well. Chill until serving time. Yield: 4 servings.

Photograph for this recipe on page 122.

SPICED PEACH SLICES

2   12-oz. packages frozen sliced peaches,
 thawed
2 cinnamon sticks
1 tbsp. whole cloves
1/4 c. cider vinegar
1/3 c. seedless raisins

Drain juice from peaches into saucepan. Add
cinnamon, cloves, vinegar and raisins; mix well.
Simmer for 5 minutes. Pour hot syrup over sliced
peaches in bowl. Let stand until cool. Chill until
serving time. Yield: 4 servings.

Photograph for this recipe on page 122.

PEAR CHUTNEY

8 c. chopped peeled pears
2 c. seedless white raisins
2 oranges, peeled, chopped
1 c. chopped pecans
3 c. sugar
1/2 c. vinegar
1/3 tsp. ground cloves

Combine pears, raisins, oranges and pecans in
glass container. Mix sugar, vinegar and cloves in
bowl. Add to fruit; mix well. Store in refrigerator. Yield: 24 servings.

Carol Furey, Fort Lauderdale, FL

STRAWBERRY-RHUBARB MEDLEY

1 pkg. frozen whole strawberries, thawed
1 pkg. frozen rhubarb, thawed
Cornstarch
1/2 c. slivered blanched almonds
1 tsp. grated lemon rind

Drain juice from strawberries and rhubarb into
measuring cup. Measure 1 1/2 tablespoons
cornstarch for each measured cup of juice into
saucepan. Gradually stir juice into cornstarch.
Cook over low heat until smooth and thickened,
stirring constantly. Stir in almonds and lemon
rind. Cool slightly. Fold in strawberries and
rhubarb gently. Chill until serving time.
Yield: 4 servings.

Photograph for this recipe on page 122.

HOMEMADE BUTTER WITHOUT THE COW

1 lb. margarine, softened
4 oz. cream cheese, softened
2 sm. cans evaporated milk

Combine margarine, cream cheese and
evaporated milk in mixer bowl; beat until
smooth. Store in refrigerator or freezer.
Yield: 1 1/2 pounds.

Pat Johnson, LaVergne, TN

CRANBERRY AND ORANGE BUTTER

1 c. butter, softened
1/3 c. whole cranberry sauce
2 tbsp. sweet orange marmalade

Cream butter in mixer bowl until fluffy. Add
cranberry sauce and marmalade; beat until well
mixed. Store in covered container in refrigerator
for up to 3 weeks. Yield: 12 servings.

Betty Berglund, Covina, CA

*Tip: Frosted grapes make a beau-
tiful garnish. Dip in egg white
and coat with sugar. Dry on
waxed paper-lined surface.*

RAISIN SAUCE FOR HAM

3/4 c. packed brown sugar
3 tbsp. cornstarch
1 1/2 c. ham stock
1/4 c. vinegar
1/2 c. raisins
1 lemon, thinly sliced
1 tbsp. oil

Combine brown sugar and cornstarch in top of double boiler. Mix in ham stock gradually, stirring constantly. Stir in vinegar, raisins, lemon and oil. Cook until raisins plump and sauce thickens, stirring constantly. Serve hot with ham. May also serve with tongue. Yield: 6 servings.

Janice Berglund, Indianapolis, IN

SWEET AND SOUR SAUCE

1/2 c. sugar
1/2 c. vinegar
2 tbsp. soy sauce
3 tbsp. tomato sauce
1   8-oz. can pineapple chunks
2 tbsp. cornstarch

Combine sugar, vinegar, soy sauce and tomato sauce in saucepan. Bring to a boil, stirring constantly. Drain pineapple, reserving juice. Stir pineapple into hot sauce. Dissolve cornstarch in reserved juice; add to sauce. Simmer until thickened, stirring constantly. May substitute catsup for tomato sauce. Yield: 18 servings.

Eleanor Jean Cook, Mount Vernon, IL

ANTIPASTO

1 clove of garlic, crushed
1/4 c. olive oil
1/4 c. wine vinegar
1   16-oz. can artichoke hearts,
   drained
1   16-oz. can asparagus spears,
   drained
1 cantaloupe, peeled, cut into wedges
1/2 lb. baked ham, thinly sliced

Combine garlic, olive oil and vinegar in bowl; mix well. Add artichoke hearts and asparagus spears. Chill in refrigerator. Wrap cantaloupe

wedges with ham slices. Arrange on lettuce-lined serving platter. Drain artichoke hearts and asparagus. Arrange drained vegetables around cantaloupe. Garnish with black olives.
Yield: 8 servings.

Bev Cooke, Navasota, TX

CREAM CHEESE AND OLIVE BALLS

8 oz. cream cheese, softened
1   6-oz. jar stuffed olives
Finely chopped pecans

Divide cream cheese into small portions. Shape ball of cream cheese around each olive; roll in pecans. Place on baking sheet. Chill, covered, for several hours to overnight. Slice each ball into halves. Serve with crackers.
Yield: 4 servings.

Marcelle Jones, Atlanta, GA

ITALIAN CHEESE BALL

1 env. Italian salad dressing mix
8 oz. cream cheese, softened
Crushed parsley flakes

Blend salad dressing mix and cream cheese in bowl. Shape into ball; roll in parsley flakes to coat. Chill for several hours. Let stand at room temperature for 30 minutes before serving. Serve with crackers. Yield: 8 servings.

Allison Cummings, Furman, SC

ONION CHEESE BALL

16 oz. cream cheese, softened
6 tbsp. Cheez Whiz
1 env. dry onion soup mix
1/2 c. chopped walnuts

Beat cream cheese in mixer bowl until light and fluffy. Add Cheez Whiz and soup mix; beat well. Shape into 3 balls; roll in walnuts to coat. Wrap in plastic wrap. Chill for 1 hour or longer before serving. Yield: 16 servings.

Doris Williams, Kansas City, MO

CHEESE BLINTZES

8 oz. cream cheese, softened
1 egg yolk
1/4 c. sugar
15 slices white bread
1/4 c. melted butter
Cinnamon to taste

Combine cream cheese, egg yolk and sugar in mixer bowl; mix well. Trim crusts from bread; flatten bread with rolling pin. Spread evenly with cream cheese mixture. Roll to enclose filling. Cut rolls into halves. Place on 10x15-inch baking sheet. Brush with melted butter; sprinkle with cinnamon. Bake at 350 degrees for 10 minutes. Yield: 2 1/2 dozen.

Helen Wenger, Denton, KY

BAKED CHICKEN NUGGETS

8 chicken breast filets
2 c. bread crumbs
1 c. Parmesan cheese
1 1/2 tsp. salt
4 tsp. each thyme and basil
1 c. melted butter

Cut chicken into 1 1/2-inch pieces. Combine bread crumbs, cheese, salt, thyme and basil in bowl; mix well. Dip chicken into butter; roll in bread crumb mixture to coat. Place in single layer on baking sheet. Bake at 400 degrees for 20 minutes or until tender and brown.
Yield: 16 servings.

Julie Fabry, Durham, NC

RANCH BUFFALO WINGS

24 chicken wing drumettes
1/2 c. melted butter
1/4 c. (or less) hot pepper sauce
3 tbsp. vinegar
2 env. ranch salad dressing mix
1/2 tsp. paprika
Celery sticks

Dip chicken in mixture of butter, hot pepper sauce and vinegar. Arrange in baking pan; sprinkle with 1 envelope salad dressing mix. Bake at 350 degrees for 25 to 30 minutes or until brown. Sprinkle with paprika. Prepare remaining envelope of salad dressing mix using package directions. Serve dressing as dip for chicken and celery sticks. Yield: 2 dozen.

Sandra Boyd, Murfreesboro, TN

CARAMEL APPLE DIP

8 oz. cream cheese, softened
1 c. packed brown sugar
1 tsp. vanilla extract

Combine cream cheese, brown sugar and vanilla in small bowl; mix well. Store in refrigerator. Serve with crisp apple slices. Yield: 16 servings.

Jan Bowers, Emporia, KS

EASY CHILI DIP

8 oz. cream cheese, softened
1   15-oz. can chili without beans

Combine cream cheese and chili in microwave-safe bowl. Microwave on Medium-High until cream cheese is melted, stirring once. Serve with tortilla chips. Yield: 12 servings.

Eura Sherman, Eureka Springs, AR

CRAB AND ARTICHOKE DIP

1 c. chopped canned artichoke hearts
1 c. mayonnaise
1 c. chopped crab meat
1 c. Parmesan cheese

Combine artichoke hearts, mayonnaise, crab meat and Parmesan cheese in 1-quart casserole; mix well. Bake at 350 degrees for 25 minutes or until heated through. Serve with assorted crackers. Yield: 20 servings.

Ed Radford, Kansas City, MO

Tip: Serve dips in hollowed-out vegetables such as green, red or yellow bell peppers, eggplant or cabbage.

VEGETABLE CURRY DIP

1 c. mayonnaise
1 tsp. each garlic salt and curry powder
1/2 tsp. onion juice
1/2 tsp. horseradish
1 tsp. vinegar

Combine mayonnaise, garlic salt, curry powder, onion juice, horseradish and vinegar in bowl; mix well. Chill until serving time. Serve with assorted fresh vegetables. Yield: 8 servings.

Lorene Leebrick, Shelbyville, TN

INCREDIBLE EGG DIP

1 pkg. dry vegetable soup mix
2 c. sour cream
4 hard-boiled eggs, chopped

Combine all ingredients in bowl; mix well. Chill in refrigerator. Yield: 3 cups.

Nancy Smith, Duluth, MN

FRUIT DIP

16 oz. whipped topping
16 oz. sour cream
1 10-oz. package frozen strawberries, thawed

Blend whipped topping and sour cream in bowl. Stir in strawberries. Serve with bite-sized fresh fruit. Yield: 16 servings.

Ruth Phillips, Midway, FL

NUTTY GUACAMOLE

2 ripe avocados, mashed
1 tomato, chopped
3/4 c. chopped dry roasted unsalted peanuts
1 sm. onion, finely chopped
2 tbsp. lemon juice
Red pepper to taste
Tortilla chips

Combine avocados, tomato, peanuts, onion, lemon juice and red pepper in bowl; mix well.

Chill for 1 hour or longer. Serve with tortilla chips. Yield: 28 servings.

PIÑA COLADA FRUIT DIP

1 8-oz. can crushed pineapple
3/4 c. milk
1 3-oz. package coconut instant pudding mix
1/2 c. sour cream

Combine pineapple, milk, pudding mix and sour cream in food processor container. Process for 30 seconds or until smooth. Spoon into serving bowl. Chill for several hours to overnight. Serve with bite-sized fresh fruit. Yield: 20 servings.

Gayle Spalding, Paris, ID

TUNA DIP

8 oz. cream cheese, softened
2 6-oz. cans tuna, drained
1 6-oz. jar tartar sauce
1/4 tsp. celery salt
Lemon pepper to taste

Combine first 3 ingredients in bowl; mix well. Add celery salt and lemon pepper; mix well. Serve with assorted crackers. Yield: 8 servings.

Nadine F. Marcum, Little Rock, AR

FROSTY VEGETABLE DIP

1 med. cucumber, chopped
2 tsp. lemon juice
White pepper to taste
8 oz. low-sodium cream cheese, softened
3/4 c. chopped dry roasted unsalted mixed nuts
1/3 c. finely shredded carrot
2 tbsp. chopped parsley

Combine first 3 ingredients in blender container. Process until cucumber is mashed. Add cream cheese. Process until smooth. Stir in mixed nuts, carrot and parsley. Chill for 1 hour or longer before serving. Yield: 12 servings.

HAM APPETIZERS

1/2 c. butter, softened
1 tbsp. poppy seed
1 tsp. each mustard and
  Worcestershire sauce
1 sm. onion, finely chopped
1 24-count pkg. dinner rolls
1 6-oz. can chunk ham
6 oz. Swiss cheese, sliced

Combine butter, poppy seed, mustard, Worcestershire sauce and onion in bowl; mix well. Slice rolls in half horizontally; spread cut sides with butter mixture. Layer ham and cheese over bottom layers of rolls. Replace top layers. Place rolls in original foil baking pan. Bake at 400 degrees for 10 minutes. Bake, covered with foil, for 10 minutes longer. May prepare ahead and refrigerate until baking time or bake and reheat in microwave. Yield: 2 dozen.

Lynette Miller, Tupelo, MS

HAM ROLL-UPS

1 lb. boiled ham, sliced
8 oz. cream cheese, softened
4 dill pickles

Spread ham slices with cream cheese. Cut pickles into quarters lengthwise. Place 1 pickle on each ham slice. Roll to enclose filling. Cut into bite-sized pieces. Yield: 16 servings.

Sherri Wenger, Greybull, WY

DEVILED BISCUITS

1 10-count pkg. refrigerator biscuits
1/4 c. margarine
1 4 1/2-oz. can deviled ham
1/4 c. Parmesan cheese

Cut each biscuit into quarters. Arrange on baking sheet. Combine margarine and deviled ham in saucepan; mix well. Heat until margarine melts, stirring frequently. Pour ham mixture over biscuits, coating well. Sprinkle with cheese. Bake at 400 degrees for 15 minutes or until golden brown. Yield: 40 servings.

Joan Leebrick, Antioch, TN

HOT DOG WRAP-UPS

1 pkg. hot dogs
8 oz. sliced bacon
1 8-oz. can pineapple chunks, drained
1 c. packed brown sugar

Cut hot dogs into 1-inch pieces. Cut bacon slices into halves. Wrap each hot dog piece and 1 pineapple chunk together with 1/2 bacon slice, securing with pick. Place in 9x13-inch baking dish. Sprinkle with brown sugar. Bake at 375 degrees for 20 minutes or until brown. Yield: 36 servings.

Arlene Sherman, Clarksville, TN

TOMATOES CAPRI

1 lg. tomato, sliced
Mozzarella cheese, thinly sliced
2 tbsp. basil
Crushed garlic, oregano and parsley
  to taste
Olive oil

Arrange tomato slices on serving plate. Top with cheese. Sprinkle basil, garlic, oregano and parsley over cheese. Drizzle with olive oil. Chill until serving time. Yield: 2 servings.

Jennie Chandler, Everett, WA

ZIPPY TOMATO BITES

1 10-oz. package frozen chopped
  spinach, thawed, drained
1/2 c. dry roasted unsalted sunflower
  seed
1/2 c. low-sodium mayonnaise
2 tbsp. prepared horseradish
30 cherry tomatoes

Combine spinach, sunflower seed, mayonnaise and horseradish in bowl; toss well. Cut tops from cherry tomatoes; scoop out pulp to form shell; drain well. Stuff each tomato with spinach mixture. Chill for 1 hour before serving. Yield: 2 1/2 dozen.

TUNA BROILER APPETIZERS

1   10-count can flaky baking powder
    biscuits
2 egg whites
1/2 tsp. salt
1   6 1/2-oz. can tuna in oil, drained, flaked
1/2 c. mayonnaise
1 tbsp. finely chopped celery
1 tbsp. pickle relish

Separate each biscuit into 3 thin layers; place on
10x15-inch baking sheet. Bake at 400 degrees
for 8 to 10 minutes or until golden brown. Beat
egg whites and salt in mixer bowl until stiff but
not dry. Stir in tuna, mayonnaise, celery and
pickle relish. Spread 1 tablespoon tuna mixture
on each biscuit. Broil 6 inches from heat source
for 2 to 3 minutes or until golden brown. Serve
hot. Appetizers may be prepared ahead of time
and refrigerated up to 3 hours, broiling just
before serving. Yield: 2 1/2 dozen.

Photograph for this recipe below.

SHRIMP ROCKEFELLER

1 1/2 lb. shrimp
1   10-oz. package frozen chopped
    spinach, drained
1 c. sour cream
1/2 c. catsup
Parsley to taste
Salt and pepper to taste
Lemon juice to taste
1/2 c. bread crumbs

Cook shrimp in water to cover in saucepan until
opaque; drain and peel. Combine with spinach,
sour cream, catsup, parsley, salt, pepper and
lemon juice in bowl; mix well. Spoon into
buttered 8-inch casserole. Sprinkle with crumbs.
Bake in preheated 450-degree oven for 15
minutes. Yield: 6 servings.

Debbie Allison, Boston, MA

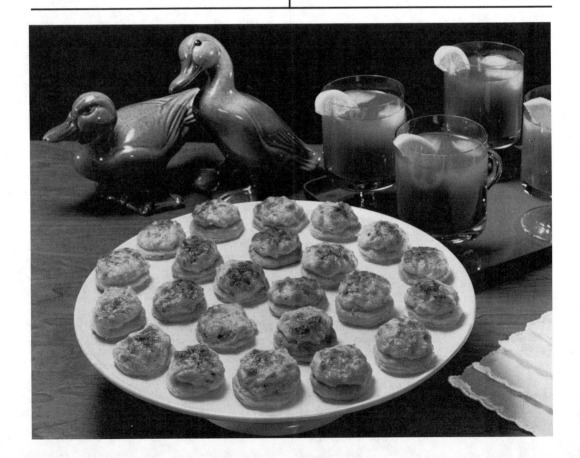

MINI REUBENS

1 8-oz. bottle of Thousand Island
     dressing
1 loaf party rye bread
1 16-oz. can sauerkraut, drained
8 oz. sliced corned beef
1 lb. Swiss cheese, thinly sliced

Spread salad dressing on bread. Arrange bread on 10x15-inch baking sheet. Layer sauerkraut, corned beef and cheese over bread. Broil 6 inches from heat source until cheese is melted. Yield: 20 servings.

Debra Schamberg, Nashville, TN

SPICY JAZZABELLS

1 18-oz. jar pineapple preserves
1 18-oz. jar apple jelly
1 sm. can dry mustard
1 sm. jar horseradish
1 tbsp. cracked pepper
8 oz. cream cheese

Combine first 5 ingredients in bowl; mix well. Chill in refrigerator. Pour 1/3 of the sauce over cream cheese on serving plate just before serving. Serve with crackers. Yield: 6 servings.

Marion Paquette, Blackwood, NJ

NACHOS

1 8-oz. package tortilla chips
1 1/2 c. shredded Cheddar cheese
1 11-oz. can jalapeño peppers

Arrange 10 chips at a time on paper plate. Sprinkle with cheese; top with peppers. Microwave on High for 1 minute. Serve hot. Yield: 4 servings.

Cindy Blanco, Stroud, OK

PARMESAN-BACON STIX

5 slices bacon, cut into halves
1/2 c. Parmesan cheese
10 thin bread sticks

Dredge 1 side of bacon strips in cheese. Roll around bread stick diagonally. Place sticks on paper plate lined with paper towels. Microwave on High for 4 1/2 to 6 minutes. Roll in remaining cheese. Store in airtight container. Yield: 10 servings.

Debbie Sherman, Edgewood, SC

HONEY-GLAZED SNACK MIX

4 c. Chex cereal
1 1/2 c. mini pretzels
1 c. mixed nuts
1/3 c. margarine
1/4 c. honey

Combine cereal, pretzels and nuts in large bowl. Melt margarine in saucepan; stir in honey. Pour over cereal mixture; toss to coat. Spread in 10x15-inch baking pan. Bake at 350 degrees for 12 to 15 minutes, stirring occasionally. Cool slightly. Spread on waxed paper to cool completely. Store in airtight container. Yield: 8 servings.

Asa Helmersson, Venice, UT

MICROWAVE PARTY SNAX

2 c. corn Chex cereal
2 c. wheat Chex cereal
2 c. Crispix cereal
4 oz. thin pretzel sticks
1 1/2 c. salted Spanish peanuts
1/2 c. butter
2 tbsp. Worcestershire sauce
1 tsp. each celery salt, onion salt
     and garlic salt

Combine cereals, pretzel sticks and peanuts in 3-quart casserole. Combine butter, Worcestershire sauce and seasonings in glass bowl. Microwave on High for 1 1/2 to 2 minutes or until melted. Drizzle over cereal mixture, stirring to coat evenly. Microwave on High for 10 to 11 minutes or until flavors are blended, stirring occasionally. Serve hot or cold. Store in airtight container. Yield: 12 servings.

Wendy Johnson, North Bridgton, ME

CAFÉ BOURBON

1 tbsp. orange and spice iced coffee mix
¼ c. Bourbon
Vanilla ice cream

Stir iced coffee mix into ½ cup water. Add Bourbon; mix well. Pour into glasses. Top each with scoop of ice cream if desired. May use whipped topping instead of ice cream.
Yield: 2 servings.

Photograph for this recipe below.

COFFEE AND SPICE SODA

3 tbsp. cinnamon iced coffee mix
Vanilla ice cream
Club soda, chilled

Combine iced coffee mix and 1 cup water in pitcher; stir until dissolved. Place scoop of ice cream in 4 tall glasses. Pour coffee mixture over ice cream. Fill each glass with club soda. Serve with iced beverage spoons and straws. May substitute orange and spice for Anisette iced coffee mix. Yield: 4 servings.

Photograph for this recipe below.

ICED CAFÉ AU LAIT

2 tbsp. Anisette iced coffee mix
1 c. milk

Stir iced coffee mix into 1 cup water; stir until dissolved. Add milk; mix well. Pour over ice in goblets or glasses. Yield: 2 servings.

Photograph for this recipe below.

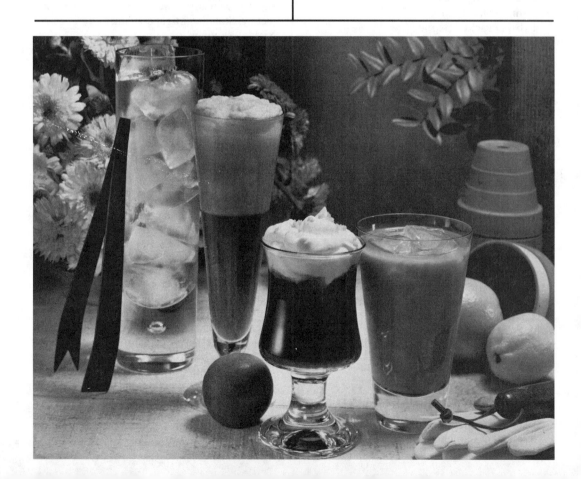

CAFÉ AU CHOCOLAT

1 c. instant cocoa mix
1/3 c. instant coffee
1/2 pt. heavy cream, whipped
Nutmeg to taste

Mix cocoa, coffee and 4 cups boiling water in large pan. Pour into coffeepot. Heat to serving temperature. Serve in demitasse cups topped with whipped cream and nutmeg.
Yield: 6 servings.

Elizabeth Livingston, Little Rock, AR

VIENNESE COFFEE

1/2 c. heavy cream
1/2 tsp. vanilla extract
1 tbsp. confectioners' sugar
3 c. hot strong coffee

Combine cream, vanilla and confectioners' sugar in mixer bowl; beat until soft peaks form. Pour hot coffee into 4 coffee mugs. Spoon whipped cream on top. Garnish with orange rind and cinnamon stick. Serve immediately.
Yield: 4 servings.

Margaret Irwin, Muncie, IN

MEXICAN HOT CHOCOLATE

1 c. milk
1/4 c. baking cocoa
1/4 c. sugar
3/4 tsp. cinnamon
Salt to taste
3 c. milk
3/4 tsp. vanilla extract
1/4 c. light cream

Heat 1 cup milk just to the boiling point in saucepan. Combine cocoa, sugar, cinnamon and salt in bowl; mix well. Add to milk; beat until smooth. Bring to a boil over low heat, stirring constantly. Add remaining 3 cups milk. Heat just to the boiling point. Stir in vanilla and cream. Heat to serving temperature. Beat with rotary beater until frothy. Yield: 6 servings.

Walter Sherman, Antioch, TN

HOT SPICED PERCOLATOR DRINK

3 c. unsweetened pineapple juice
2 c. cranberry juice
1/3 c. packed brown sugar
1 1/2 tsp. whole cloves
1 stick cinnamon
1/8 tsp. salt

Combine pineapple juice, cranberry juice and brown sugar in 10-cup percolator. Place cloves, cinnamon and salt in basket. Brew as for coffee for 5 to 6 minutes. Yield: 8 servings.

Colleen Paul, Monrovia, CA

APPLE COOLER

1 qt. apple juice, chilled
1 pt. vanilla ice cream, softened
1 8-oz. can crushed pineapple, drained
1/2 tsp. cinnamon

Combine apple juice, ice cream, pineapple and cinnamon in blender container. Process until frothy. Pour into glasses. Garnish with pineapple cubes on skewers and mint sprigs.
Yield: 8 servings.

Linda Norton, Flintstone, GA

BERRY AND TEA FIZZ

1/3 c. instant tea powder
2 6-oz. cans frozen lemonade
   concentrate, thawed
1 10-oz. package frozen raspberries,
   thawed
1 12-oz. can lemon soda, chilled

Combine tea powder, 5 cups water, lemonade and raspberries in glass pitcher; mix well. Chill until serving time. Stir in lemon soda just before serving. Serve over ice. Yield: 8 servings.

Katherine Paquette, St. Louis, MO

Tip: For an easy coffee cooler, blend 3 cups cold water, 1 tablespoon instant coffee powder and 2 cups coffee ice cream in blender.

BOHEMIAN TEA

3 tea bags
2 c. sugar
Juice and grated rind of 3 lemons

Pour 2 cups boiling water over tea bags in teapot. Steep, covered, for 20 minutes. Remove tea bags. Add sugar and lemon rind, stirring until sugar dissolves. Let stand for 15 minutes, stirring occasionally. Remove lemon rind. Add lemon juice; stir well. Combine 3 cups water to 1 cup lemon syrup in pitcher; mix well. Serve over ice. Yield: 4 servings.

Ann Charlton, Birmingham, AL

BLENDER BANANA NOG

1 banana, chopped
1 egg
3/4 c. milk
1 tsp. sugar
1/2 tsp. vanilla extract
Nutmeg to taste

Combine banana, egg, milk, sugar, vanilla and nutmeg in blender container. Process until smooth. Pour into serving glass. Yield: 1 serving.

Julie Yost, New York, NY

DIXIE BOILED CUSTARD

1/4 c. sugar
1/8 tsp. salt
4 egg yolks, well beaten
2 c. milk, scalded

Beat sugar, salt and egg yolks in bowl until frothy. Stir in a small amount of scalded milk; stir egg mixture into scalded milk. Cook over low heat until thickened, stirring frequently. Do not boil. Chill in refrigerator. Serve with vanilla extract and grated lemon rind. Yield: 4 servings.

Judy Calvin, Atlanta, GA

CHOCOLATE RICKY

8 oz. chocolate milk
1 tsp. sugar

1/2 tsp. vanilla extract
Crushed ice

Combine chocolate milk, sugar and vanilla in tall glass; stir to mix well. Add crushed ice. Serve immediately. May vary by using strawberry-flavored milk. Yield: 1 serving.

Richard Snitzer, Pulaski, TN

ICED CHOCOLATE

4 oz. unsweetened chocolate, broken
1 c. sugar
Salt to taste
1 tsp. vanilla extract
1 pt. whipping cream, partially whipped

Combine chocolate, 4 cups hot water, sugar and salt in saucepan. Boil for 5 minutes, stirring constantly. Add vanilla. Pour chocolate over whipped cream in bowl. Beat until frothy. Pour into glasses half-filled with crushed ice. Garnish with additional whipped cream.
Yield: 6 servings.

Beverly Adams, Westminster, CA

CITRUS COOLER

2 c. orange juice
2 tbsp. lemon juice
1/8 tsp. salt
1/2 c. crushed ice

Combine orange juice, lemon juice and salt in pitcher; mix well. Stir in crushed ice. Serve immediately. Yield: 2 servings.

Ginger Phillips, Seattle, WA

CRANBERRY SPRITZERS

1 c. cranberry-apple drink
1/2 c. white grape juice
1/4 c. club soda

Combine cranberry-apple drink and grape juice in small pitcher; mix well. Pour over ice in glasses. Add club soda just before serving. Garnish with lemon wedges. Yield: 2 servings.

Photograph for this recipe on page 140.

FRUITY FLOATS

**1 6-oz. can frozen fruit punch
concentrate
1 pt. vanilla ice cream**

Dilute punch using package directions. Chill for several hours. Place small scoop of ice cream in chilled tall glass. Add 1/2 to 3/4 cup chilled punch; stir slightly. Top with additional ice cream. Yield: 4 servings.

Haley Green, Fort Walton, FL

FRUITY GINGER COOLER

**Juice of 2 lemons
Juice of 2 oranges
2 bananas, mashed
1 c. crushed pineapple with juice
3/4 c. sugar
Ginger ale, chilled**

Combine first 5 ingredients and 1 cup water in blender container. Process for several seconds. Pour into 2 ice cube trays. Freeze until firm. Place 3 to 4 cubes in glass; pour chilled ginger ale over cubes. Yield: 4 servings.

Lois Clark, Richmond, MO

PARTY GRAPE PUNCH

**1 2 oz. can frozen lemonade concentrate
4 c. grape juice
1 tsp. whole cloves
1 c. sugar
4 cinnamon sticks**

Prepare lemonade using concentrate directions. Combine all ingredients in saucepan. Bring to a boil stirring constantly; strain. Serve hot or cold. Yield: 12 cups.

Donna Tignor, Garden City, IA

PICNIC LEMONADE

**1/2 c. light corn syrup
1/2 c. sugar
2 tbsp. grated lemon rind
1 1/4 c. lemon juice**

Combine corn syrup, sugar, 2/3 cup water and lemon rind in saucepan. Bring to a boil. Boil for 5 minutes, stirring constantly. Strain; cool. Pour into ice-filled pitcher. Add lemon juice and 7 cups water; mix well. Garnish with maraschino cherries and lemon slices. Yield: 8 servings.

Lisa Gaither, Pray, MT

LIME FLOAT

**1 qt. lime sherbet, softened
1 c. pineapple juice
1 qt. vanilla ice cream, softened
1 c. 7-Up**

Blend lime sherbert, pineapple juice and vanilla ice cream in glass pitcher. Stir in 7-Up just before serving. Yield: 8 servings.

Karon Soderland, Ypsilanti, MI

ORANGE BREAKFAST DRINK

**1 6-oz. can frozen orange juice
concentrate
1 c. milk
1/2 c. sugar
1 tsp. vanilla extract
2 eggs
6 to 8 ice cubes**

Combine all ingredients in blender container. Process until blended. Serve in chilled glasses. Yield: 2 servings.

Carla Seippel, Blue Springs, MO

ORANGE FRAPPÉ

**1 6-oz. can frozen orange juice
concentrate
1 c. milk
1/2 c. sugar
1 tsp. vanilla extract
12 ice cubes**

Combine orange juice concentrate, milk, sugar, vanilla, ice cubes and 1 cup water in blender container. Process until thickened and smooth. Yield: 2 servings.

Deena Ferguson, Houston, TX

ORANGE JULIUS

1 6-oz. can frozen orange juice
   concentrate
12 ice cubes
1 tsp. vanilla extract
1/2 c. nonfat dry milk powder
1/4 c. sugar

Combine orange juice, 1 3/4 cups water, ice cubes, vanilla, milk powder and sugar in blender container. Process at medium speed until frothy. May add scoop of ice cream during processing if desired. Yield: 2 servings.

Stephen Lee, Pomona, CA

ORANGE SLUSH

1 pt. vanilla ice cream, softened
1/4 c. frozen orange juice concentrate,
   thawed

Combine ice cream and orange juice concentrate in blender container. Process until thick and smooth. Pour into glasses. Garnish with orange slices and mint. Yield: 2 servings.

Robin Dixon, Longmont, CO

PEACHY VANILLA SHAKE

2 env. Alba vanilla shake mix
6 ice cubes
1 peach, peeled, chopped
Nutmeg to taste

Combine 1 cup ice water and shake mix in blender container. Add ice cubes 1 at a time, processing at low speed constantly. Process at high speed for 60 seconds or until mixture is thickened and ice cubes are completely crushed. Add peach and nutmeg. Process until smooth. Yield: 2 servings.

Betty Joanne Howes, Hartford, CT

PEAR YOGURT COOLER

1 fresh Bartlett pear, cored
2 fresh purple plums, seeded
1/2 c. plain yogurt

2 tbsp. sugar
1/4 tsp. vanilla extract

Combine all ingredients in blender container. Process for 2 minutes or until smooth. Serve over crushed ice. Yield: 1 serving.

Betty Mijares, Abilene, TX

PIÑA COLADA FRAPPÉ

8 oz. piña colada yogurt
1 8-oz. can juice-pack crushed
   pineapple
1 tbsp. shredded coconut
4 ice cubes

Combine all ingredients in blender container. Process at high speed until smooth. Pour into tall glasses. Yield: 2 servings.

Judy Chisenall, Jamestown, RI

PINEAPPLE-GINGER ALE COOLER

2 tbsp. puréed crushed pineapple
8 oz. ginger ale, chilled
2 tbsp. (heaping) whipped topping

Place 1 tablespoon pineapple in each of two 4-ounce glasses. Pour ginger ale over pineapple. Top each with tablespoonful whipped topping. Serve with straw. Yield: 2 servings.

Jane Carter, Arcanum, OH

PINEAPPLE MINT SHAKE

3 c. cold milk
2 c. pineapple juice, chilled
3/4 c. cream
1/4 c. sugar
1 1/2 tsp. lemon juice
1/8 tsp. salt
12 drops of peppermint extract

Combine milk, pineapple juice, cream, sugar, lemon juice, salt and peppermint extract in 2-quart shaker. Shake until foamy. Pour into tall glasses. Garnish with mint leaves. Serve immediately. Yield: 6 servings.

Vicki Barnes, Madison, TN

Cooking For Two

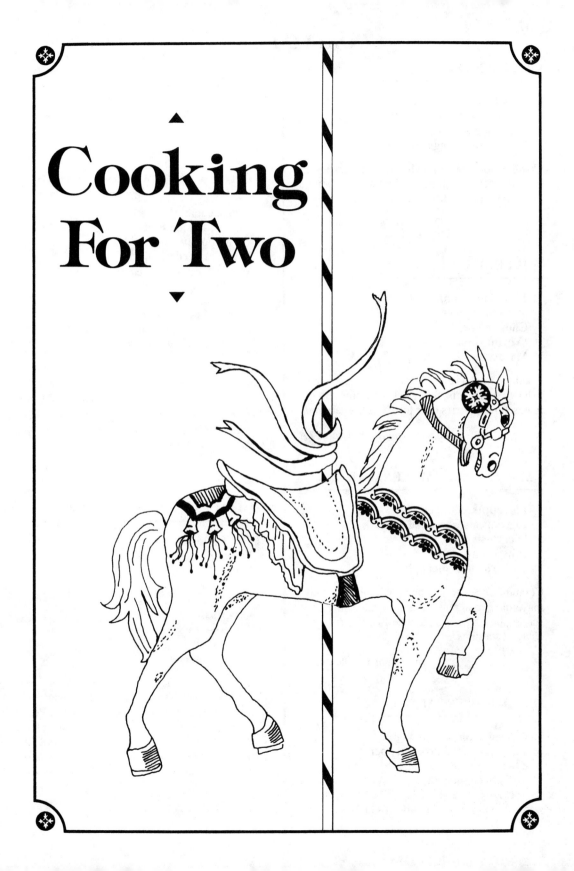

FRUIT MEDLEY

2 med. oranges, peeled, sectioned
1 c. fresh strawberry halves
1 c. grape halves
2 to 3 tbsp. orange liqueur

Combine oranges, strawberries and grapes in bowl. Drizzle with liqueur. Garnish with orange twist and mint. Yield: 2 servings.

Sharyl Fuller, Coleman, TX

WALDORF SALAD

1 c. chopped unpeeled apple
1/3 c. chopped celery
Chopped pecans
1/3 c. mayonnaise
Maraschino cherries

Combine apple, celery, pecans and mayonnaise in bowl; toss to mix. Serve in lettuce cups. Spoon maraschino cherries over top. Yield: 2 servings.

Renee B. Stephens, Provencal, LA

CARROT-RAISIN-APPLE SALAD

1 lg. apple, chopped
2 lg. carrots, shredded
1/4 c. raisins
2 tbsp. mayonnaise
1/4 c. crushed pineapple

Combine apple, carrots and raisins in bowl. Add mayonnaise and pineapple; mix well. Chill until serving time. Serve on lettuce-lined plate. Yield: 2 servings.

Jean Jackson, Uniontown, KS

CAULIFLOWER SALAD

1/2 head cauliflower, chopped
2 tbsp. chopped green pepper
2 tbsp. chopped carrot
2 tbsp. chopped onion
1/2 c. mayonnaise
Seasoned salt and pepper to taste

Combine cauliflower, green pepper, carrot, onion, mayonnaise and seasoned salt and pepper in bowl; toss to mix. Chill until serving time. Yield: 2 servings.

Bonnie Edgell, Ligonier, IN

SPINACH AND STRAWBERRY SALAD

2 tbsp. sugar
1 1/2 tsp. sesame seed
3/4 tsp. poppy seed
1/2 tsp. minced onion
Worcestershire sauce and paprika
   to taste
2 tbsp. oil
1 tbsp. cider vinegar
1/2 bunch fresh spinach, washed, dried
1/2 c. fresh strawberries

Combine sugar, sesame seed, poppy seed, onion, Worcestershire sauce and paprika in blender container. Process until well blended. Add oil and vinegar gradually, processing constantly. Arrange spinach and strawberries on salad plates; drizzle with dressing. Yield: 2 servings.

Sarah Holloway, Camden, NJ

TOMATOES WITH RAISIN SLAW

1/8 c. California raisins
3/4 c. shredded cabbage
1/8 c. buttermilk
3/4 tsp. vinegar
3/4 tsp. sugar
1/8 tsp. salt
2 lg. tomatoes
2 hard-boiled eggs
Parsley to taste

Combine raisins and cabbage in bowl. Drizzle with mixture of buttermilk, vinegar, sugar and salt; toss to mix well. Chill in refrigerator. Peel tomatoes; hollow out the inside to form cup. Turn upside down on plate to drain. Chill in refrigerator for several minutes. Spoon slaw into tomatoes on salad plates. Garnish with sliced egg and parsley. Yield: 2 servings.

Photograph for this recipe on page 137.

CUBE STEAK STROGANOFF

1 med. onion, thinly sliced
3 tbsp. oil
2 cubed steaks
2 tbsp. flour
1/2 tsp. salt
1/4 c. sour cream
1   2-oz. can mushroom pieces

Sauteé onion in 1 tablespoon oil in skillet for 4 minutes. Remove from skillet. Add 2 tablespoons oil. Coat steaks with flour. Place in skillet. Cook over medium heat for 4 minutes on each side. Sprinkle with salt. Place steaks on warm plates. Drain drippings. Add sautéed onion, sour cream and undrained mushrooms to skillet. Heat to serving temperature. Serve with steaks. Yield: 2 servings.

Lora Lynn Adams, Bentley, LA

STIR-FRY BEEF WITH BROCCOLI

3/4 c. thinly sliced beef
1 clove of garlic, minced
2 tbsp. soy sauce
3 tbsp. oil
1/3 bunch broccoli, sliced
2 tbsp. sugar

Marinate beef with garlic in soy sauce in bowl. Heat oil just to the smoking point in wok. Stir-fry marinated beef for 3 minutes; remove to platter. Add broccoli with 1/3 cup water and sugar to wok. Cook, covered, over medium-high heat for 6 minutes, stirring occasionally. Add beef; mix well. Any available meat, cooked or uncooked, may be substituted, as well as a variety of vegetables to suit individual taste and appetite. Yield: 2 servings.

Jeanne Shirley, Wynnewood, OK

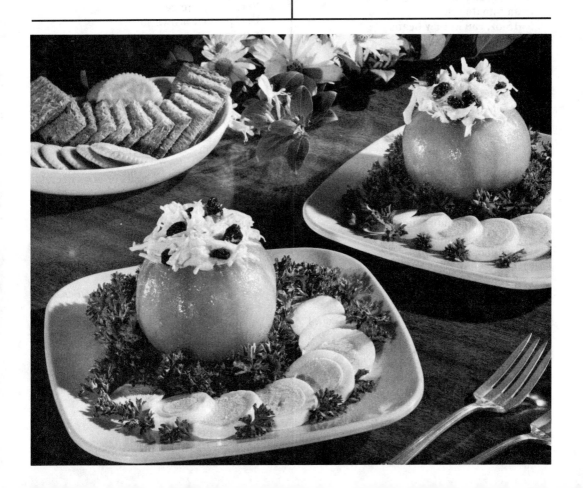

BARBECUE CUPS

1/2 lb. ground beef
1/4 c. barbecue sauce
2 tsp. instant onion
Garlic powder to taste
1   5-oz. package refrigerator biscuits
1/2 c. shredded Cheddar cheese

Brown ground beef in skillet, stirring until crumbly; drain. Add barbecue sauce, onion and garlic powder; mix well. Flatten each biscuit; press into greased muffin cups. Spoon in ground beef mixture. Top with cheese. Bake at 400 degrees for 10 to 12 minutes or until browned. Yield: 2 servings.

Carla Seippel, Blue Springs, MO

CHILI

1/2 lb. ground beef
1 can tomato soup
1   15-oz. can kidney beans
1 pkg. taco seasoning mix

Brown ground beef in skillet, stirring until crumbly. Add soup, beans and seasoning mix; mix well. Heat to serving temperature. Garnish with shredded cheese or onion. Yield: 2 servings.

Joyce Grohmann, Cypress, CA

SPAGHETTI SAUCE FOR TWO

1/2 lb. ground beef
1   8-oz. can tomato sauce
1   6-oz can tomato paste
3 tbsp. chopped onion
1 tsp. oregano
1 tsp. basil
Salt and pepper to taste

Brown ground beef in skillet, stirring until crumbly. Add mixture of tomato sauce and tomato paste. Stir in onion, oregano, basil, salt and pepper. Simmer for 15 minutes. Serve over cooked spaghetti. May cook in Crock•Pot for 6 hours. Yield: 2 servings.

Denise Schares, LaPorte City, IA

CHEESEBURGER CHOWDER

1/4 lb. ground beef
1/4 c. chopped onion
2 tbsp. chopped green pepper
1 can Cheddar cheese soup
1 soup can milk
Worcestershire sauce to taste

Brown ground beef with onion and green pepper in skillet, stirring until crumbly. Add soup, milk and Worcestershire sauce. Simmer for 5 minutes. Yield: 2 servings.

Beth Neeley, Abilene, TX

GINGERED HAM SLICE

1 fully cooked 1-in. thick center-cut
   ham slice
1/2 c. ginger ale
1/2 c. orange juice
1/4 c. packed brown sugar
1 tbsp. oil
1 1/2 tsp. wine vinegar
1 tsp. dry mustard
1/4 tsp. ginger
1/8 tsp. cloves

Cut fat edge of ham; place in shallow dish. Combine ginger ale, orange juice, brown sugar, oil, vinegar, dry mustard, ginger and cloves in bowl; mix well. Pour over ham. Marinate at room temperature for 2 hours or in refrigerator overnight, spooning marinade over ham several times. Bake at 350 degrees for 30 minutes, brushing frequently with marinade. Serve with remaining marinade. May grill ham over low coals for 15 minutes on each side, basting frequently. Yield: 2 servings.

Norma Dabney, Orlando, FL

PORK CHOPS AND POTATOES

2 pork chops
Oil
4 potatoes, peeled, sliced
1 sm. onion, sliced
Salt and pepper to taste
1 can cream of mushroom soup
1/2 soup can milk

Brown pork chops in a small amount of oil in skillet. Layer potatoes and onion in 2-quart casserole; season with salt and pepper. Place pork chops on top. Combine soup and milk in bowl; mix well. Pour over pork chops. Bake, covered, at 375 degrees for 1 hour. Yield: 2 servings.

Sharon Petersen, Westland, MI

STUFFED PORK CHOPS

2 slices bread, cubed
1/4 c. chopped onion
2 tbsp. melted margarine
2 double-thick pork chops with pockets
Salt and pepper to taste
2 tbsp. melted margarine
2 med. unpeeled baking potatoes

Spoon mixture of first 3 ingredients into pockets in pork chops; secure with picks. Season with salt and pepper. Brown in 2 tablespoons margarine in skillet. Place in casserole. Cut potatoes in half. Arrange around pork chops. Bake, covered, at 350 degrees for 50 minutes. Bake, uncovered, for 10 minutes longer.
Yield: 2 servings.

Emily B. Fallaw, Lockhart, SC

KRAUT FRANKFURTER ROLL-UPS

2 c. buttermilk baking mix
2/3 c. milk
2 tsp. mustard
4 turkey frankfurters
1/3 c. minced onion
1/3 c. minced fresh parsley
3 c. sauerkraut
2 tbsp. butter
2 tbsp. flour
Pepper and paprika to taste
1 c. milk
1 c. shredded Cheddar cheese

Combine baking mix and milk in bowl. Stir until soft dough forms; beat vigorously for 30 seconds. Add additional baking mix if dough is too sticky. Turn dough onto well-floured surface; form into ball, coating all sides with flour. Knead dough 10 times. Roll dough into 8x12-inch rectangle. Spread mustard over dough. Cut into 4 quarters; sprinkle with onion and parsley.

Place 1 frankfurter on each dough section; roll dough tightly around frankfurter jelly-roll style, sealing ends and seam. Place on greased baking sheet. Bake at 400 degrees for 15 minutes or until golden brown. Heat sauerkraut to serving temperature in saucepan. Melt butter in medium saucepan over medium heat. Stir in flour, pepper and paprika, stirring until smooth and bubbly. Add milk gradually. Cook until sauce is thickened and smooth, stirring constantly. Stir in cheese. Cook over low heat until cheese melts, stirring constantly. Arrange frankfurters over sauerkraut on serving plate. Spoon cheese sauce over top. Yield: 2 servings.

BAKED CHICKEN PARMESAN

1 egg, beaten
1/4 c. sour cream
1/4 c. Italian-style bread crumbs
2 tbsp. Parmesan cheese
2 chicken breasts, skinned

Combine egg with sour cream in shallow bowl; mix well. Combine bread crumbs and cheese in shallow bowl. Dip chicken in egg mixture; coat with crumb mixture. Place in greased 6x10-inch baking dish. Bake at 350 degrees for 45 minutes or until tender. Yield: 2 servings.

Wanda Benzing, Erlanger, KY

CHICKEN SCALLOPINE

2 chicken breast filets
1/4 c. flour
1 tbsp. oil
2 tbsp. butter
1 tbsp. lemon juice

Pound chicken breasts between waxed paper to 1/4-inch thickness. Coat with flour. Cook in mixture of oil and 1 tablespoon butter in skillet over medium heat for 4 minutes on each side. Remove chicken to warm platter. Add remaining 1 tablespoon butter to skillet; stir in lemon juice. Pour over chicken. Garnish with parsley and lemon slices. Yield: 2 servings.

Sharyl Fuller, Coleman, TX

CHICKEN SUPREME

1 whole chicken breast, split
1/2 tsp. salt
Pepper to taste
3 tbsp. margarine
1 c. sliced mushrooms
1 c. milk
1 tbsp. cornstarch
2 tbsp. dry Sherry

Sprinkle chicken with salt and pepper. Place chicken skin side down in 8-inch baking dish. Dot with margarine. Bake at 350 degrees for 20 minutes. Add mushrooms. Bake for 5 minutes longer. Combine milk and cornstarch in small saucepan. Bring to a boil over medium heat. Cook for 1 minute, stirring constantly. Stir in Sherry. Pour over chicken, stirring well to incorporate pan juices and mushrooms. Bake for 5 minutes or until hot and bubbly.
Yield: 2 servings.

Photograph for this recipe below.

FANCY CHICKEN BROIL

2 chicken breasts
Salt and pepper to taste
1 tbsp. lemon juice
1 clove of garlic, minced
1/4 c. oil
2 tbsp. soy sauce
1/2 tsp. ginger
2 tbsp. sesame seed

Sprinkle chicken breasts with salt, pepper and lemon juice in bowl. Mix garlic, oil, soy sauce and ginger in bowl. Pour over chicken, coating well. Let stand for 30 minutes. Drain, reserving marinade. Place on rack in broiler pan. Broil for 30 minutes, brushing occasionally with marinade. Turn chicken over; baste. Broil until tender. Sprinkle with sesame seed. Broil until sesame seed is golden. Serve with tossed salad and French bread. Yield: 2 servings.

Dorothy Weirick, Salt Lake City, UT

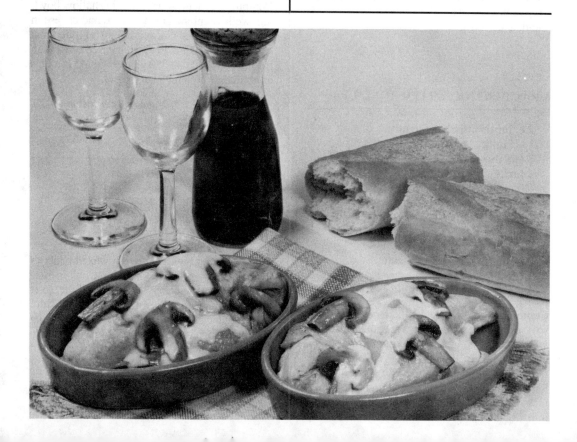

IMPERIAL CHICKEN

2 chicken breasts
Garlic powder to taste
1 egg
1/2 c. bread crumbs
2 tbsp. melted margarine

Sprinkle chicken breasts with garlic powder. Dip in mixture of egg and 2 tablespoons water; roll in bread crumbs to coat. Place skin side down in baking dish. Drizzle with margarine. Bake at 300 degrees for 30 minutes. Turn chicken over. Bake for 30 minutes longer. Yield: 2 servings.

Meryl Weiss, Chicago, IL

MICROWAVE ITALIAN CHICKEN

2 chicken breasts
1/2 tsp. salt
1/4 tsp. each pepper, garlic powder and
    oregano
1/4 med. onion, sliced
1/4 med. green pepper, sliced
1/4 c. drained canned sliced mushrooms
1/4 to 1/2 c. tomato juice

Arrange chicken breasts with meaty portion toward outer edge of 2-quart glass baking dish. Sprinkle with salt, pepper, garlic powder and oregano. Layer onion, green pepper and mushrooms over chicken. Pour tomato juice over all. Microwave, covered, on high for 8 minutes per pound, turning once. Let stand for 5 to 10 minutes. Yield: 2 servings.

Shelley Wagner, Wichita, KS

CHICKEN PASTA SALAD

1 pkg. vinegar and oil salad dressing mix
1/2 head lettuce, shredded
1 sm. can chicken
1/2 c. pasta, cooked
1 sm. can crushed pineapple

Prepare salad dressing mix using package directions. Combine remaining ingredients in bowl. Drizzle with dressing; toss lightly. Serve with favorite soup and breadsticks. Yield: 2 servings.

Joy Hemphill, Fletcher, NC

STIR-FRIED CHICKEN AND VEGETABLES

2 tbsp. chopped green bell pepper
1 oz. sliced canned mushrooms, drained
2 tbsp. melted margarine
2 tbsp. flour
1/2 tsp. salt
1/8 tsp. pepper
1/2 c. canned chicken broth
1/2 c. milk
1 can boned chicken
2 tbsp. chopped pimento
1 c. cooked rice

Sauté green pepper and mushrooms in margarine in large skillet until tender. Add mixture of flour, salt and pepper to vegetables; mix well. Cook for 1 minute, stirring constantly. Stir in chicken broth and milk gradually. Cook over medium heat until thickened, stirring constantly. Stir in chicken and pimento. Heat to serving temperature. Serve over hot rice. Yield: 2 servings.

Donna Biggs, Canby, OR

FRENCH-BROILED GAME HENS

1/2 sm. onion, chopped
2 tbsp. butter
Juice of 1 lime
2 Cornish game hens, split
Paprika to taste

Combine onion, butter and lime juice in saucepan. Cook for several minutes or until onion is tender, stirring constantly. Place game hens skin side down on rack in broiler pan. Brush with half the lime juice mixture. Broil 8 to 10 inches from heat source for 10 minutes. Turn game hens; brush with remaining sauce. Broil for 4 to 5 minutes longer or until tender. Sprinkle with paprika. Serve with hot cooked rice pilaf. Yield: 2 servings.

Julie Baskin, Dallas, TX

> *Tip: Spread chicken breasts with Dijon mustard, drizzle with honey and sprinkle with fresh rosemary. Bake at 350 degrees for 1 hour.*

GROUND TURKEY AND CHEESE ENCHILADAS

8 oz. ground turkey
Garlic salt and pepper to taste
1 med. white onion, chopped
6 corn tortillas
1 c. oil
1½ c. mild enchilada sauce
1½ c. shredded Cheddar cheese

Brown ground turkey seasoned with garlic salt and pepper in skillet over low heat, stirring until crumbly. Add onion. Cook for several minutes, stirring constantly; drain. Soften tortillas in warm oil. Dip in enchilada sauce; drain excess sauce. Place 1 tablespoon each turkey mixture and cheese on each tortilla; roll to enclose filling. Place seam side down in baking dish. Top with remaining sauce and cheese. Bake at 350 degrees for 20 minutes. Ground turkey must be cooked at low temperature to avoid toughness. Yield: 2 servings.

Brenda Montgomery, Grandfield, OK

TURKEY SUPREME

1 c. chopped cooked turkey
1 c. chopped celery
½ c. mayonnaise
¼ c. slivered almonds
1 tbsp. lemon juice
¼ c. shredded sharp cheese
½ c. crushed potato chips

Combine turkey, celery, mayonnaise, almonds and lemon juice in bowl; toss lightly. Spoon into greased individual custard cups or small casserole. Top with cheese and potato chips. Bake at 450 degrees for 10 minutes. Yield: 2 servings.

Josephine Catron, Luray, VA

SUNSHINE FILLETS

1 lb. fresh fish fillets
1½ tsp. oil
1 tbsp. fresh orange juice
1 tsp. grated orange rind
1 tsp. salt
Pepper and nutmeg to taste

Cut fillets into serving-sized portions. Place skin side down in greased baking dish. Combine oil, orange juice, orange rind, salt, pepper and nutmeg in bowl; mix well. Pour over fillets. Bake at 350 degrees for 25 minutes or until fish flakes easily. Yield: 2 servings.

Mary Sue Flentge, Cape Girardeau, MO

POACHED FISH

2 halibut steaks
¼ tsp. salt
1 tbsp. melted butter
1 tbsp. flour
½ c. milk
2 tbsp. dry white wine
½ c. shredded Swiss cheese

Place halibut in skillet with enough water to just cover; add salt. Bring to a boil; reduce heat. Simmer, covered, for 7 minutes or until fish flakes easily; drain. Place in heated serving dish. Blend butter and flour in saucepan. Stir in milk and wine gradually. Cook until bubbly, stirring constantly. Add cheese. Cook until melted, stirring constantly. Spoon over halibut. Garnish with paprika. Yield: 2 servings.

Maxine H. Warren, Walkertown, NC

TUNA CASSEROLE

1 2¼-oz. package potato chips
1 can cream of mushroom soup
1 7-oz. can tuna
Pepper to taste

Alternate layers of potato chips, soup and tuna in buttered casserole, ending with potato chips. Sprinkle with pepper. Bake, covered, at 375 degrees for 20 minutes. Bake, uncovered, for 10 minutes longer or until brown. Yield: 2 servings.

Hassie Hunter Rodgers, Goshen, AL

Tip: Grill fish fillets over hot coals after brushing with oil and sprinkling generously with garlic salt and white pepper.

SCALLOP CASSEROLE

1/2 lb. scallops
1/4 c. light cream
1/2 c. dry bread crumbs
1/4 c. melted butter
1 tsp. celery seed
1/2 tsp. salt
Pepper to taste
1/4 c. light cream
Paprika

Cut scallops into 1 1/2-inch pieces. Arrange in greased 8x8-inch baking dish. Pour 1/4 cup cream over scallops. Combine bread crumbs, butter, celery seed, salt and pepper in bowl; mix well. Sprinkle over scallops. Pour remaining 1/4 cup cream over top. Sprinkle with paprika. Bake at 375 degrees for 25 to 30 minutes or until tender. Yield: 2 servings.

Marie Lohman, Stroudsburg, PA

CRAB NEWBURG

1 tbsp. melted margarine
1 tbsp. flour
1/2 c. skim milk
2 tsp. dry Sherry
1/8 tsp. salt
White pepper to taste
8 oz. crab meat, flaked
4 lemon wedges

Blend margarine and flour in saucepan. Cook over low heat for 1 minute, stirring constantly. Stir in milk. Cook until thickened, stirring constantly. Stir in Sherry, salt and white pepper; remove from heat. Fold in crab meat. Spoon onto serving plates. Arrange lemon wedges on plates. Garnish with pimento and parsley. Yield: 2 servings.

Francis Bruce, Abilene, TX

SHRIMP CREOLE

1 sm. onion, chopped
1/2 green bell pepper, chopped
1 stalk celery, chopped
1 clove of garlic, crushed
1 1/2 tsp. oil
1 15-oz. can tomato sauce

1 tsp. oregano
1 bay leaf
1 8-oz. package frozen shrimp, thawed

Sauté onion, green pepper, celery and garlic in oil in skillet until tender. Add tomato sauce, oregano and bay leaf. Simmer for 20 minutes, stirring frequently. Stir in shrimp. Simmer for 5 minutes longer, stirring frequently. Remove bay leaf. Serve over hot cooked rice. Yield: 2 servings.

Alma Lee Hicks, Murphysboro, IL

ASPARAGUS CASSEROLE

1 16-oz. can cut asparagus
1/2 c. shredded Cheddar cheese
2 eggs, beaten
1/4 c. chopped pimento
1/4 c. milk
3/4 c. cracker crumbs
2 tbsp. melted butter

Combine asparagus, cheese, eggs, pimento, milk, cracker crumbs and butter in bowl; mix gently. Spoon into greased 1-quart casserole. Bake at 350 degrees for 20 to 25 minutes or until set. Do not overcook. Yield: 2 servings.

Margaret A. Ramsdale, Hutchinson, KS

GOURMET GREEN BEANS

1 env. dry chicken-noodle soup mix
1 10-oz. package frozen French-style
   green beans
1/3 c. sliced blanched almonds

Dissolve soup mix in 1/2 cup hot water in saucepan. Add green beans. Bring to a boil. Cook, covered, until tender-crisp. Spoon into serving bowl. Top with almonds. Yield: 2 servings.

Anna Fargo, Toledo, OH

Tip: Dress up cooked green beans by arranging in bundles and "tying" each bundle with a long strip of pimento.

CARROT AND APPLE MEDLEY

¹/₂ onion, sliced
1¹/₂ tbsp. margarine
3 med. carrots, sliced
2 tbsp. maple syrup
¹/₄ tsp. salt
1 med. tart apple, cut into wedges

Sauté onion in margarine in skillet. Add carrots, syrup and salt; stir well. Cook, covered, over low heat for 15 minutes. Add apple. Simmer, covered, until tender. Yield: 2 servings.

June Sherwin, Liberty, MO

GINGER CARROTS

1¹/₂ c. carrot strips
1 tsp. diet margarine
1 tsp. brown sugar
¹/₈ tsp. ginger

Cook carrots in a small amount of boiling water in saucepan until tender-crisp; drain. Melt margarine in small saucepan; stir in brown sugar and ginger. Cook over medium-low heat until sugar is dissolved, stirring constantly. Add carrots. Cook until carrots are well coated and heated through, stirring gently. Yield: 2 servings.

Joann Brown, Hattiesburg, MS

POTATO PUFFS

¹/₂ c. mashed potatoes
1 egg
¹/₄ c. finely chopped onion
2 tbsp. flour
Oil for frying

Combine mashed potatoes, egg, onion and flour in bowl; mix well. Drop by teaspoonfuls into hot oil in skillet. Brown on both sides. Drain on paper towels. Serve hot. Yield: 2 servings.

Audrey S. Bowers, Greer, SC

CRISP-TOP POTATOES

2 potatoes, sliced ¹/₂ in. thick
2 tbsp. melted margarine

Salt, pepper and paprika to taste
¹/₂ c. shredded Cheddar cheese
Cornflake crumbs

Coat potato slices on both sides with margarine. Place in single layer on 10x15-inch baking sheet. Season with salt, pepper and paprika. Sprinkle with cheese and cornflake crumbs. Bake at 375 degrees for 30 minutes. Yield: 2 servings.

Katie Ramfield, Scottsdale, AZ

BAKED POTATOES PARMESAN

¹/₃ c. Parmesan cheese
1 tbsp. dried parsley
2 potatoes, baked

Combine cheese, parsley and ¹/₃ cup water in bowl; mix well. Spoon into hot baked potatoes. Yield: 2 servings.

Debbie Stanioch, Greensboro, NC

MUSHROOMS IN SOUR CREAM

2 lb. fresh mushrooms, sliced
¹/₂ c. minced green onions
1 tsp. each salt and pepper
¹/₂ c. butter
¹/₂ c. sour cream

Sauté mushrooms and onions with salt and pepper in butter in skillet for 10 minutes. Add sour cream. Heat until well mixed. Do not boil. Serve warm or chilled. Yield: 2 servings.

Debi Moore, Atoka, OK

MARINATED TOMATOES

¹/₄ c. oil
2 tbsp. vinegar
Garlic salt to taste
1¹/₂ tsp. sugar
2 tomatoes, cut into quarters

Combine first 4 ingredients in bowl; mix well. Add tomatoes. Chill until serving time. Yield: 2 servings.

Lois Pentel, Dundee, OR

BROILED CHEESE TOMATOES

2 firm ripe tomatoes, cored
1/2 tsp. salt
1/8 tsp. pepper
2 tbsp. cracker crumbs
2 tbsp. shredded Cheddar cheese
Butter

Cut tomatoes in half crosswise. Sprinkle with salt, pepper and mixture of crumbs and cheese. Dot with butter. Place on rack in broiler pan. Broil 6 inches from heat source for 10 minutes or until cheese is melted. Yield: 2 servings.

Audrey Cordes, Montgomery, AL

RICE VERDE

1/4 c. sour cream
2 tbsp. chopped green chilies
1/2 c. shredded Cheddar cheese
1 1/3 c. cooked rice

Combine sour cream, chilies and half the cheese in bowl; mix well. Layer half the rice and all the sour cream mixture in buttered casserole. Top with remaining rice and cheese. Bake at 350 degrees for 15 minutes. May prepare and store in refrigerator for up to 24 hours before baking. Yield: 2 servings.

Jean Jackson, Uniontown, KS

HOT BISCUITS

2 tbsp. shortening
1 c. sifted self-rising flour
1/3 c. milk

Cut shortening into flour in bowl until crumbly. Add milk; mix with fork. Turn onto lightly floured surface. Knead until smooth. Roll dough 1/2-inch thick; cut with biscuit cutter. Place on ungreased baking sheet. Bake at 450 degrees for 10 to 12 minutes or until browned. May substitute all-purpose flour for self-rising and add 1 1/4 teaspoons baking powder and 3/8 teaspoon salt. May double recipe, partially bake biscuits, then freeze. Yield: 1/2 dozen.

Delieda McCormick, Princeton, KY

CORN BREAD FOR TWO

1/4 c. cornmeal
1 tsp. baking powder
3 tbsp. flour
1/2 tsp. salt
1 tbsp. (heaping) mayonnaise
5 tbsp. milk

Combine cornmeal, baking powder, flour and salt in bowl. Add mayonnaise; mix well. Stir in milk gradually. Pour into generously greased preheated 6-inch iron skillet. Bake at 425 degrees for 15 minutes. Cut into wedges. Yield: 2 servings.

Robbie McKinnon, Gurdon, AR

SOUR CREAM BISCUITS

1/4 c. margarine, softened
1/4 c. sour cream
1/2 c. self-rising flour

Combine margarine and sour cream in bowl; blend well. Add flour; mix well. Fill greased muffin cups 3/4 full. Bake at 425 degrees for 12 to 15 minutes or until brown. Serve hot. Yield: 2 servings.

Alycia Outlaw, Newnan, GA

EASY KOLACHES

1   5-count pkg. refrigerator biscuits
2 1/2 tsp. jam
2 tbsp. flour
2 tbsp. sugar
1 tbsp. margarine
1/4 c. confectioners' sugar
1 tsp. orange juice

Place biscuits on greased baking sheet. Make imprint in center of each biscuit. Fill with 1/2 teaspoon jam. Mix flour, sugar and margarine in bowl until crumbly. Sprinkle on top of biscuits. Bake at 350 degrees for 20 minutes or just until lightly browned. Combine confectioners' sugar and orange juice in small bowl. Drizzle over top of hot biscuits. Yield: 2 servings.

Shelley Wagner, Wichita, KS

BATTER BUNS

1 pkg. dry yeast
2 tbsp. sugar
1/2 tsp. salt
1 egg
1/4 c. shortening
1 2/3 c. flour

Dissolve yeast in 2/3 cup warm water in bowl. Add sugar, salt, egg, shortening and 1 cup flour; mix well. Add remaining 2/3 cup flour; beat until smooth. Fill greased muffin cups 1/2 full. Let rise in warm place until doubled in bulk. Bake at 375 degrees for 20 to 25 minutes or until light golden brown. Yield: 2 servings.

Carla Seippel, Blue Springs, MO

PANCAKES FOR TWO

1/4 c. melted butter
2 eggs
1 c. self-rising flour
1/3 c. (about) milk

Combine butter and eggs in bowl; beat by hand until mixed well. Add flour; beat well. Add enough milk to make of desired consistency. Pour about 1/4 cup batter on hot greased griddle. Cook until brown on both sides. Yield: 2 servings.

Marlo Marie Little, Greenville, NC

ADAM AND EVE WAFFLES

1/2 c. flour
1/2 tsp. each salt and baking powder
2 eggs, beaten
1/2 c. milk
1 tbsp. oil
1 apple, chopped

Mix flour, salt and baking powder in bowl. Add eggs, milk, oil and apple; mix well. Bake in waffle iron using manufacturer's directions or bake as for pancakes on greased griddle. Yield: 2 servings.

Sr. M. M. Clarke, Sioux Falls, SD

MINI WHITE BREAD

1/2 c. flour
1 tbsp. sugar
2 tsp. dry yeast
1 tsp. salt
1/2 c. milk
2 tsp. shortening
1 3/4 to 2 c. flour
Melted butter

Combine 1/2 cup flour, sugar, yeast and salt in large mixer bowl; mix well. Combine milk, 1/3 cup water and shortening in small saucepan. Heat over low heat to 120 degrees. Stir into yeast mixture gradually. Beat at medium speed for 2 minutes. Add enough remaining flour to make stiff dough. Knead on floured surface for 5 to 7 minutes or until smooth and elastic. Shape into loaf. Place in greased miniature loaf pan. Let rise until doubled in bulk. Bake at 375 degrees for 45 to 55 minutes or until deep golden brown. Remove from pan to wire rack. Brush top with melted butter. Yield: 2 servings.

Cynthia Warren, Kernersville, NC

BLUEBERRY COBBLER

1/2 can blueberry pie filling
1/2 tsp. shredded orange rind
1/2 c. buttermilk baking mix
2 tsp. sugar
2 tbsp. orange juice
2 tsp. butter, softened

Mix pie filling and orange rind in ungreased 2 1/2-cup casserole. Bake at 400 degrees for 15 minutes. Combine baking mix, sugar, orange juice and butter in bowl; mix with fork. Drop dough by spoonfuls onto hot blueberry mixture. Bake for 15 to 20 minutes longer or until topping is lightly browned. Serve warm with light cream or ice cream. Serve remaining 1/2 can pie filling in tart shells or use as topping for ice cream, pancakes or pudding. Yield: 2 servings.

Ann Frisbie, Minco, OK

Tip: Heat 1 can whole cranberry sauce or 1 package frozen cranberry-orange relish and serve over vanilla ice cream.

CRANBERRY CRUNCH

³/4 c. oats
¹/4 c. flour
6 tbsp. brown sugar
3 tbsp. butter
1 c. cranberry sauce

Mix oats, flour and brown sugar in bowl. Cut in butter until crumbly. Press half the mixture into 6x6-inch baking pan. Spread with cranberry sauce. Top with remaining crumb mixture. Bake at 350 degrees for 30 minutes. Serve warm topped with ice cream. Yield: 2 servings.

Nancy W. Anderson, Clarklake, MI

MARMALADE CREAMWICHES

4 frozen waffles
¹/2 jar orange marmalade
1 tbsp. chopped pecans
¹/2 pt. vanilla ice cream

Toast waffles. Cool to room temperature. Mix marmalade and pecans in bowl. Spread mixture on 1 side of waffles. Cut ice cream into 2 slices. Sandwich between marmalade spread waffles. Top with marmalade. Yield: 2 servings.

Donna McBride, Abilene, TX

MINT PATTY ALASKAS

2 egg whites
¹/4 tsp. cream of tartar
¹/4 tsp. vanilla extract
¹/4 c. sugar
2 individual sponge cake cups
2 chocolate-coated peppermint
    ice cream patties

Beat egg whites with cream of tartar and vanilla in mixer bowl until soft peaks form. Add sugar gradually, beating until stiff. Place cake cups on wooden cutting board. Top with ice cream patty. Spread meringue thickly over ice cream and thinly over cake, sealing completely to board. Bake in preheated 500-degree oven for 2 to 3 minutes or until browned. Garnish with crushed peppermint candy. Yield: 2 servings.

Joyce Titus, New Knoxville, OH

STRAWBERRY AND RICE PARFAITS

¹/2 c. strawberry yogurt
³/4 c. cooked rice, chilled
5 oz. frozen strawberries, thawed
Whipped topping

Combine yogurt and rice in bowl; mix well. Chill, covered, in refrigerator. Layer rice and strawberries alternately in parfait glasses. Garnish with whipped topping and whole strawberries. Yield: 2 servings.

Lynn Tartan, Topeka, KS

PERSIAN PEACHES

4 c. sliced peaches
1 c. orange juice
6 tbsp. honey
1 tbsp. finely chopped candied ginger
Salt to taste

Mix peaches, orange juice, honey, ginger and salt in bowl. Chill, covered, in refrigerator. Spoon into chilled sherbet glasses.
Yield: 2 servings.

Sharon Haywood, Dallas, TX

PEANUT BUTTER PARFAITS

1 c. packed brown sugar
¹/3 c. milk
¹/4 c. light corn syrup
1 tbsp. butter
¹/4 c. peanut butter
Vanilla ice cream
Peanuts

Combine brown sugar, milk, corn syrup and butter in saucepan; mix well. Cook over medium heat until sugar dissolves and butter melts, stirring constantly. Remove from heat. Add peanut butter; beat until smooth. Cool. Alternate layers of peanut butter sauce and ice cream in parfait glasses, beginning and ending with ice cream. Top with peanuts. Serve immediately.
Yield: 2 servings.

Morgan Liane Jones, Goodlettsville, TN

Microwave Time Savers

PRODUCT	QUANTITY	UTENSIL	SETTING & TIME
Baby bottle	8 oz.	Remove lid and nipple	Med-High for 1 to 1^1/$_2$ min.
Baby food	4-oz. jar	Remove lid	Med-High for 20 to 30 sec.
Bacon	4 slices	7x12-in. glass dish	High for 4 to 6 min.
Bread (frozen)	1 slice 1 loaf	Paper towel or napkin (remove twist tie from bag)	Med-Low for 15 to 25 sec. Med-Low for 1^1/$_2$ to 4 min.
Buns and rolls	2	Paper plate, paper towel	Med-High for 20 to 25 sec.
Butter	2 tbsp. melted 2 tbsp. softened ^{1}/$_2$ cup melted ^{1}/$_2$ cup softened	1-cup glass measure 1-cup glass measure 2-cup glass measure 2-cup glass measure	Med-High for 45 sec. Low for 45 sec. to 1 min. Med-High for 1^1/$_2$ to 2 min. Warm for 1^1/$_2$ to 2^1/$_2$ min.
Casseroles (refrigerated)	1 serving 1 quart	Glass or china dish (cover with waxed paper)	Med-High for 3 to 4 min. Med-High for 10 to 14 min.
Chocolate	1 or 2 oz.	1-cup glass measure	High for 1 to 2 min.
Chocolate chips (to melt)	6 oz. 12 oz.	2-cup glass measure 4-cup glass measure	High for 2 to 2^1/$_2$ min. High for 2^1/$_2$ to 3 min.
Coffee and tea	1 cup	Glass or china cup	High for 1 to 2 min.
Cream cheese (to soften)	3 oz. 8 oz.	Glass plate (remove from foil package)	Warm for 2 to 2^1/$_2$ min. Warm for 4 to 4^1/$_2$ min.
Hot dogs	2	In bun (wrap in paper)	Med-High for 1 to 1^1/$_2$ min.
Juice (frozen concentrate)	6 oz. 12 oz.	Original container (remove lid)	Low for 2 to 2^1/$_2$ min. Low for 5 to 6 min.
Leftovers	1 plate or bowl	Cover with waxed paper	Med-High for 4 to 5 min.
Meat	1 slice 1 plate	Glass or china plate (cover with waxed paper)	Med-High for 1 to 2 min. Med-High for 6 to 7 min.
Pie	1 slice	Glass or china plate	Med. for 25 to 35 sec.
Pizza	1 to 2 slices	Paper plate, paper towel	Med-High for 1 to 2 min.
Potatoes, to bake	4 medium	Pierce skin	High for 10 to 15 min.
Rice, cooked	1 cup	Covered glass dish	Med-High for 1^1/$_2$ to 2^1/$_2$ min.
Sandwich	1 2	Wrap in paper towel	Med-High for ^{1}/$_2$ to 1 min. Med-High for 1^1/$_2$ to 2 min.
Syrups and sauces	1 cup	2-cup glass measure	Med-High for 2 to 3 min.
TV dinner (frozen)	2 trays	Original ^{3}/$_4$-in. foil tray or paper carton	Med-High for 14 to 16 min.

Microwave Tips

- Always choose the minimum cooking time. Remember, food continues to cook after it is removed from the microwave.
- Keep your microwave clean. Built-up grease or food spatters can slow cooking times.
- When poaching or frying an egg in a browning dish, always prick the center of the yolk with a fork to keep the egg from exploding.
- Do not try to hard-cook eggs in the shell in a microwave. The eggs will build up pressure and burst.
- Do not use metal dishes or aluminum foil except as specifically recommended by the manufacturer of your microwave.
- Never use a foil tray over 3/4 inch deep in your microwave.
- When heating TV-style dinners, remove the foil cover, then place tray back in carton. Food will heat only from the top.
- Be sure to prick potatoes before baking to allow steam to escape.
- Cut a small slit in pouch-packed frozen foods before heating in microwave to allow steam to escape.
- When placing more than one food item in microwave, arrange foods in a circle near edges of oven.
- Cover foods that need to be steamed or tenderized.
- Do not try to pop popcorn without a microwave-approved corn popper.

Did You Know You Can...?

(Use High setting for the following unless otherwise indicated.)

- Use your microwave oven to melt chocolate, to soften cream cheese and to soften or melt butter or margarine.
- Roast shelled nuts for 6 to 10 minutes, stirring frequently.
- Peel fruit or tomatoes by placing in 1 cup hot water. Microwave for 30 to 45 seconds; remove skins easily.
- Plump dried fruit by placing in a dish with 1 to 2 teaspoons water. Cover tightly with plastic wrap. Microwave for 1/2 to 1 1/2 minutes.
- Precook barbecued ribs or chicken until almost done, then place on the grill to sear and add a charcoal flavor.
- Soften brown sugar by placing in a dish with a slice of bread or apple and microwaving for 30 to 45 seconds, stirring once.
- Dry bread for crumbs or croutons. Place cubed or crumbled bread on paper towels. Microwave for 6 to 7 minutes, stirring occasionally.
- Warm baby food or baby bottles by removing metal lid and microwaving for 10 to 20 seconds. Be sure to test temperature before feeding baby.
- Freshen chips and crackers by microwaving for 15 to 30 seconds. Let stand for 2 to 3 minutes before serving.
- Dry herbs by placing on paper towels and microwaving for 2 to 3 minutes or until the herbs are dry.
- Ripen an avocado by microwaving on Low for 2 to 4 minutes.

Sauces in Minutes

You can miraculously transform meat, poultry or fish into a masterpiece by adding a simple sauce. These quick and easy sauces use creamed soups as a base.

SAUCE	SOUP BASE	ADDITIONS
Cheese	Cream of celery, chicken or mushroom	3 tablespoons milk 1/2 cup Cheddar cheese Seasonings to taste
Mock Hollandaise	Cream of celery, chicken or mushroom	1/4 cup mayonnaise 3 tablespoons water 1 tablespoon lemon juice Seasonings to taste
Mushroom	Cream of mushroom	Chopped mushrooms Seasonings to taste
Peppery Cheese	Cheddar cheese	Cayenne pepper to taste Tabasco sauce to taste
Sour Cream	Cream of celery	1/2 cup sour cream Chicken or mushrooms Milk if needed Seasonings to taste
Tomato	Tomato	Sautéed onions and peppers Dash of Worcestershire sauce Seasonings to taste

BASIC WHITE SAUCE

Ingredient	Thin	Medium	Thick
Margarine	2 tbsp.	1/4 cup	6 tbsp.
Flour	2 tbsp.	1/4 cup	6 tbsp.
Milk	2 cups	2 cups	2 cups
Salt	1 tsp.	1 tsp.	1 tsp.

Melt margarine in saucepan over low heat. Stir in flour until smooth. Add milk gradually, stirring constantly. Cook over medium heat until bubbly, stirring constantly. Season with salt. Add 1 or more of the following ingredients.

- Mustard: 1/2 teaspoon dry mustard mixed with 2 teaspoons water
- Curry: 1/2 to 1 teaspoon curry mixed with 2 teaspoons water
- Parsley: 2 tablespoons chopped fresh parsley or 2 teaspoons parsley flakes
- Chives: 2 tablespoons chopped fresh chives or 2 teaspoons dried flakes
- Dill: 1 to 2 teaspoons dillweed
- Cheese: Use less flour. Stir in shredded cheese, heating until melted. Cheese will thicken sauce as it melts

Refrigeration Chart

Food	Refrigerate	Freeze
Beef steaks	1-2 days	6-12 months
Beef roasts	1-2 days	6-12 months
Corned beef	7 days	2 weeks
Pork chops	1-2 days	3-4 months
Pork roasts	1-2 days	4-8 months
Fresh sausage	1-2 days	1-2 months
Smoked sausage	7 days	Not recommended
Cured ham	5-7 days	1-2 months
Canned ham	1 year	Not recommended
Ham slice	3 days	1-2 months
Bacon	7 days	2-4 months
Veal cutlets	1-2 days	6-9 months
Stew meat	1-2 days	3-4 months
Ground meat	1-2 days	3-4 months
Luncheon meats	3-5 days	Not recommended
Frankfurters	7 days	1 month
Whole chicken	1-2 days	12 months
Chicken pieces	1-2 days	9 months

FREEZING TIPS

- Date all items before placing them in the freezer.
- Frozen canned hams become watery and soft when thawed. Processed meats have a high salt content which speeds rancidity when thawed.
- Do not freeze stuffed chickens or turkeys. The stuffing may suffer bacterial contamination during the lengthy thawing process.
- Partially thawed food which still has ice crystals in the package can be safely refrozen. A safer test is to determine if the surface temperature is 40° F. or lower.

Equivalent Chart

	When the recipe calls for	Use
Baking	1/2 cup butter	4 ounces
	2 cups butter	1 pound
	4 cups all-purpose flour	1 pound
	4 1/2 to 5 cups sifted cake flour	1 pound
	1 square chocolate	1 ounce
	1 cup semisweet chocolate chips	6 ounces
	4 cups marshmallows	1 pound
	2 1/4 cups packed brown sugar	1 pound
	4 cups confectioners' sugar	1 pound
	2 cups granulated sugar	1 pound
Cereal – Bread	1 cup fine dry bread crumbs	4 to 5 slices
	1 cup soft bread crumbs	2 slices
	1 cup small bread cubes	2 slices
	1 cup fine cracker crumbs	28 saltines
	1 cup fine graham cracker crumbs	15 crackers
	1 cup vanilla wafer crumbs	22 wafers
	1 cup crushed cornflakes	3 cups uncrushed
	4 cups cooked macaroni	8 ounces uncooked
	3 1/2 cups cooked rice	1 cup uncooked
Dairy	1 cup shredded cheese	4 ounces
	1 cup cottage cheese	8 ounces
	1 cup sour cream	8 ounces
	1 cup whipped cream	1/2 cup heavy cream
	2/3 cup evaporated milk	1 small can
	1 2/3 cups evaporated milk	1 13-ounce can
Fruit	4 cups sliced or chopped apples	4 medium
	1 cup mashed bananas	3 medium
	2 cups pitted cherries	4 cups unpitted
	3 cups shredded coconut	8 ounces
	4 cups cranberries	1 pound
	1 cup pitted dates	1 8-ounce package
	1 cup candied fruit	1 8-ounce package
	3 to 4 tablespoons lemon juice plus 1 tablespoon grated lemon rind	1 lemon
	1/3 cup orange juice plus 2 teaspoons grated orange rind	1 orange
	4 cups sliced peaches	8 medium
	2 cups pitted prunes	1 12-ounce package
	3 cups raisins	1 15-ounce package

	When the recipe calls for	Use
Meats	4 cups chopped cooked chicken 3 cups chopped cooked meat 2 cups cooked ground meat	1 5-pound chicken 1 pound, cooked 1 pound, cooked
Nuts	1 cup chopped nuts	4 ounces shelled 1 pound unshelled
Vegetables	2 cups cooked green beans 2¹/2 cups lima beans or red beans 4 cups shredded cabbage 1 cup grated carrot 8 ounces fresh mushrooms 1 cup chopped onion 4 cups sliced or chopped potatoes 2 cups canned tomatoes	¹/2 pound fresh or 1 16-ounce can 1 cup dried, cooked 1 pound 1 large 1 4-ounce can 1 large 4 medium 1 16-ounce can

Measurement Equivalents

1 tablespoon = 3 teaspoons
2 tablespoons = 1 ounce
4 tablespoons = ¹/4 cup
5¹/3 tablespoons = ¹/3 cup
8 tablespoons = ¹/2 cup
12 tablespoons = ³/4 cup
16 tablespoons = 1 cup
1 cup = 8 ounces or ¹/2 pint
4 cups = 1 quart
4 quarts = 1 gallon

1 6¹/2 to 8-ounce can = 1 cup
1 10¹/2 to 12-ounce can = 1¹/4 cups
1 14 to 16-ounce can = 1³/4 cups
1 16 to 17-ounce can = 2 cups
1 18 to 20-ounce can = 2¹/2 cups
1 20-ounce can = 3¹/2 cups
1 46 to 51-ounce can = 5³/4 cups
1 6¹/2 to 7¹/2- pound can or Number
   10 = 12 to 13 cups

Metric Equivalents

Liquid	Dry
1 teaspoon = 5 milliliters 1 tablespoon = 15 milliliters 1 fluid ounce = 30 milliliters 1 cup = 250 milliliters 1 pint = 500 milliliters	1 quart = 1 liter 1 ounce = 30 grams 1 pound = 450 grams 2.2 pounds = 1 kilogram

NOTE: The metric measures are approximate benchmarks for purposes of home food preparation.

Substitution Chart

	Instead of	Use
Baking	1 teaspoon baking powder	$1/4$ teaspoon soda plus $1/2$ teaspoon cream of tartar
	1 tablespoon cornstarch (for thickening)	2 tablespoons flour or 1 tablespoon tapioca
	1 cup sifted all-purpose flour	1 cup plus 2 tablespoons sifted cake flour
	1 cup sifted cake flour	1 cup minus 2 tablespoons sifted all-purpose flour
	1 cup dry bread crumbs	$3/4$ cup cracker crumbs
Dairy	1 cup buttermilk	1 cup sour milk or 1 cup yogurt
	1 cup heavy cream	$3/4$ cup skim milk plus $1/3$ cup butter
	1 cup light cream	$7/8$ cup skim milk plus 3 tablespoons butter
	1 cup sour cream	$7/8$ cup sour milk plus 3 tablespoons butter
	1 cup sour milk	1 cup milk plus 1 tablespoon vinegar or lemon juice or 1 cup buttermilk
Seasoning	1 teaspoon allspice	$1/2$ teaspoon cinnamon plus $1/8$ teaspoon cloves
	1 cup catsup	1 cup tomato sauce plus $1/2$ cup sugar plus 2 tablespoons vinegar
	1 clove of garlic	$1/8$ teaspoon garlic powder or $1/8$ teaspoon instant minced garlic or $3/4$ teaspoon garlic salt or 5 drops of liquid garlic
	1 teaspoon Italian spice	$1/4$ teaspoon each oregano, basil, thyme, rosemary plus dash of cayenne
	1 teaspoon lemon juice	$1/2$ teaspoon vinegar
	1 tablespoon mustard	1 teaspoon dry mustard
	1 medium onion	1 tablespoon dried minced onion or 1 teaspoon onion powder
Sweet	1 1-ounce square chocolate	$1/4$ cup cocoa plus 1 teaspoon shortening
	$1 2/3$ ounces semisweet chocolate	1 ounce unsweetened chocolate plus 4 teaspoons granulated sugar
	1 cup honey	1 to $1 1/4$ cups sugar plus $1/4$ cup liquid or 1 cup corn syrup or molasses
	1 cup granulated sugar	1 cup packed brown sugar or 1 cup corn syrup, molasses or honey minus $1/4$ cup liquid

Index

All microwave recipe page numbers are preceded by an M.

TO ADD TO YOUR COOKBOOK COLLECTION
OR
TO GIVE AS GIFTS

Write to :
Favorite Recipes® Press
a division of Great American Opportunites, Inc.
P.O. Box 305142, Nashville, TN 37230
or
Call Toll-free
1-800-251-1542